MACMILLAN WORK OUT SERIES

Engineering Materials

The titles in this series

MACMILLAN WORK OUT SERIES

Engineering Materials

V. B. John

MACMILLAN

First published 1990
Reprinted 1990, 1991

Published by
MACMILLAN EDUCATION LTD
Houndmills, Basingstoke, Hampshire RG21 2XS
and London
Companies and representatives
throughout the world

Printed in Hong Kong

British Library Cataloguing in Publication Data
John, Vernon. 1931–
Engineering Materials
1. Materials
I. Title
620.1'1
ISBN 0–333–46372–2

Contents

Acknowledgements

Grateful acknowledgement is made by the author and publishers to the following Institutions who kindly gave permission for the use of questions from their first year examination papers:

City University
Kingston Polytechnic
Polytechnic of Central London
University of Salford
Sheffield City Polytechnic
University of Sheffield
University of Southampton
Trent Polytechnic.

Any errors or omissions remain the responsibility of the author and publishers.

Introduction

Materials Science or Engineering Materials is a core subject in all engineering degree courses. This volume is designed to be used by students on engineering degree courses but it may also prove helpful to those studying for a specialist degree in materials science or materials engineering.

One of the aims of this book is to provide a guide for revision study of materials at first year undergraduate level. The content of this volume may appear to be very wide and contain more than first year work. This is because there is a wide variation between the curricula operated in different colleges. Topics which, in some institutions, feature in the second year of a course may be introduced in the first year of study at other colleges. Materials selection is one of the study topics which is introduced in a simple way at an early stage of some courses and this is reflected in this volume.

The summaries at the beginning of each chapter are intentionally neither greatly detailed, nor completely comprehensive. They are simply reminders of the more important facts or concepts with which you should be familiar. If this is not the case for a particular topic, you should refer back to your lecture notes and/or textbooks before going on to the worked examples.

Bear in mind that often there is not just one 'correct' answer to the examination question. Many questions could be successfully answered in several different ways. Thus, the 'worked examples' are not intended to be 'model answers', but are more of a guide to what the examiner is looking for. They also contain additional comments and discussion of particular points of interest or difficulty which should help to clear up some of the more common misconceptions or misunderstandings.

Symbols Used in the Text

Symbol	Quantity	Preferred Units	Alternative Units
a	lattice parameter	m	Å $(1\ \text{Å} = 10^{-8}\text{m})$
D	diffusion coefficient	$\text{m}^{-2}\,\text{s}^{-1}$	
E	modulus of elasticity (Young's modulus)	Pa	N m^{-2}
F	force	N	
G	modulus of rigidity	Pa	N m^{-2}
K_c	fracture toughness	$\text{Pa m}^{1/2}$	$\text{N m}^{-3/2}$
M	atomic mass number		
N_0	Avogadro's number	$6.023 \times 10^{26}\ \text{kmol}^{-1}$	
Q	activation energy	J kmol^{-1}	
R_0	universal constant	$8314\ \text{J kmol}^{-1}\,\text{K}^{-1}$	
T	temperature	K	°C
T_g	glass transition temperature		
T_m	melting temperature		
t	time	s	min
Z	atomic number		
γ	surface energy	J m^{-2}	
ε	direct strain		
ε_n	nominal strain		
ε_t	true strain		
η	viscosity	Pa s	poise $(1\ \text{poise} = 10^{-1}\ \text{Pa s})$
λ	wavelength	m	Å
ν	Poisson's ratio		
ρ	density	kg m^{-3}	
σ	direct stress	Pa	N m^{-2}
σ_{FL}	fatigue limit	Pa	N m^{-2}
σ_{TS}	tensile strength	Pa	N m^{-2}
σ_Y	yield stress	Pa	N m^{-2}
τ	shear stress	Pa	N m^{-2}
ΔK	stress intensity factor	$\text{Pa m}^{1/2}$	$\text{N m}^{-3/2}$
$\Delta\sigma$	cyclic stress range	Pa	N m^{-2}

1 Atomic Structure and Bonding

1.1 Fact Sheet

(a) Sub-atomic Particles

The main sub-atomic particles are the proton, electron and neutron.

Particle	Mass (kg)	Relative mass	Charge (C)	Relative charge
Proton	1.672×10^{-27}	1	1.602×10^{-19}	$+1$
Electron	0.905×10^{-30}	0	1.602×10^{-19}	-1
Neutron	1.675×10^{-27}	1	0	0

The protons and neutrons form a small compact nucleus and the electrons are arranged in orbital shells around the nucleus.

(b) Electron States

The energy state of an orbital electron is given by four quantum numbers. These are:

- the principal quantum number, n, having positive integral values and is a description of the general energy level or shell,

- the secondary quantum number, l, having integral values, including 0, up to $(n-1)$. l indicates the sub-shell and values of l are denoted by the letters s, p, d and f, as $l = 0 \equiv s; l = 1 \equiv p; l = 2 \equiv d; l = 3 \equiv f$,

- the third quantum number, m_l, can have integral values, including 0, from $+l$ to $-l$,

- the fourth quantum number, m_s, the spin number, can have two values, $\pm \frac{1}{2}$.

The Pauli exclusion principle states that no two electrons within an atom can have the same set of four quantum numbers. From this the electron capacities of shells and sub-shells can be stated.

Shell	Sub-shell	Capacity of sub-shell	Capacity of shell
1 ($n = 1$)	s ($l = 0$)	2	2
2 ($n = 2$)	s ($l = 0$)	2	
	p ($l = 1$)	6	8
3 ($n = 3$)	s ($l = 0$)	2	
	p ($l = 1$)	6	
	d ($l = 2$)	10	18
4 ($n = 4$)	s ($l = 0$)	2	
	p ($l = 1$)	6	
	d ($l = 2$)	10	
	f ($l = 3$)	14	32

(c) Atomic Number, Atomic Mass Number and Isotopes

The atomic number, Z, is the number of protons in the nucleus of an atom. The atomic number is characteristic of the chemical element.

The atomic mass number (atomic weight), M, is the sum of the protons and neutrons in a nucleus.

Isotopes of an element have the same number of nuclear protons but a differing number of neutrons, hence different mass numbers.

(d) Avogadro's Number N_0

N_0 is the number of atoms of an element in one kilomole (the mass number expressed in kg). $N_0 = 6.023 \times 10^{26}$/kmol (or 6.023×10^{23}/mol).

(e) Interatomic Bonding

Bonding between atoms involves inter-action between the outermost electron shells (the valence electrons). The primary bond types are: ionic, based on electron transfer; covalent, based on electron sharing; and metallic, in which the valence electrons are shared between all atoms. In addition to these strong primary bonds, weaker secondary bonding forces, based on the electrostatic attraction between weak dipoles, exist. These secondary bonds are known as van der Waal's forces.

(f) Interatomic Forces and Bond Energies

When two atoms are in close proximity, there are several forces acting on the atoms. These are: a gravitational attractive force between dense nuclei, an electrostatic attractive force (in the cases of ions of opposite sign or if there are weak dipoles), and an electrostatic force of repulsion when the electron clouds of both atoms are close to one another. There will be one value of atom separation distance at which the forces are in balance and the net potential energy will be a minimum.

The Mie equation for the net potential energy is:

$$P.E. = -\frac{A}{r^m} + \frac{B}{r^n}$$

where A and B are constants, r is interatomic distance, and m and n are powers of r. The negative first term is the potential energy of attraction while the second term is that due to repulsion. (The form of the curve showing the variation of potential energy with interatomic distance is given in Solution 1.3.) The values of the indices m and n are: for primary bonds $m \simeq 1$, n being between 2 and 9 depending on the nature of the atoms and the type of bond; for van der Waal's bonds $m \simeq 6$ and $n \simeq 12$. Bond energies for primary bonds are of the order of 8 eV $(1.2 \times 10^{-18}\text{J})$ per bond and those for secondary bonds are between 1 and 10 per cent of this.

1.2 Worked Examples

Example 1.1

The ground state electron configuration of the first twenty elements in the periodic table, as predicted by wave mechanics, is given in the accompanying table.

Z	Symbol	Electrons in each sub-shell									
		1s	2s	2p	3s	3p	3d	4s	4p	4d	4f
1	H	1									
2	He	2									
3	Li	2	1								
4	Be	2	2								
5	B	2	2	1							
6	C	2	2	2							
7	N	2	2	3							
8	O	2	2	4							
9	F	2	2	5							
10	Ne	2	2	6							
11	Na	2	2	6	1						
12	Mg	2	2	6	2						
13	Al	2	2	6	2	1					
14	Si	2	2	6	2	2					
15	P	2	2	6	2	3					
16	S	2	2	6	2	4					
17	Cl	2	2	6	2	5					
18	Ar	2	2	6	2	6					
19	K	2	2	6	2	6		1			
20	Ca	2	2	6	2	6		2			

(a) Show, by using the appropriate quantum numbers, why an s state never has more than two electrons associated with it, and a p state never more than six.

(b) Explain what the filling of the 4s state before the 3d state tells one concerning the associated energy levels, and why this effect arises.

(c) Describe the variation one would expect in the ionisation potential of the last electron in each atom, up to element Z = 20, expected from the table.

(d) Group together those atoms which behave chemically the same as:
   (i)   He (Z = 2)
   (ii) Li (Z = 3)
   (iii) F (Z = 9)
   and state the names by which these groups are classified.

(e) Show whether or not Br (Z = 35) belongs to any of the groups listed in part (d).

(Sheffield City Polytechnic)

Solution 1.1

(a) The energy of an orbital electron is designated by four quantum numbers, n, l, m_l and m_s. The electron states s, p, d and f correspond to secondary quantum number values of $l = 0$, $l = 1$, $l = 2$ and $l = 3$ respectively. The third quantum number m_l may only have integral values, including zero, between $+ l$ and $- l$. Therefore in an s state, $l = 0$, m_l can have one value only, namely 0. The fourth quantum number m_s may have the values $+ \frac{1}{2}$ and $- \frac{1}{2}$. This gives two combinations of quantum numbers only and an s state is filled with two electrons. For a p state, $l = 1$, therefore there are three possible values for m_l, $+ 1$, 0 and $- 1$. With two possible values for m_s this gives six possible quantum number combinations for a p state.

(b) The fact that a 4s state fills before a 3d state indicates that the energy level of the 4s state is lower than that of the 3d state, in other words a 4s electron is more tightly bound to the nucleus than a 3d one. According to the Rutherford–Bohr model of an atom, a 3d orbital is circular whereas a 4s orbital is elliptical with high eccentricity. In the latter case, the orbital at one point lies very close to the nucleus, a condition for strong binding.

(c) The ionization potential is a measure of the energy required to remove an electron from an atom to infinity so that a positive ion results. The variation in ionization potential is as follows: for elements 1–2, 3–10 and 11–18, namely a series in which the number of outer shell electrons is increasing, the ionisation potentials increase as the number of outer shell electrons increases. For each series, the element with the highest potential is the one with an s^2, p^6 consideration, a noble gas. However, within each group, that is elements with the same outer shell configuration, for example, H, Li, Na and K, all with one s state electron in the outer shell, the ionisation potential reduces as the atomic number increases. As the number of inner shell electrons increases the outer electrons are more screened from the nucleus and are less tightly bound.

(d) (i) The other elements which behave, chemically, in the same manner as He, $Z = 2$, are those elements with completely filled s and p states, namely, neon, Ne, ($Z = 10$) and argon, Ar ($Z = 18$). These elements form part of the group known as the noble or inert gases.

(ii) The elements which behave similarly to Li ($Z = 3$) are those with the same outer shell electron structure, namely, one s state electron. These are Na ($Z = 11$) and K ($Z = 19$). These form part of the group termed the alkali metals.

(iii) The elements which behave similarly to F ($Z = 9$) are those with an outer electron shell configuration of s^2, p^5. In the table shown, only Cl ($Z = 17$) has this configuration. These form part of the halogen group of elements.

(e) Br ($Z = 35$) has 35 electrons per atom. The electronic configuration, following the pattern shown in the data table, is $1s^2$, $2s^2$, $2p^6$, $3s^2$, $3p^6$, $3d^{10}$, $4s^2$, $4p^5$. This is the same outer shell configuration as F and Cl. Br is a member of the halogen group.

Example 1.2

The following data are given for fluorine and magnesium:

	Atomic No.	Atomic mass (amu)	Electron configuration
Fluorine	9	19.00	$1s^2$, $2s^2\ 2p^x$
Magnesium	12	24.31	$1s^2$, $2s^2\ 2p^y$, $3s^z$

(a) What are the chemical symbols for fluorine and magnesium, and the values of x, y and z?

(b) How many atoms are there in 19 g of fluorine?

(c) From the above data, show how the valencies of the two elements are found and hence give the chemical formula of magnesium fluoride.

(d) What is the molecular mass of magnesium fluoride?

(e) Explain why the atomic mass of magnesium is not a whole number.

(f) With the aid of simple illustrations show the structure of the magnesium atom.

(g) With simple reasoning, identify the possible properties of magnesium fluoride.

(City University)

Solution 1.2

(a) The chemical symbols for fluorine and magnesium are F and Mg, respectively.

Fluorine, atomic number = 9, has 9 nuclear protons. In a neutral atom, these are balanced by 9 orbital electrons. Therefore $x = 9 - 4 = 5$. (There are two $1s$, two $2s$ and 5 $2p$ electrons in fluorine.) Similarly, magnesium must have 12 orbital electrons. $y = 6$ (the third electron shell does not begin to fill until the second shell is filled with two $2s$ and six $2p$ electrons). Therefore $z = 12 - (2 + 2 + 6) = 2$.

(b) The atomic mass number of fluorine is given as 19 (19 amu) therefore 19 g is one gramme atom and the number of atoms contained is Avogadro's number, $N_0 = 6.023 \times 10^{23}$.

(c) The valence of an element is equal to n or $(8 - n)$, where n is the number of outer shell electrons. For fluorine there are seven outer shell electrons (two $2s$ and five $2p$) so the valency is $8 - 7 = 1$. Magnesium has two outer shell electrons (two $3s$) and its valency is 2. On the basis of these valencies, two atoms of fluorine are required for every atom of magnesium. The chemical formula for magnesium fluoride is, therefore, MgF_2.

(d) The molecular mass of magnesium fluoride is $24.31 + (2 \times 19.00) = 62.31$

(e) There are three isotopes of magnesium having mass numbers of 24, 25 and 26. The relative proportions of these isotopes in any sample of magnesium is constant. The most abundant isotope is Mg-24. The average atomic mass number of any sample of magnesium is 24.31.

(f)

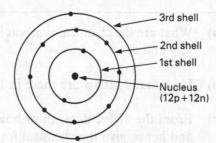

Figure 1.1 *Structure of magnesium atom*

(g) Magnesium atoms will lose their two valency electrons to become Mg^{2+} ions while fluorine atoms will each gain an electron forming F^- ions. Ionic bonding will occur between ions of opposing sign, and the ions will form a crystalline lattice in which Mg^{2+} and F^- ions are present in the ratio 1:2. This ionic compound will have a relatively high melting point, be non-ductile and electrically non-conductive. As an ionic compound, it will dissolve in a polar solvent, such as water. In the form of a solution and in the molten state, the ions will have mobility and, in these states, be electrically conductive, that is, be electrolytes.

Example 1.3

Describe the principal types of bond which exist between atoms and discuss the influence of bond type on the electrical and mechanical properties of solids.

Solution 1.3

There are three main types of primary interatomic bond, namely ionic (or electrovalent), covalent (or homopolar) and metallic. In addition, there are weaker secondary bonds based on electrostatic attraction between polarised molecules. Known as van der Waal's bonds, this type of secondary bond occurs between atoms of the noble gases at very low temperatures.

Ionic bond.   A bond based on electron transfer. Atoms with a small number of outer shell electrons may ionise by losing these, so exposing a filled electron shell. Conversely, atoms with almost complete outer shells may become negatively charged ions by capturing one or more electrons. As an example:

$$Na \rightarrow Na^+ + e^- \text{ and } Cl + e^- \rightarrow Cl^-.$$

Ions of opposing sign attract one another. There are other forces acting also. These are a gravitational attractive force between adjacent nuclear masses and, when the electron shells of atoms are in close proximity, an electrostatic repulsive force between these. At one specific separation distance, the forces of attraction and repulsion will be equal and opposite. At this separation distance, the potential energy of the system is a minimum, and of negative sign, and an energy input would be necessary either to separate the ions or move them closer together. The potential energies due to attraction and repulsion are inversely proportional to some power of the distance r between nuclei. The energy due to attraction is negative and is equal to $-A/r^m$ while the potential energy of repulsion equals $+B/r^n$, A and B are constants dependent on factors such as nuclear masses and quantity of charge and m and n are powers with $m < n$. The net potential energy is given by $-A/r^m + B/r^n$. The variation of potential energy with interatomic distance is shown in figure 1.2. The solid curve is the resultant showing a minimum energy value at distance r_0, the stable nuclear separation distance. In the solid state the ions build up into a strongly bonded crystalline solid.

Covalent bond.   A bond based on electron sharing. Chlorine, Cl, has an outer shell configuration of s^2, p^5. Two chlorine atoms combine with one electron from each atom being shared, and orbiting both nuclei, giving each nucleus in effect a filled outer shell. One pair of shared electrons forms one covalent bond. Atoms of carbon, with four outer shell electrons, form four covalent bonds. In diamond, each carbon atom is covalently bonded to four other atoms building a giant molecular crystal.

Metallic bond.   Generally, metal atoms have one, two or three outer shell electrons. In an aggregate of metal atoms, the forces acting between adjacent atoms will be a gravitational attraction and an electrostatic repulsion similar to that described above for the ionic bond. The atoms form a compact crystal structure and the outer shell, or valence, electrons are shared by all the atoms in the assembly. This has similarities to covalent bonding but the strength of the bond is weaker than a true covalent bond. The metallic state can be likened to an array of positive ions permeated by an electron 'gas'.

Van der Waal's bonding.   This is an electrostatic attraction between atoms or molecules which are polarised, namely the centre of positive charge and the centre

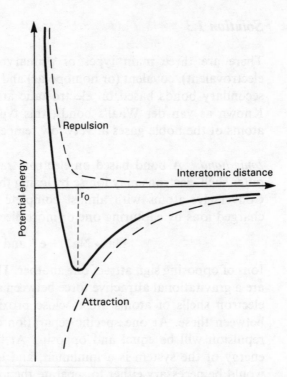

Figure 1.2 *Variation of potential energy with interatomic distance*

of negative charge do not coincide and a dipole exists. The monatomic noble gases condense into liquids and solids at very low temperatures. In atoms, with a continual movement of electrons, at any instant the centroid of negative charge need not coincide with the centre of positive charge and the atom may become slightly polarised and become attracted to a similarly polarised atom. At extremely low temperatures, the kinetic energies of the atoms will be insufficient to overcome these weak attractions and the gas can condense. Dipoles may be large in some polarised molecules and van der Waal's forces of attraction may be relatively large.

The ionic bond is relatively strong and ionic solids are crystalline and have relatively high melting points. The solid material is non-ductile and also electrically insulating. Many ionic compounds will dissolve in a polar solvent, such as water. The solution will conduct electricity, that is, is an electrolyte, as the dissolved ions have mobility. Similarly, a molten ionic compound is an electrolyte because the ions have mobility. The covalent bond is the strongest primary bond. Covalently bonded compounds are electrically non-conductive. The mechanical strength of covalently bonded materials ranges from extremely hard and strong—diamond, quartz—to soft and flexible—polythene and other thermoplastics. The former types are crystalline giant molecules while the polymers consist of large covalently bonded molecules with relatively weak secondary bonds existing between molecules. Metals are electrically conductive because of the mobile electron 'gas'. They are relatively strong materials but show plasticity because of the relative ease with which the metallic bond can be broken and remade.

Example 1.4

Write a concise account of the electron configuration in atoms of the various elements and explain how the electronic structure of atoms affects the manner in which atoms of elements bond together.

State, briefly, the influence that the type of interatomic bond has on the physical properties of a material.

Solution 1.4

Electrons enter orbitals, or energy states, around the nucleus. The lowest energy states are filled first and, as the number of electrons increases, so higher states of energy are filled progressively. The energy state of an electron is expressed as a series of four quantum numbers and no two electrons in an atom can have the same set of quantum numbers (the Pauli exclusion principle). The four quantum numbers are:

- principal quantum number n having integral values 1, 2, 3, 4, etc.

- secondary quantum number l. The permissible values of l are 0, 1, 2, 3, with a maximum value $= (n - 1)$. (Note: $l = 0 \equiv s$ state, $l = 1 \equiv p$ state, $l = 2 \equiv d$ state, $l = 3 \equiv f$ state.)

- magnetic quantum number m_l. Permissible values are integers, including zero, from $+ l$ to $- l$.

- spin quantum number m_s, which has two possible values, namely $\pm \frac{1}{2}$.

For the first electron shell $n = 1$ therefore $l = 0$ and $m_l = 0$. There are 2 values for m_s, $\pm \frac{1}{2}$, therefore two electrons only, both s state, fill the first electron shell.

For the second electron shell $n = 2$ therefore $l = 0$ or 1. When $l = 0$ (s state), $m_l = 0$, $m_s = \pm \frac{1}{2}$, giving two electrons. When $l = 1$ (p state), m_l may be $+ 1$, 0 or $- 1$. In each case m_s may be $\pm \frac{1}{2}$ giving a maximum of six electrons in the p state. Therefore the capacity of the second electron shell is eight electrons, two in the s state and six in the p state.

Similarly, for the third electron shell $n = 3$, so $l = 0$, 1 or 2. When $l = 2$ (d state) there are five possible values for m_l. This means, taking two values for m_s into account, that up to ten electrons can exist in the d state. The total capacity of the third electron shell is 18 electrons, 2 in the s state, 6 in the p state and 10 in the d state.

For the fourth electron shell, $n = 4$, so $l = 0$, 1, 2 or 3. When $l = 3$ (f state) the maximum number of electrons for this state is 14 and the total capacity of the fourth shell is 32 electrons.

Each element is characterised by an atomic number, Z, which is equal to the number of protons in the nucleus. In a neutral atom this also equals the number of orbital electrons. The electron configurations for the various elements can be built up using the principles outlined above, at least up to element $Z = 18$. Beyond this point, a complication arises as the energy level of the $4s$ state is slightly lower than that of the $3d$ state and the former state is filled first. (The electron configuration of the first 20 elements is given in example 1.1)

The configuration with filled s and p states in the outermost electron shell is a very stable arrangement. This is the configuration of the noble gases. Atoms of elements with incomplete outer shells attempt, by combination with other atoms, to satisfy this condition for stability. The bonding which occurs is the result of a rearrangement of outer shell or valence electrons and, consequently, is dependent on the electronic configurations of the atoms. There are three main types of primary bond. These are the ionic, the covalent and the metallic bond.

The ionic bond is based on electron transfer. An atom may lose one or more electrons exposing a filled $s^2 p^6$ arrangement and becoming a positive ion in the process. Other elements may gain one or more electrons to obtain an $s^2 p^6$ outer shell becoming a negative ion. Ions of opposite sign will be attracted to one another. (For greater detail see solution 1.3)

The covalent bond is based on electron sharing with one pair of electrons shared between two atoms constituting one covalent bond. Each atom achieves an outer shell arrangement of eight electrons by sharing. This type of bond occurs between atoms possessing 4, 5, 6 or 7 outer shell electrons (see solution 1.3). The atoms of most metals have 1, 2 or 3 outer shell electrons and an aggregate of metal atoms form densely-packed crystalline arrangements with all valence electrons shared between them (see solution 1.3).

Atoms of the noble gases with an $s^2 p^6$ outer shell configuration do not bond with one another except by a weak van der Waal's bonding at very low temperatures (see solution 1.3).

The influence of bond type on properties has already been covered in solution 1.3.

Example 1.5

The electronic structure, atomic weight and ionic radius of sodium are $1s^2 2s^2 2p^6 3s^1$, 22.99 and 0.098 nm respectively while for chlorine they are $1s^2 2s^2 2p^6 3s^2 3p^5$, 35.45 and 0.181 nm.

(a) Describe the form of bonding in solid sodium chloride.

(b) Describe the arrangement of sodium and chlorine ions in the unit cell of the crystalline solid if chlorine ions form a face-centred cubic arrangement and estimate the lattice parameter.

(c) What is the molecular weight of sodium chloride and how many sodium and chlorine ions are present in a mole of the material?

(d) Why are the atomic weights of the two elements not whole numbers?

(e) Explain why solid sodium chloride is electrically insulating and yet when dissolved in water it is electrically conducting.

(City University)

Solution 1.5

(a) The electronic structures given show that sodium has one outer shell electron ($3s^1$) while chlorine has seven outer shell electrons ($3s^2$ and $3p^5$). A sodium atom can lose its $3s$ electron to become a Na^+ ion; a chlorine atom can gain one electron, giving a filled third shell, to become a Cl⁻ ion. These ions of opposing sign will be attracted to one another and will form an ionic crystalline solid. They combine in the ratio 1:1 and the molecular formula can be expressed as NaCl.

(b) The arrangement of sodium and chlorine ions in the unit cell is shown in the diagram. The lattice parameter, a, of the unit cell can be calculated as $(2 \times 0.181) + (2 \times 0.098) = 0.558$ nm.

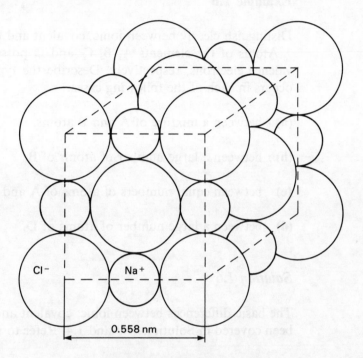

Figure 1.3 *Unit cell of NaCl*

(c) With a chemical formula NaCl, the molecular weight is the sum of the atomic weights of each element $= 22.99 + 35.45 = 58.44$.

A mole, the molecular weight in grams, contains N_0 (Avogadro's number) molecules. Total number of ions in a mole of NaCl is equal to $2 \times 6.023 \times 10^{23} = 1.2046 \times 10^{24}$.

(d) There are two reasons for atomic weights of elements not being whole numbers. One is the existence of *isotopes*. There are two isotopes of chlorine with mass numbers of 35 and 37. The other is *mass defect*. The measured mass of an atomic nucleus is less than the sum of the masses of the protons and neutrons present. The discrepancy is termed mass defect and this represents the nuclear binding energy. (Mass and energy are related by Einsteins' expression $E = mc^2$.) In the case of sodium, only one isotope exists (mass number = 23). The atomic weights of elements are determined relative to a standard. The standard used is the isotope of carbon, C-12. The atomic weight of this is taken as 12.000. Relative to this, the atomic weight of sodium is 22.99.

(e) In the solid state, the ions of sodium and chlorine are in fixed positions within a crystal lattice. As these charged particles cannot move significantly, even in a strong electrical field, the solid is electrically insulating. When dissolved in water,

11

the individual ions are mobile and can move preferentially in an electrical field. When two electrodes, with a potential difference between them, are introduced into the solution Na^+ ions, *cations*, will move toward the cathode and Cl^- ions, *anions*, will move toward the anode. This movement of charge carrying particles constitutes an electric current.

Example 1.6

Distinguish clearly between ionic, covalent and metallic bonding in solids.

Atoms of the elements A, B, C, and D possess 2, 3, 6, and 4 outer shell, or valence electrons, respectively. Describe the type of interatomic bonding which occurs in each of the following cases:

(a) between a mixture of A and B atoms,

(b) between a large number of atoms of B,

(c) between equal numbers of atoms of A and C, and

(d) between a large number of atoms of D.

Solution 1.6

The basic differences between ionic, covalent and metallic bonding in solids have been covered in Solutions 1.3 and 1.4. Refer to these for details.

(a) Elements A and B with two and three outer shell electrons, respectively, could ionise to give A^{2+} and B^{3+} ions, but could not bond with one another by either an electron transfer (ionic bond) or balanced electron sharing (covalent bond) mechanism. They are both metallic elements and an aggregate of A and B atoms will be held together by metallic bonding. (See solution 1.3 for metallic bond details)

(b) As stated in (a) above element B is a metal and metallic bonding occurs.

(c) Element A can ionise to A^{2+} ions while element C, with six outer shell electrons, can ionise to form C^{2-} ions. Electron transfer occurs giving an ionically bonded substance with the two ion types in a 1/1 ratio. (See solution 1.3 for ionic bond details)

(d) The atoms of element D, each with four outer shell electrons, will form covalent bonds. Each atom will be bonded to four other atoms, each covalent bond consisting of one pair of shared electrons. An example of this is the diamond structure (carbon atoms have four outer shell electrons). (See solution 1.3 for covalent bond details)

Example 1.7

State, with reasons, the type of bonding that occurs in each of the following substances:

(a) common salt, NaCl,

(b) methane, CH_4,

(c) diamond, and

(d) brass containing 70 per cent copper and 30 per cent zinc.

Methane is a gas at ordinary temperatures and pressures while diamond is the hardest known solid. Account for the properties of these materials on the basis of interatomic bonding.

Solution 1.7

(a) Ionic bonding. The electronic configuration of sodium is $1s^2, 2s^2, 2p^6, 3s^1$, while that for chlorine is $1s^2, 2s^2, 2p^6, 3s^2, 3p^5$. Sodium can readily ionise by losing its $3s$ electron while chlorine needs to gain one electron for a completed outer shell, becoming a negative ion in the process.

(b) Covalent bonding. The electronic configuration of hydrogen is $1s^1$ and it requires one electron to achieve the helium structure. Carbon has the configuration $1s^2 2s^2 2p^2$ and requires four electrons to obtain the neon structure. The structure of the methane molecule can be written as:

$$
\begin{array}{ccc}
 & H & \\
 & \cdot\cdot & \\
H : C : H & \text{or} & H-C-H \\
 & \cdot\cdot & \\
 & H & \\
\end{array}
$$

where : represents a pair of electrons shared between the carbon atom and a hydrogen atom. One pair of shared electrons is one covalent bond —.

(c) Covalent bonding. Each carbon atom bonds covalently to four other atoms of carbon giving each atom effectively eight outer shell electrons. This arrangement builds up into a crystalline array as shown in the figure below.

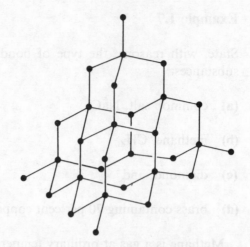

Figure 1.4 *Structure of diamond*

(d) Metallic bonding. Both copper and zinc possess two outer shell electrons and cannot form either ionic or covalent bonds with one another. When mixed together they form a common crystalline arrangement of atoms held together by metallic bonding. This type of mixture is termed a solid solution. (See chapter 3 for explanation of solid solution)

Both methane and diamond are substances which are covalently bonded yet their properties differ greatly. Methane is an easily liquifiable gas while diamond is the hardest known substance. In methane, four hydrogen atoms and one carbon atom bond covalently form a small discrete molecule. The bonding within the molecule is strong but only weak van der Waal's forces of attraction exist between methane molecules. In diamond, all the carbon atoms are covalently bonded to one another forming a continuous crystalline structure (giant molecule).

Example 1.8

Describe the origins of the interatomic forces of attraction in ionic crystals, valence crystals, metals and van der Waal's crystals. Show how the forces affect the physical properties of each type.

The energy, $E(r)$, of a two-atom bond can be expressed in terms of the bond separation, r, as follows:

$$E(r) = -\frac{\alpha}{r^m} + \frac{\beta}{r^n}$$

where α, β, m and n are all positive constants.

Identify the contributions of the repulsive and attractive forces and show that the requirement for the stability of the bond is $m < n$.

Give a graphical representation of the variation of $E(r)$ with r.

(Sheffield City Polytechnic)

14

Solution 1.8

Ionic crystals. Ions of opposing charge are attracted to one another by the Coulomb force of attraction. When ions are close to one another the interaction of electron clouds generates a repulsive force.

Valence crystals. This term means substances in which the bonding is of the covalent type. The covalent bond means a sharing of a pair of outer orbital electrons between two atoms. These electrons tend to spend more time in the region between the two atoms than outside it and the resulting concentration of a negative charge between two positive nuclei gives a force of attraction between them. Covalent bonds are directional.

Metallic crystals. The outer, or valence, electrons of a metal are easily freed and in a metal crystal they are not 'fixed' to their parent atoms. The metal structure is a lattice of positive ions permeated by an 'electron gas'. The force of attraction is between the positive ions and the free electrons.

Van der Waal's crystals. Many molecules show some degree of polarisation and form weak dipoles. It is the force of attraction which exists between the oppositely charged ends of dipoles which holds the crystals together.

The forces of attraction in the primary bonds are high, giving rise to stable materials with high melting points and strengths. The covalent bond strength is the highest making solids such as silica and diamond harder and of higher melting point than ionic compounds. It is the presence of free and mobile valence electrons in metallic structures that confers the property of electrical conductivity.

The potential energy of a two atom bond is:

$$E(r) = -\frac{\alpha}{r^m} + \frac{\beta}{r^n}$$

The potential energy due to attraction is $-\alpha/r^m$ and that of repulsion is β/r^n.

At the stable interatomic distance the net force is zero and the net potential energy will be negative (energy of attraction). This condition for bond stability, that the net energy is negative, will only be achieved if $\alpha/r^m > \beta/r^n$ and the criterion for this is that $m < n$.

The graphical representation of $E(r)$ with r is as shown below.

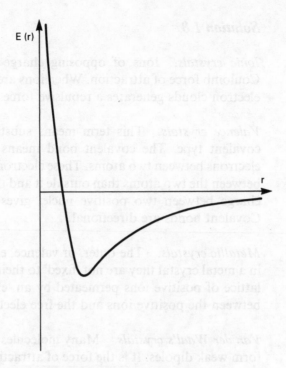

Figure 1.5 *Variation of* E(r) *with* r

Example 1.9

(a) Give a brief description of the three main sub-atomic particles.

(b) Describe the arrangement of sub-atomic particles in an atom of the element with atomic number, $Z = 19$, and atomic mass number, $M = 39$.

(c) If atoms of element, $Z = 19$, are reacted with atoms of element, $Z = 17$, and a compound formed:

   (i) explain the type of interatomic bonding forces within the compound, and

   (ii) describe a possible crystal structure for the compound.

(Polytechnic of Central London)

Solution 1.9

(a) The three main sub-atomic particles are the proton, neutron and electron. A proton has a mass of 1.672×10^{-27} kg and carries an electrical charge of 1.602×10^{-19} C (referred to as unit mass and unit charge respectively). A neutron has a mass almost identical to that of a proton but carries no charge while an electron has an extremely small mass (1/1847 that of a proton) but carries a quantity of charge identical to that of a proton though of opposite sign.

(b) Atomic number, Z, is the number of protons in a nucleus. $Z = 19$ indicates 19 nuclear protons. Atomic mass number, M, is the total number of nucleons, so that

16

the number of neutrons is $M - Z = 39 - 19 = 20$. In a neutral atom the number of orbital electrons equals the number of nuclear protons. The electronic arrangement for an atom with 19 nuclear electrons is: $1s^2, 2s^2, 2p^6, 3s^2, 3p^6, 4s^1$.

(c) (i) Element $Z = 19$ has one outer shell electron ($4s^1$, see (b) above) while element $Z = 17$ has seven outer shell electrons, the third shell configuration being $3s^2, 3p^5$. These are the conditions for the formation of ions by electron transfer with element 19, potassium, losing an electron forming K^+ and element 17, chlorine, gaining an electron forming Cl^-. The compound formed will be bonded ionically (see solution 1.3).

(ii) The two types of ion will be attracted to one another and form an ionically bonded compound with the two types of ion present in the ratio 1/1. The type of crystal structure will be cubic and of the same form as that of NaCl (see solution 1.5(b)).

Example 1.10

The table below gives the melting points of five commonly used materials:

Material	Melting Point (°C)
Mild steel	1530
Low density polyethylene	100
Nylon 66	265
Magnesium chloride	714
Argon	-189

Identify the bonding system(s) operating in each case and explain why the range of melting points shown above is so wide.

(Trent Polytechnic)

Solution 1.10

The bonding in mild steel (an alloy between iron and a small amount of carbon) is metallic. Both polyethylene and nylon are carbon-based polymer materials and the interatomic bonding in these substances is covalent. Intermolecular bonding of the van der Waal's type can also exist in these materials and in nylon, a polyamide, hydrogen bonds are also formed between molecules.

Magnesium chloride is an ionic compound in which Mg^{2+} ions are bonded ionically to Cl^- ions. The crystalline arrangement is composed of Mg and Cl ions in the ratio 1:2.

Argon is a monatomic noble gas. Very weak van der Waal's forces of attraction may occur between atoms. At very low temperatures, when atom kinetic energies are low, the attractive forces are sufficient to cause the gas to condense.

Argon has a very low melting point because it requires quite low levels of energy to exceed the bond strength of the weak van der Waal's forces.

Polyethylene and nylon 66 are both covalently bonded linear polymers. Van der Waal's forces of attraction exist between molecules in each of these materials. In addition hydrogen bonds occur between N—H and C=O groups in adjacent molecular chains. (Hydrogen can only form one normal covalent bond but the electrostatic field surrounding the proton nucleus of hydrogen is very strong and in some situations a bond can occur due to attraction between the proton nucleus of hydrogen and the electrons of an adjacent atom. This is the hydrogen bond, a secondary bond.) The presence of an additional intermolecular bonding system means that the energy required to disrupt the bonding and melt the substance is higher in the case of nylon than for polyethylene, hence the higher melting point.

Magnesium chloride has a crystalline structure (giant molecule) and the ionic bond has a relatively high strength, so giving the compound a relatively high melting temperature at 714°C.

Although the strength of the metallic bond is generally rated as being less than either ionic or covalent bonds the crystals of metals, such as mild steel, tend to have densely packed structures. This closeness of atomic packing tends to give relatively high melting temperatures.

1.3 Questions

Question 1.1

Magnesium, $Z = 12$, contains three isotopes in the following proportions: 78.7 per cent of atoms contain 12 neutrons, 10.13 per cent of atoms contain 13 neutrons and 11.17 per cent of atoms contain 14 neutrons. Calculate the atomic mass number of magnesium.

Question 1.2

Copper, $Z = 29$, has a mass number of 63.54 and contains two isotopes, Cu-63 and Cu-65. State the number of neutrons in each isotope and the percentage of each isotope present in copper.

Question 1.3

Indium, $Z = 49$, has all of its linear electron states filled, apart from the $4f$, which is empty. What would be the expected valence of indium?

Question 1.4

(a)   Calculate the number of valence electrons in 1 kg of aluminium. (Atomic mass number of aluminium is 26.98; $Z = 13$)

(b)   Assuming that the number of electrons free to move in 100 g of silicon semiconductor is 5×10^{10}, what fraction of the total number of valence electrons does this represent? (for silicon $Z = 14$, $M = 28.09$)

Question 1.5

The potential energy–interatomic separation distance curves for an ionically bonded substance and a material bonded by van der Waal's forces and a metal are shown below. Which curve relates to which type of material?

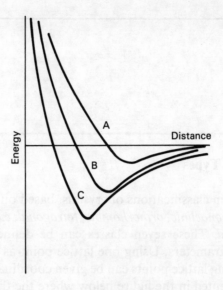

Figure 1.6

Question 1.6

What would be the expected formulae when the following ionic compounds are formed:
(a) when magnesium combines with (i) fluorine, (ii) sulphur,
(b) when the following metals are oxidised: (i) aluminium, (ii) beryllium, (iii) potassium. (atomic numbers are: Al = 13, Be = 4, F = 9, K = 19, Mg = 12, O = 8, S = 16)

1.4 Answers to questions

1.1 24.325.
1.2 Cu-63—34 neutrons, Cu-65—36 neutrons; 73 per cent of Cu-63, 27 per cent of Cu-65.
1.3 3 (filled $1s$, $2s$, $2p$, $3s$, $3p$, $3d$, $4s$, $4p$ and $4d$ states $\equiv$ 46 electrons, so outer shell (the fifth) must contain three electrons).
1.4 **(a)** 6.7×10^{25}; **(b)** 5.8×10^{-15}
1.5 Curve A—van der Waal's bonding; Curve B—metallic bonding; Curve C—ionic bonding.
1.6 **(a)** (i) MgF_2, (ii) MgS, **(b)** (i) Al_2O_3, (ii) BeO, (iii) K_2O.

2 Crystallography

2.1 Fact Sheet

(a) Crystal Types

There are seven classifications of crystals, based on the degree of symmetry. These are *triclinic*, *monoclinic*, *orthorhombic*, *tetragonal*, *cubic*, *rhombohedral* (or *trigonal*), and *hexagonal*. These seven classes can be defined using the Miller system by quoting six parameters. Using one lattice point as a point of reference, or origin, the surrounding lattice points can be given coordinates on suitably orientated axes. This is represented in the figure below where the three reference axes are OX, OY and OZ. The nearest lattice points to the origin, O, on these axes are A, B and C at distances a, b and c respectively. The angles between the reference axes are α, β and γ.

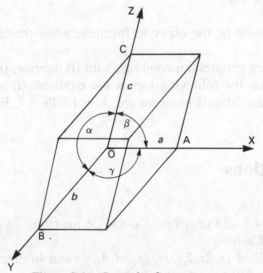

Figure 2.1 *Crystal reference axes*

The tetragonal, cubic and hexagonal crystal systems are important and these can be defined on the Miller system as:

Tetragonal	$a = b \neq c$;	$\alpha = \beta = \gamma = 90°$
Cubic	$a = b = c$;	$\alpha = \beta = \gamma = 90°$
Hexagonal	$a = b \neq c$;	$\alpha = \beta = 90°, \gamma = 60°$

There is an alternative method for defining the hexagonal class, namely the Miller–Bravais system, which uses four reference axes. This system uses three co-planar axes of equal length with an angular separation of 120°C and a fourth axis perpendicular to them (see figure below). It will be seen that the Miller–Bravais unit cell is equivalent to three unit cells of the Miller system.

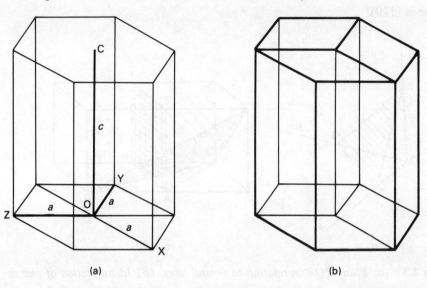

(a)   (b)

Figure 2.2   *Miller–Bravais system. (a) reference axes, (b) unit cell, showing equivalence to three Miller cells*

It should be observed that it is only necessary to quote two parameters, the axis lengths a and c, to define a specific tetragonal or hexagonal crystal as b is equal to a and, in tetragonal, all angles are right angles, while in hexagonal it is known that α and β are right angles and $\gamma = 60°$. Similarly, only one parameter, axis length a, is needed to fully define a cubic crystal.

(b)   Miller Indexing System

Planes and directions within crystals can be identified using the Miller notation. Three indices, h, k and l are necessary to denote a plane or direction. (Four indices are needed when using the Miller–Bravais system for hexagonal crystals.) When enclosed within ordinary brackets, (hkl), the indices signify a plane and when enclosed within square brackets, $[hkl]$, they indicate a direction.

(i)   Planes

For the identification of planes the indices h, k and l are defined as the reciprocals of the intercepts made between the plane and the reference axes. Plane PQR in Figure 2.3(a) below intercepts the three axes OA, OB and OC at P, Q and R respectively. The indices are:

$$h = \frac{\text{length OA}}{\text{length OP}}, \; k = \frac{\text{length OB}}{\text{length OQ}}, \; l = \frac{\text{length OC}}{\text{length OR}}$$

In Figure 2.3(b), the plane ABDE intercepts the OA and OB axes at A and B respectively but is parallel to the OC axis and intercepts it at infinity. Therefore

$$h = \frac{OA}{OA} = 1, \ k = \frac{OB}{OB} = 1, \ l = \frac{OC}{\infty} = 0.$$

The plane is (110).

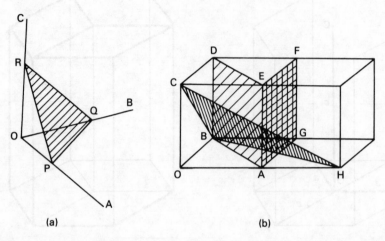

Figure 2.3 *(a) Plane PQR in relation to crystal axes, (b) Identification of planes*

Similarly, for plane AEFG, it intercepts the OA axis at A and the OB and OC axes at infinity so: $h = OA/OA$, $k = OB/\infty$, $l = OC/\infty$. The plane is (100).

Plane OBDC, or indeed any plane which contains the origin, poses a slight problem. This can be resolved by transposing the origin temporarily from O to A. Now the plane can be said to intercept the new OA axis at unit distance in the negative direction. The indices of the plane become ($\bar{1}$00). Plane BCH intercepts the axes at H, B and C. The indices for plane BCH are $h = OA/OH$, $k = OB/OB$, $l = OC/OC$ or ($\frac{1}{2}$11). Fractions are not usually quoted as indices. Multiplying to remove fractions gives plane BCH = (122).

A family of planes, as opposed to a unique plane, can be referred to using curly brackets, for example, the family of cube face planes as {100}.

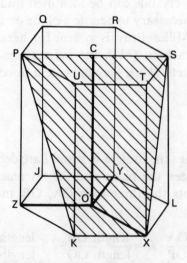

Figure 2.4 *Miller–Bravais indices*

The Miller–Bravais notation for the hexagonal crystal system uses four axes of reference and therefore four indices must be quoted to identify planes and directions. Examples are given in figure 2.4.

The four reference axes are OX, OY, OZ and OC. The top plane of the cell, plane PQRSTU is parallel to the axes OX, OY and OZ and intercepts them at infinity, but intercepts the OC axis at C. The indices for the plane are (0001). Considering the plane PSXK, this plane intercepts the OX axis at X, the OY axis at K (which is at unit distance from O but in the negative direction) and the OC axis at C. It is parallel to the OZ axis, intercepting it at infinity. The indices of plane PSXK are (1$\bar{1}$01).

(ii) Directions

The indices for directions within crystals are obtained as follows. The cartesian coordinates of the start of the direction line are subtracted from the coordinates of the point at which the direction line emerges from the unit cell. Consider line AP in the accompanying figure. The coordinates of point A are 1,0,0, and the coordinates of point P are 1,1,$\frac{1}{2}$. The indices for direction AP are given by 1,1,$\frac{1}{2}$ − 1,0,0 = 0,1,$\frac{1}{2}$. Multiplying to remove fractions gives direction AP = [021].

The reciprocal of this, namely direction PA would be 1,0,0 − 1,1,$\frac{1}{2}$ = 0, − 1, − $\frac{1}{2}$ giving direction PA = [0$\bar{2}\bar{1}$]

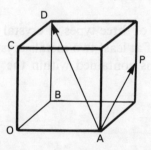

Figure 2.5 *Directions in crystals*

Similarly, direction AD would be 0,1,1 − 1,0,0 = [$\bar{1}$11] and its reciprocal, DA, would be [1$\bar{1}\bar{1}$].

To refer to a family of similar directions, brackets ⟨ ⟩ thus are used ⟨*hkl*⟩. Directions in the hexagonal system using the Miller–Bravais system are obtained in a similar manner to the Miller system. (Refer to figure for Miller–Bravais indices above.) Direction OX would be [1000] and its reciprocal [$\bar{1}$000]. Direction OC would be [0001].

(c) Analysis of cubic crystals

For face-centred cubic, $a = D\sqrt{2}$ or $D = a/\sqrt{2}$ where a is the lattice parameter and D is the atomic diameter, and for body centred cubic $a = 2D/\sqrt{3}$ or $D = \frac{1}{2}a\sqrt{3}$. See example 2.2 for derivation of above expressions.

The interplanar spacing d, written as $d_{(hkl)}$, for planes (*hkl*) in the cubic system is given by:

$$d_{(hkl)} = \frac{a}{\sqrt{(h^2 + k^2 + l^2)}}$$

The index number for plane $(hkl) = h^2 + k^2 + l^2$.

(d) Bragg equation

The Bragg equation is $n\lambda = 2d \sin\theta$, where λ is the wavelength of the incident radiation, d is the interplanar spacing, θ is the Bragg angle and n is a small integer. (Assume, unless told otherwise, that all Bragg reflections are first order, i.e. $n = 1$.)

With cubic crystals, Bragg reflections occur as follows:

   (i)   for simple cubic—reflections from all planes,

  (ii)   for body-centred cubic—reflections from all planes with even index numbers,

 (iii)   for face-centred cubic—reflections from those planes where h, k, and l are either all odd numbers or all even numbers (0 is taken as an even number).

2.2   Worked Examples

Example 2.1

Sketch the unit cells of three types of crystal structure commonly found in metals and give examples of at least two metals crystallising in each of these forms. State the number of atoms contained within the unit cells of each of the three types considered.

Solution 2.1

Three types of crystal structure frequently found in metals are body centred cubic, BCC, face centred cubic, FCC, and hexagonal close-packed, HCP. These can be sketched as follows:

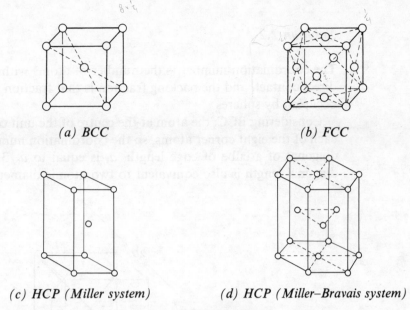

(a) BCC

(b) FCC

(c) HCP (Miller system)

(d) HCP (Miller–Bravais system)

Figure 2.6

Some of the metals which crystallise in these forms are:

BCC—chromium, α-iron, molybdenum, β-titanium and tungsten.
FCC—aluminium, copper, gold, γ-iron and nickel.
HCP—beryllium, magnesium, α-titanium and zinc.

When determining the number of atoms in each of the unit cells it should be noted that when one unit cell is drawn not all of the atoms shown in the sketch belong exclusively to that cell. For example, in a cubic system eight adjacent unit cells meet at a cube corner point. Therefore only one-eighth part of any corner atom is effectively within one unit cell.

In BCC, the centre atom is wholly contained within the unit cell, therefore a BCC unit cell contains $(8 \times 1/8) + 1 = 2$ atoms.

In FCC, each of the six atoms at face centre positions is shared between two adjacent cells, therefore a FCC unit cell contains $(8 \times 1/8) + (6 \times 1/2) = 4$ atoms.

In HCP (using the Miller–Bravais cell), six cells meet at any of the twelve corner points. Each of the atoms at the centre of end faces is shared equally between two cells, while the three atoms situated on the centre plane are wholly contained within the cell. Therefore a Miller–Bravais HCP unit cell contains $(12 \times 1/6) + (2 \times 1/2) + 3 = 6$ atoms. (A Miller unit cell of the HCP system would contain two atoms.)

Example 2.2

Assuming that within metal crystals the atoms can be considered as hard spheres in contact, determine the coordination number and packing fraction for BCC, FCC and HCP crystal types.

Solution 2.2

The coordination number is the number of atoms with which any one atom is in direct contact, and the packing fraction is that fraction of the total space which is occupied by spheres.

Considering BCC, the atom at the centre of the unit cell is in direct contact with each of the eight corner atoms, so the coordination number is 8. The length of the diagonal of a cube of edge length, a, is equal to $a\sqrt{3}$. In the BCC system, the diagonal length is also equivalent to two atomic diameters, $2D$.

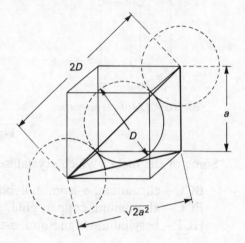

Figure 2.7 *BCC—relation between a and D*

Therefore $2D = a\sqrt{3}$ or $a = 2D/\sqrt{3}$. The BCC cell contains two atoms (solution 2.1).

The packing fraction is

$$\frac{\text{volume of 2 atoms}}{\text{volume of unit cell}} = 2 \times \pi D^3/6 \div \left(\frac{2D}{\sqrt{3}}\right)^3 = 0.68$$

The coordination number in FCC is 12. This can be shown by examining the packing in the most densely packed planes, which are those of the (111) type. It will be seen that within such a plane any one atom is in direct contact with six other atoms.

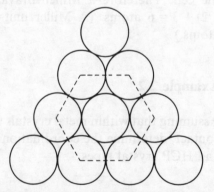

Figure 2.8 *Close packing in FCC (111) type plane*

An atom will also be in contact with three atoms in each of the planes of similar

26

packing situated immediately above and below this plane. The length of the diagonal of a square face in a cube of edge length, a, is equal to $a\sqrt{2}$. In an FCC cell, this is equivalent to the diameter of two atoms. So, $2D = a\sqrt{2}$ or $a = D\sqrt{2}$. An FCC unit cell contains 4 atoms. (see solution 2.1)

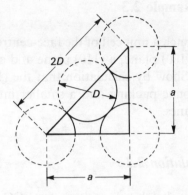

Figure 2.9 *FCC—relation between a and D*

The packing fraction is

$$\frac{\text{volume of 4 atoms}}{\text{volume of unit cell}} = 4 \times \pi D^3/6 \div (D\sqrt{2})^3 = 0.74.$$

The coordination number for HCP is also twelve. The basal planes (0001) are the most closely packed and the atoms in these planes are arranged in the same manner as in the FCC (111) planes.

There are two lattice parameters for the HCP system, a and c. It will be seen in the accompanying figure that parameter a is equal to one atomic diameter, D, and that the parameter c is equal to $2h$, where h is the height of a regular tetrahedron of edge length a.

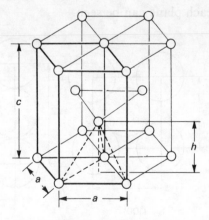

Figure 2.10 *HCP—relation between a, c and h*

$$h = \frac{a\sqrt{2}}{\sqrt{3}} \qquad \therefore 2h = \frac{2a\sqrt{2}}{\sqrt{3}} = c$$

The area of a regular hexagon of side equal to a is $a^2 3\sqrt{3}/2$ and so the volume of a hexagonal prism is $\frac{1}{2}a^2 3\sqrt{3} \times 2a\sqrt{2}/\sqrt{3} = 3\,a^3\sqrt{2} = 3D^3\sqrt{2}$ as $a = D$.

A Miller–Bravais HCP cell contains six atoms (see solution 2.1). The packing fraction for HCP = volume of 6 atoms/volume of unit cell = $6 \times \pi D^3/6 \div 3D^3\sqrt{2} = 0.74$.

Example 2.3

Sketch a unit cell of the face-centred cubic crystal system and show the positions of a (100) plane, a (110) plane and a (111) plane.

Show by calculation that the (111) planes in FCC possess a greater density of atomic packing and a smaller interplanar spacing than either the (100) or (110) planes.

Solution 2.3

The sketch below shows an FCC unit cell with the three planes identified.

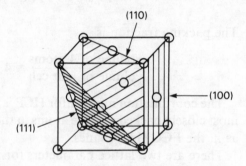

Figure 2.11

These three planes are now shown in plan view and the arrangement of atoms in each plane can be seen.

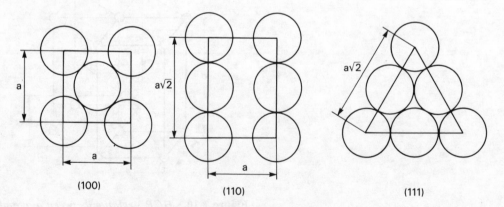

Figure 2.12 *Atom packing within planes in FCC*

It can be seen that the number of circles (atoms) contained within each of the planes is two. For (100) $(4 \times 1/4) + 1 = 2$, for (110) $(4 \times 1/4) + (2 \times 1/2) = 2$, and for (111) $(3 \times 1/6) + (3 \times 1/2) = 2$.

The density of packing in each plane is given by area of circles/area of plane. The areas of the three planes are: $(100) - a^2$, $(110) - a^2\sqrt{2}$, $(111) - \frac{1}{2}a^2\sqrt{3}$. Since

$a^2\sqrt{2} > a^2 > \frac{1}{2}a^2\sqrt{3}$, the packing density in the (111) plane is greater than that for either the (100) or (110) planes.

The interplanar spacing is given by $d_{(hkl)} = a/\sqrt{(h^2 + k^2 + l^2)}$. Therefore,

$$d_{(111)} = \frac{a}{\sqrt{3}} < d_{(110)} = \frac{a}{\sqrt{2}} < d_{(100)} = a$$

Example 2.4

The atomic radius of an iron atom is 1.238×10^{-10} m. Iron crystallises as BCC. Calculate the lattice parameter, a, of the unit cell.

Solution 2.4

For the BCC unit cell $a = 2D/\sqrt{3} = 4r/\sqrt{3}$ and $r = 1.238 \times 10^{-10}$ m. Therefore $a = (4 \times 1.238 \times 10^{-10})/\sqrt{3} = 2.859 \times 10^{-10}$ m.

Example 2.5

Given that the radius of the nickel atom is 0.124 nm, calculate the volume of one unit cell of nickel (FCC). Given, further, that the atomic mass number of nickel is 58.69 and Avogadro's number is 6.023×10^{26} kmol^{-1}, determine the density of nickel.

Experimental determination of the density of a polycrystalline sample of nickel gives a value of 8887 kg/m^3. Why is there a difference between the calculated value and that found by experiment? State three structural features that could account for the discrepancy.

(Trent Polytechnic)

Solution 2.5

The lattice parameter, a, of a FCC unit cell is $= 2\sqrt{2} \times r$.
Volume of a unit cell of nickel, $a^3 = (2 \times 0.124 \times 10^{-9} \times \sqrt{2})^3$ m^3

$$= 4.314 \times 10^{-29} \text{ m}^3$$

A unit cell of the FCC system contains 4 atoms (see solution 2.1). 1 kmol of nickel (58.69 kg) contains N_0 atoms.

$$\text{Mass of four nickel atoms} = \frac{4 \times 58.69}{N_0} = \frac{4 \times 58.69}{6.023 \times 10^{26}} \text{ kg}$$

$$\text{Density of nickel} = \frac{\text{mass}}{\text{volume}} = \frac{4 \times 58.69}{6.023 \times 10^{26} \times 4.314 \times 10^{-29}}$$

$$= 9.035 \times 10^3 \text{ kg/m}^3$$

The theoretical density of nickel, as calculated is greater than the experimentally determined density of nickel. The reasons for this are that the calculation is based on the assumption that the crystal lattice is perfect and does not contain lattice defects, such as vacancies, dislocations, grain boundaries and small voids.

Example 2.6

The structure of iron changes from BCC to FCC when it is heated through 910°C. By how much would a 1 m length of iron wire contract as the structure changes? Ignore any change in the radius of the wire and take the radius of the iron atom in the BCC structure to be 0.1258 nm and 0.1292 nm in the FCC structure at the transition temperature.

(Polytechnic of Central London)

Solution 2.6

A BCC unit cell contains two atoms whereas a FCC unit cell contains four atoms. So, at the transition temperature, two BCC cells will transform into one FCC cell. In the BCC system $a = 2D/\sqrt{3} = 4r/\sqrt{3}$ and in the FCC system $a = D\sqrt{2}$.

Therefore, the volume of two BCC cells is $\dfrac{(4 \times 0.1258 \times 10^{-9})^3}{3\sqrt{3}} \times 2$

$$= 49.04 \times 10^{-30} \text{ m}^3$$

and the volume of a FCC cell is $(2 \times 0.1292 \times 10^{-9} \times \sqrt{2})^3$

$$= 48.80 \times 10^{-30} \text{ m}^3.$$

The volume change during the transformation is $(49.04 - 48.80)/49.04 = 0.0049$. Assuming no change of diameter a 1 m length of wire would contract by 0.0049 m or 4.9 mm.

Example 2.7

(a) Derive the Bragg equation which relates the interplanar spacing, d, for a set of parallel planes to the wavelength of incident radiation, λ, and the diffraction angle, θ.

(b) Describe a diffraction camera which can be used for obtaining X-ray diffraction patterns from powder metal specimens.

Solution 2.7

(a) The wavelengths of X-radiation are of the same order of magnitude as the interplanar spacings in crystals. When monochromatic X-radiation is directed at a crystalline material it will be reflected by atomic planes, both surface and sub-surface.

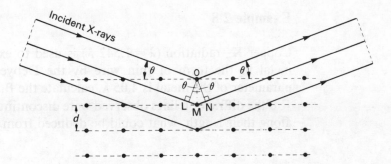

Figure 2.13 *Reflection of X-rays by crystal planes*

For radiation striking atomic planes at some angle, θ, as in the diagram, there will be effective reflection only when the various ray paths differ by an amount that is equal to one wavelength, or an integral number of wavelengths. Under these conditions, the reflected rays will be in phase. From the diagram, this condition will be satisfied when distance LMN is equal to $n\lambda$, where λ is the wavelength of the radiation and n is a small integer.

OM = d, the interplanar spacing, so LM = MN = $d\sin\theta$ and LMN = $2d\sin\theta$. The condition for reflection is, therefore: $n\lambda = 2d\sin\theta$.

(b) The Debye–Scherrer method is used to determine crystal interplanar spacings. A powdered metal sample is placed in the centre of a circular diffraction camera and monochromatic X-radiation directed at it. A strip of X-ray sensitive film is mounted around the circumference of the camera. The incident beam is diffracted by crystal planes, according to Bragg's law, giving a series of emerging cones of radiation. A series of lines are recorded on the film. The cone angle is equal to 4θ. After exposure and development measurements are taken on the strip of film and the Bragg angles calculated.

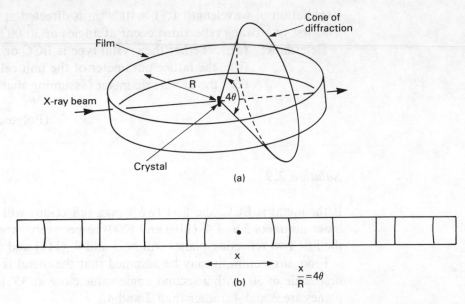

Figure 2.14 *(a) Principle of Debye–Scherrer camera; (b) Diffraction pattern*

If the distance between a pair of lines is x then $x/R = 4\theta$ (in radians), where R is the radius of the camera.

31

Example 2.8

Copper K_α radiation ($\lambda = 1.542$ Å) is used to examine specimens of a pure FCC metal in the form of thin wire by the Debye–Scherrer method. If the lattice parameter of the metal is 4.05 Å, calculate the Bragg angles for the first four lines.

If the diffraction lines observed were discontinuous (spotty) or varied in intensity along their length, what could be deduced from this?

(Kingston Polytechnic)

Solution 2.8

The first four reflecting planes in the FCC system are: 3 (111), 4 (200), 8 (220) and 11 (311).

Using

$$d_{(hkl)} = \frac{a}{\sqrt{(h^2 + k^2 + k^2)}} \quad \text{so } d_{(111)} = \frac{4.05}{\sqrt{3}} = 2.338 \text{ Å}$$

Similarly, $d_{(200)} = 2.025$ Å, $d_{(220)} = 1.432$ Å and $d_{(311)} = 1.221$ Å.

From the Bragg equation $\theta = \sin^{-1}(\lambda/2d)$, so $\theta_{(111)} = 19.25°$, $\theta_{(200)} = 22.38°$, $\theta_{(220)} = 32.58°$ and $\theta_{(311)} = 39.16°$.

Discontinuous lines or lines which varied in intensity would indicate that the sample was in the cold worked condition, rather than annealed.

Example 2.9

X-radiation of wavelength 1.71×10^{-10} m is directed at a cubic crystalline metal. The first two Bragg reflections occur at angles of 30°00′ and 35°17′ respectively.

Determine: (a)   whether the crystal type is BCC or FCC,
                (b)   the lattice parameter of the unit cell, and
                (c)   the atomic diameter (assuming that all atoms are identical).

(Polytechnic of Central London)

Solution 2.9

If the metal is BCC, the first two Bragg reflections will be from the planes with index numbers 2 and 4, (110) and (200) respectively, whereas if the metal is FCC the first two reflecting planes will be 3 and 4, (111) and (200).

From inspection, it may be assumed that the metal is FCC. (A relatively large first angle of 30° with a second angle value close at 35° indicate that the first two planes are 3 and 4, rather than 2 and 4.)

Hence, $d_{(111)} = 1.71 \times 10^{-10}$ m and $d_{(200)} = 1.48 \times 10^{-10}$ m

giving $a = 1.71 \times 10^{-10} \times \sqrt{3} = 2.96 \times 10^{-10}$ m and $a = 1.48 \times 10^{-10} \times 2 = 2.96 \times 10^{-10}$ m

These two values are the same, showing that the metal is FCC with a lattice parameter of 2.96×10^{-10} m.

In the FCC system, the relationship between atomic diameter, D, and the lattice parameter, a, is given by: $D = a \div \sqrt{2}$. Therefore

$$D = \frac{(2.96 \times 10^{-10})}{\sqrt{2}} = 2.093 \times 10^{-10} \text{ m}$$

Example 2.10

Bragg reflections may occur from the following planes in BCC crystals: (110), (200), (211), (220), (310), (222), (321), (400), (411), (420), (332), (422).

Which of these planes will give reflections when X-radiation of wavelength 0.154 nm is directed at a sample of chromium? Assume that the atomic diameter of chromium is 0.2494 nm.

(Polytechnic of Central London)

Solution 2.10

$$\lambda = 2d \sin\theta \quad \text{or} \quad \frac{\lambda}{2d} = \sin\theta$$

$$\sin\theta \not> 1 \quad \text{therefore} \quad d \not< \frac{\lambda}{2}$$

$$d_{(hkl)} \not< \frac{1.54 \times 10^{-10}}{2} \text{ m}$$

But

$$d_{(hkl)} = \frac{a}{\sqrt{(h^2 + k^2 + l^2)}}$$

Therefore $\quad \sqrt{(h^2 + k^2 + l^2)} \not> \frac{2a}{1.54 \times 10^{-10}}$

In BCC crystals $a = \dfrac{2D}{\sqrt{3}}$

Therefore, lattice parameter for chromium, $a = \dfrac{2 \times 2.494 \times 10^{-10}}{\sqrt{3}}$

$$= 2.88 \times 10^{-10} \text{ m}$$

Therefore $\sqrt{(h^2 + k^2 + l^2)} \not> \dfrac{2 \times 2.88 \times 10^{-10}}{1.54 \times 10^{-10}} \not> 3.74$

So $\qquad h^2 + k^2 + l^2 \not> 13.98$

and the highest reflecting plane index number will be 12. The highest possible values of (hkl) are therefore (222).

Bragg reflections will occur from the first six reflecting planes, that is, up to and including plane (222).

Example 2.11

(a) A diffraction pattern has been obtained from a pure BCC metal using a Debye–Scherrer type X-ray camera. Indicate the appearance of the film for low angle lines. Use the information given below to determine the interplanar spacing for the planes giving rise to the lowest angle lines on the film.

Distance between closest pair of lines on film = 44.52 mm
Wavelength of radiation, $\lambda = 1.541 \times 10^{-10}$ m
Diameter of camera = 57.5 mm

(b) Calculate the radius of the metal atoms in the sample.

(c) It is proposed to alloy the original BCC metal with up to 5 atomic per cent of another metal, the alloying element being FCC and having an atomic radius of 1.35×10^{-10} m. Assuming the metals form a substitutional solid solution with a solubility limit of 5 atomic per cent, discuss whether the X-ray diffraction method could be used to estimate the composition of the alloy. Suggest what is likely to be the appearance of the X-ray diffraction pattern if the amount of added element exceeds 5 atomic per cent.

(Trent Polytechnic)

Solution 2.11

(a) The arc subtended by first pair of lines is 44.52 mm and radius, R, of the camera is $57.5 \div 2 = 28.75$ mm.

The angle included, $4\theta = 44.52 \div 28.75 = 1.549$ radians, therefore $\theta = (1.549/4) \times (180/\pi) = 22.19°$.

In BCC crystals the first reflection is from plane 2, (110), so $d_{(110)} = \lambda/(2\sin\theta) = 1.541 \times 10^{-10} \div (2 \times \sin 22.19) = 2.04 \times 10^{-10}$ m.

(b) For a BCC structure, the lattice parameter, $a = d_{(110)} \times \sqrt{2}$ and the atomic radius, $r = a\sqrt{3} \div 4$, so $a = 2.04 \times 10^{-10} \times \sqrt{2} = 2.885 \times 10^{-10}$ m and $r = (2.885 \times 10^{-10} \times \sqrt{3})/4 = 1.25 \times 10^{-10}$ m.

(c) When a substitutional solid solution is formed the lattice parameter will be altered. The effective average atomic radius for the 5 atomic per cent solid solution will be $\{(1.25 \times 0.95) + (1.35 \times 0.05)\} \times 10^{-10} = 1.255 \times 10^{-10}$ m giving a new lattice parameter, $a' = 2.898 \times 10^{-10}$ m and $d_{(110)} = 2.049 \times 10^{-10}$ m. From this the value of θ can be obtained and the distance between the closest pair of lines calculated to be 44.32 mm. This is a difference of only 0.2 mm from the distance for a pure metal sample. If one considers the outer reflecting planes, the highest plane which will give reflections in this metal, using the same wavelength radiation, will be plane 12 (222). (*Note*: The method of finding the highest index reflecting plane is given in the solution to example 2.10.) Plane 12 will give a line separation distance of 134.6 mm for the pure metal and a line separation distance of 135.9 mm for the 5 per cent alloy. The diffraction lines on an exposed film may have a thickness of 0.5–1.0 mm and so this degree of difference between the line separation distances for the pure metal and alloy is probably insufficient to use as a reliable method for estimating alloy composition. If the alloy content exceeds 5 per cent FCC solid solution will appear as a second phase. The diffraction pattern will contain lines from the FCC crystals in addition to the BCC pattern. These will be of low density as there will not be a large amount of the FCC phase present.

Example 2.12

The X-ray diffraction pattern of a cubic crystal, using radiation of wavelength 1.54×10^{-10} m, gives lines at the following angles: 21.66°, 31.47°, 39.74°, 47.58°, 55.63°, 64.71° and 77.59°.

Determine: **(a)**   the structure of the crystal,
                (b)   the Miller indices of the reflecting planes, and
                (c)   the lattice parameter.

(Polytechnic of Central London)

Solution 2.12

The material is said to be of cubic structure but the exact type is not specified and so it could be simple cubic, BCC or FCC. The first seven reflecting planes for each of these three systems are:

    simple cubic—planes 1, 2, 3, 4, 5, 6 and 8 (see note below)
    BCC—planes 2, 4, 6, 8, 10, 12 and 14
    FCC—planes 3, 4, 8, 11, 12, 16 and 19.

Note: The sum of the squares of three small integers cannot equate to 7, so there can be no plane with an index number of 7.

From inspection the angles appear to have a regular spacing, indicating simple cubic or BCC, rather than FCC.

Using the Bragg equation $\lambda = 2d \sin\theta$ or $d = \dfrac{\lambda}{2 \sin\theta}$

Considering the first two angles, $d_1 = \dfrac{1.54 \times 10^{-10}}{2 \sin 21.66°} = 2.086 \times 10^{-10}$ m

and $d_2 = \dfrac{1.54 \times 10^{-10}}{2 \sin 31.47°} = 1.475 \times 10^{-10}$ m

Using the relationship $a = d\sqrt{(h^2 + k^2 + l^2)}$

Assuming simple cubic, $a = 2.086 \times 10^{-10}$ m and $a = 1.475 \times 10^{-10} \times \sqrt{2}$
$$= 2.086 \times 10^{-10} \text{ m}$$
Assuming BCC, $a = 2.086 \times 10^{-10} \times \sqrt{2} = 2.95 \times 10^{-10}$ m and $a = 1.475 \times 10^{-10} \times 2$
$$= 2.95 \times 10^{-10} \text{ m}$$

The first two reflections are consistent with either a simple cubic or BCC structure but would be inconsistent with a FCC structure. To distinguish between simple cubic and BCC consider the seventh reflection. This could either be from plane 8 (simple cubic) or plane 14 (BCC).

$$d = \frac{1.54 \times 10^{-10}}{2 \sin 77.59°} = 0.788 \times 10^{-10}$$

If simple cubic $a = 0.788 \times 10^{-10} \times \sqrt{8} = 2.23 \times 10^{-10}$ m
If BCC $\qquad a = 0.788 \times 10^{-10} \times \sqrt{14} = 2.95 \times 10^{-10}$ m
From the above only a BCC structure would be consistent with the measured reflection angles.

The reflecting planes are: 2(110), 4(200), 6(211), 8(220), 10(310), 12(222) and 14(321).

The lattice parameter of the cell is 2.95×10^{-10} m.

2.3 Questions

Question 2.1

Give the Miller indices for the planes A, B, C, D and E in the accompanying figures.

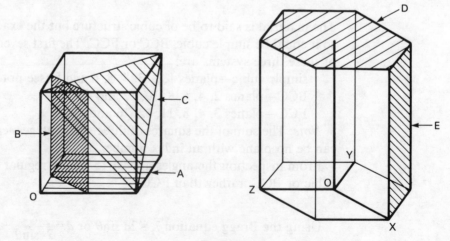

Figure 2.15

Question 2.2

Give the Miller indices for the directions A, B, C, D and E in the accompanying figures.

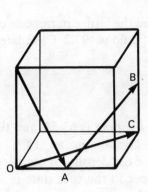
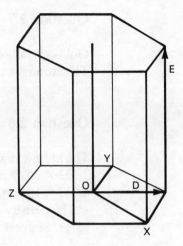

Figure 2.16

Question 2.3

Sketch a cubic unit cell and mark the positions of both a (221) and a (110) plane on the sketch. Draw a line in each of the two planes and give the Miller indices for the directions of your lines.

Question 2.4

A crystal of high purity sodium chloride is used for determining the wavelength of monochromatic X-radiation. Determine the wavelength of the radiation if a first order Bragg reflection from the (111) planes of sodium chloride occurs at an angle of 5.2°. The lattice parameter, a, for sodium chloride is 5.63×10^{-10} m.

Question 2.5

X-radiation of wavelength 6.25×10^{-11} m is directed at a metal sample showing a cubic crystallinity. The first three Bragg reflections occur at angles of 7.7°, 8.9° and 12.7°.

Determine: **(a)** the type of crystal structure and
(b) the lattice parameter of the unit cell.

Question 2.6

When X-radiation of wavelength 0.179 nm strikes a sample of copper a first order reflection from the (111) set of planes occurs at an angle of 25°25′. Calculate the atomic radius of copper atoms, given that copper crystallises as FCC.

(Polytechnic of Central London)

37

Question 2.7

Gold crystallises as FCC and the lattice parameter of the unit cell is 4.07×10^{-10} m. The atomic mass number of gold is 197.2. Calculate the theoretical density of gold.

Question 2.8

The atomic mass number of copper is 63.54, and the atomic diameter of copper is 2.552×10^{-10} m. Copper crystallises as FCC. Avogadro's number, N_0 is 6.023×10^{23}/mole. Calculate the density of copper.

The density of pure copper in the cast state is slightly less than the calculated value. Suggest reasons for this.

(Polytechnic of Central London)

Question 2.9

A powdered sample of metal M is subjected to X-rays of wavelength 1.786×10^{-10} m in a camera of diameter 5.08×10^{-2} m. The distances between the arcs for the first six reflected cones of radiation are 4.19, 6.09, 7.77, 9.42, 11.23 and 13.9×10^{-2} m respectively.

Determine the following:
(a) the crystal arrangement for metal M,
(b) the lattice parameter,
(c) the density of M if its atomic mass number $= 185.35$.
Assume Avogadro's number $= 6.023 \times 10^{26}$ kmol^{-1}.

(Salford)

Question 2.10

An X-ray diffractometer recorder chart for an element with a cubic structure shows diffraction peaks at the following 2θ angles (in degrees): 40, 58, 73, 86.8, 100.4, and 114.7.

If the wavelength of the X-rays used was 0.154 nm, determine:
(a) the cubic structure of the element, and
(b) the lattice parameter.

(Salford)

Question 2.11

Copper atoms are 2.552×10^{-10} m in diameter and form into a FCC structure. X-radiation of wavelength 1.52×10^{-10} m is used for the analysis of two samples of copper. For sample A the first order Bragg reflection from (111) planes occurred at an angle of 21°00′, while for sample B the first order Bragg reflection from (111) planes was at 21°23′.

Give an explanation for the difference between the two samples.

(Polytechnic of Central London)

Question 2.12

Copper is FCC with an atomic radius of 1.278 Å. How many atoms are there per mm² on the (100) crystal planes?

(City University)

Question 2.13

High density polyethylene shows a high degree of crystallinity and the hydrocarbon chains pack themselves into an orthorhombic form. The parameters of the unit cell are: $a = 7.41 \times 10^{-10}$ m, $b = 4.94 \times 10^{-10}$ m and $c = 2.55 \times 10^{-10}$ m. Find the number of atoms in a unit cell. Take density of HD polyethylene = 965 kg/m³, atomic mass numbers: C = 12, H = 1, formula of polyethylene $(C_2H_4)_n$, Avogadro's number = 6.023×10^{23}/mol

2.4 Answers to Questions

2.1 Plane A = (00$\bar{1}$) (obtain by transposition of origin to C), Plane B = (220), Plane C = (1$\bar{1}$1) (refer to sketch. Extend plane into next unit cell where it cuts the B axis at unit distance in the negative direction), Plane D = (0001), Plane E = (10$\bar{1}$0)

2.2 Direction A = [10$\bar{2}$], Direction B = [121], Direction C = [110], Direction D = [$\bar{1}$000], Direction E = [0001]

2.3 Refer to sketch below.

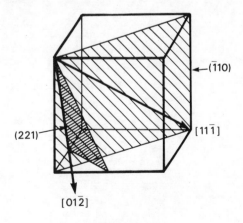

Figure 2.17

The two marked directions are [01$\bar{2}$] and [11$\bar{1}$]

2.4 $\lambda = 0.59 \times 10^{-10}$ m

2.5 Structure is FCC, lattice parameter is 4.04×10^{-10} m

2.6 $r = 1.277 \times 10^{-10}$ m.

2.7 Calculated density of gold $= 19.425 \times 10^3$ kg/m^3

2.8 Calculated density of copper $= 8.98 \times 10^3$ kg/m^3. The theoretical density of pure copper, as calculated, is slightly greater than the experimentally determined density of pure cast copper. There are two contributory reasons for this. Firstly, the calculations are based on the assumption that the crystal lattice is perfect and does not contain lattice defects, such as vacancies. Secondly, there is always the possibility of there being some porosity in a casting, be it micro-shrinkage porosity or gross gas porosity.

2.9 **(a)** BCC; **(b)** $a = 3.16 \times 10^{-10}$ m; $\rho = 19.51$ kg/m^3.

2.10 **(a)** BCC; **(b)** 0.318 nm.

2.11 The lattice parameter for sample B is the same as that calculated for pure copper. Therefore sample B is high-purity copper. The lattice parameter for sample A is 1.75 per cent greater than that for pure copper. Sample A is not pure and the presence of impurity atoms (in solid solution) has imposed strain in the crystal lattice of the copper.

2.12 1.53×10^{13}/mm^2.

2.13 Assume a unit cell contains x carbon atoms and $2x$ hydrogen atoms. Find mass of x carbon and $2x$ hydrogen atoms. Calculate volume of unit cell from data given. Knowing density x can be evaluated. $x = 3.87 \simeq 4$. Cell contains four carbon and eight hydrogen atoms.

3 Defects in Crystals and Plastic Deformation

3.1 Fact Sheet

(a)

Plastic deformation in metals takes place by a process of slip on certain crystal planes under the action of a shear stress. The slip planes are those of greatest atomic packing and slip across a slip plane occurs in specific directions, namely the lines of greatest atom density. The combination of a slip plane and a slip direction is termed a slip system.

Structure	Slip plane	Slip direction	No. of slip planes	No. of slip directions per plane	Total no. of slip systems
FCC	{111}	<110>	4	3	12
BCC	{110}	<111>	6	2	12
HCP	(0001)	[1000]	1	3	3

(Refer to Chapter 2 for details of planes and directions.)

(b)

The resolved shear stress, τ, on a slip plane within a crystal subject to a direct stress, σ, is given by: $\tau = \sigma \cos\theta.\cos\varphi$, where θ is the angle between the direct stress axis and the slip direction and φ is the angle between the direct stress axis and the normal to the slip plane. (See example 3.1 for proof.)

(c)

The theoretical value of shear stress, τ_c, necessary to initiate slip in a crystal is given by: $\tau_c \simeq G/2\pi$, where G is the modulus of rigidity.

The experimentally observed values of shear stress required to initiate slip in metals are very much lower than the theoretical values owing to the presence of lattice defects (see below).

(d)

Crystals contain certain structural defects which may be *line defects* or *point defects*.

Line defects are termed *dislocations* and the two main types are known as *edge* dislocations and *screw* dislocations. In practice, a dislocation is a loop or part of a loop and will be part edge and part screw. (Line defects are described in the solution to example 3.3.)

The main point defects in metal crystals are *vacancies*, *substitutionalcies*, *interstitialcies* and *Frenkel* defects. (These defect types are illustrated in the solution to example 3.5.)

(e)

Plastic deformation, by slip, in metal crystals occurs through the movement of dislocations across slip planes under the influence of a shear stress. The *Burger's vector*, b, gives the direction in which slip occurs and its magnitude is equal to one increment of slip.

(f)

Point defects interact with dislocations and render the movement of dislocations more difficult. The introduction of point defects into a lattice increases the yield strength of the material. There are three main strengthening mechanisms for metals. These are: *strain hardening*, *solution hardening* and *dispersion hardening*.

(g)

Crystal grain boundaries act as barriers to the movement of dislocations. Consequently, a fine-grain-sized metal is stronger than a coarse-grained sample of the same metal. The yield strength is related to the grain size by the Petch equation: $\sigma_y = \sigma_0 + K d^{-1/2}$, where σ_y is the yield strength, d is the average grain diameter in mm and σ_0 and K are constants for the metal.

(h)

Grain size is determined by counting the number of grains observed in a known area during microexamination of a prepared sample. The result may be expressed as number of grains/mm^2 or as an ASTM index number. The ASTM index number is based on the number of grains/in^2 as counted at a magnification of $\times$ 100. The ASTM index, n, is given by: $N = 2^{(n-1)}$, where N is the number of grains/in^2 at $\times$ 100.

3.2 Worked Examples

Example 3.1

(a) Derive an expression for the critical resolved shear stress required to produce plastic deformation in a single crystal.

(b) Describe the tensile behaviour of a magnesium single crystal specimen commenting on the influence of orientation on the load/elongation curve.

(c) The critical shear stress for the $\langle\bar{1}10\rangle\{111\}$ slip system of a pure FCC metal was found to be 1.5 MPa. What stress must be applied in the [001] direction to produce slip in (i) the [101] direction on the $(\bar{1}11)$ plane and (ii) in the [011] direction on the $(\bar{1}1\bar{1})$ plane?

Solution 3.1

(a) Derivation of resolved shear stress. When a material is subject to a direct stress, σ, a resolved shear stress, τ, will exist on some plane XZ inclined at some angle θ. Consider the prism XYZ. Diagram (b) shows the stresses acting on this prism. The forces, F, F_θ and F_s (diagram (c)) must be in equilibrium. Force = stress $\times$ area, so if the thickness of the prism XYZ is w then $F = \sigma \times XY \times w$, $F_\theta = \sigma_\theta \times XZ \times w$ and $F_s = \tau \times XZ \times w$.

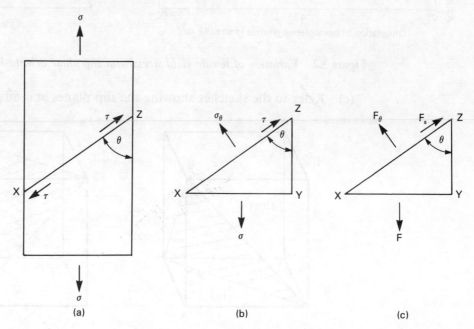

Figure 3.1 *Resolution of shear stress*

Resolving along XZ: $\tau \times XZ \times w = \sigma \times XY \times w \times \cos\theta$

$$\tau = \sigma \times (XY/XZ) \times \cos\theta$$
$$= \sigma \times \sin\theta.\cos\theta = \tfrac{1}{2}\sigma\sin2\theta$$

This expression can also be written $\tau = \sigma \times \cos\varphi.\cos\theta$, where $\varphi = 90° - \theta$, namely the angle between the line of stress and the normal to the plane.

43

The critical resolved shear stress on a plane inclined at some angle θ is $\frac{1}{2}\sigma \sin 2\theta$. This function is a maximum, $= \frac{1}{2}\sigma$, when $\theta = 45°$ and is zero when $\theta = 0°$ or $90°$. The variation of σ with θ for a constant value of τ is shown in the accompanying diagram.

(b) Magnesium crystallises as HCP and has one set of parallel slip planes, the basal planes. If these planes are aligned at $0°$ or $90°$ to the line of direct stress there will be no shear stress on the slip planes, hence no slip, and the crystal will fracture in a brittle manner when the fracture stress is exceeded. For crystals with the basal planes aligned at some other angle a shear stress will be developed and when this exceeds the critical value, slip will occur.

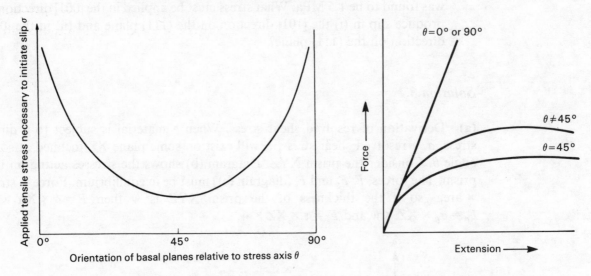

Figure 3.2 *Variation of tensile yield stress with slip plane orientation*

(c) Refer to the sketches showing the slip planes and directions.

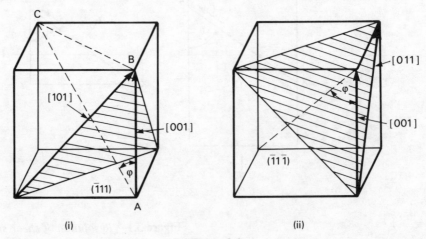

Figure 3.3

By inspection it can be seen that, in both cases, the angle θ between the line of direct stress, [001] and the direction of slip, [101] or [011], is $45°$. The angle between [001] and the normal to the slip plane in (i) is $\sin^{-1} BC/AC$. But $BC = a\sqrt{2}$ and $AC = a\sqrt{3}$, so $\varphi = \sin^{-1}\sqrt{2}/\sqrt{3} = 54.74°$. It can be shown that in (ii) φ is also $54.74°$.

From the expression $\tau = \sigma \times \cos\theta.\cos\varphi$ then $\sigma = 1.5 \div (\cos 45°.\cos 54.74°)$
$$= 3.67\ \text{MPa}.$$

Example 3.2

(a) During the elastic deformation of an annealed single crystal of an HCP metal in a tensile test, an extension of 0.1 per cent was caused by a stress of 200 N/mm^2. Estimate the theoretical strength of the material, given that $G = E/2(1 + v)$ and that v for the metal is 0.3.

(b) If the specimen in (a) starts to deform plastically at a tensile load of 8 kN, calculate the critical resolved shear stress, given that the specimen is cylindrical with a diameter of 5 mm and that the slip plane and slip direction are at 45° to the tensile axis. Briefly explain any difference between this result and that found in **(a)**.

(Trent Polytechnic)

Solution 3.2

(a) $E = \sigma/\varepsilon$, $\sigma = 200\ \text{N/mm}^2 = 200\ \text{MPa}$, $\varepsilon = 0.001$, so $E = 200\ \text{GPa}$

$G = E/2(1 + v) = 200 \div (2(1 + 0.3)) = 76.9\ \text{GPa}$

$\tau_c = G/2\pi = 76.9/2\pi = 12.24\ \text{GPa}.$

The theoretical shear strength of this metal is 12.24 GPa.

(b) The tensile stress acting, $\sigma = 8000 \div \pi 5^2/4 = 407.4\ \text{N/mm}^2 = 407.4\ \text{MPa}$

$\tau = \sigma \cos\theta.\cos\varphi = 407.4 \cos 45°.\cos 45° = 203.7\ \text{MPa}$

The critical resolved shear stress for the start of plastic deformation is 203.7 MPa, which is about 1/380 of the theoretical shear strength calculated in (a). The reason for the discrepancy is that in the theoretical calculation it is assumed that the crystal lattice is perfect. The presence of dislocation defects in the crystal permits slip by dislocation movement at much lower levels of stress.

Example 3.3

Describe, with the aid of sketches, **(a)** an edge dislocation, **(b)** a screw dislocation and **(c)** a dislocation loop.

In each case, show the relationship between the dislocation line and the Burger's vector.

Solution 3.3

(a) An edge dislocation can be regarded as an additional half-plane of atoms inserted into the crystal lattice.

(b) In a screw dislocation a portion of the lattice has been skewed,

(c) The accompanying diagram shows a portion of a curved dislocation line which is of the screw type at X and of the edge type at Y. This could be part of a complete loop.

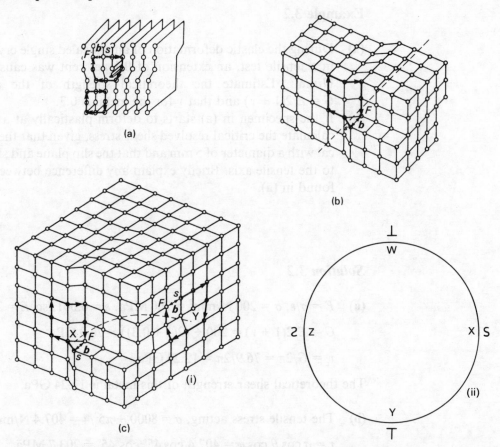

Figure 3.4 *(a) Edge dislocation, Burger's vector, **b**, normal to dislocation; (b) Screw dislocation, Burger's vector, **b**, parallel to dislocation; (c) (i) Part of dislocation loop that is screw at X and edge at Y, Burger's vector, **b**, constant at all points; (ii) complete dislocation loop, edge type at W and Y, screw type at X and Z, Burger's vector constant at all points.*

In a complete loop, it will be of edge type at two diametrically opposite points, the edge dislocations being of opposite sign. Similarly the two parts of the loop of pure screw type will be of opposing sign.

To obtain the Burger's vector, *b*, describe a circuit moving an equal number of lattice spacings in each direction. In a dislocated lattice, the closure vector necessary to complete the circuit is the Burger's vector. The Burger's vector is normal to an edge dislocation but parallel to a screw dislocation. The Burger's vector is the same at all points on a dislocation loop. The Burger's vector indicates the direction in which slip will occur.

Example 3.4

A metal crystal with a FCC structure of lattice parameter 3.61×10^{-10} m contains an edge dislocation lying in a (111) plane. Determine the magnitude and direction of the Burger's vector.

Solution 3.4

The direction of the Burger's vector is normal to the dislocation line, namely normal to a (110) plane. The direction normal to a (110) plane is [110]. The magnitude of the Burger's vector is equal to the interplanar spacing, namely $a/\sqrt{(h^2 + k^2 + l^2)} = 3.61 \times 10^{-10} \div \sqrt{2} = 2.553 \times 10^{-10}$ m.

Example 3.5

Describe with the aid of sketches four types of point defect which may occur in metal crystals and indicate the way in which they affect the lattice.

Solution 3.5

A vacancy occurs when an atom is missing from a normal lattice point.

A substitutionalcy occurs when a lattice point is occupied by a stranger atom, but one of roughly comparable size to the parent metal atoms.

An interstitialcy occurs when a stranger atom is fitted into the structure, but not at a normal lattice point. Usually interstitial atoms are very much smaller than the parent metal atoms.

A Frenkel defect is an interstitial-vacancy pair formed when an atom moves into an interstitial site, leaving behind a vacancy.

These various point defects are shown in the diagram.

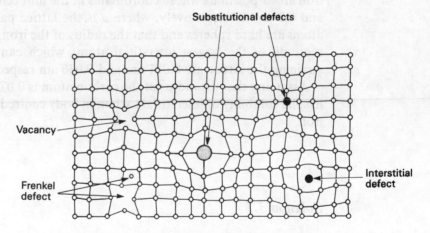

Figure 3.5 *Lattice containing several types of point defect*

All these defects cause the lattice to be strained. Substitutional atoms may be either larger or smaller than the parent metal atoms creating either positive or negative lattice strain. Interstitial atoms, although small, are usually larger than the maximum size interstice and cause positive strain.

Example 3.6

The density of a sample of pure iron is determined experimentally and found to be

7875 kg/m^3. If the radius of an iron atom is 1.24×10^{-10} m and the crystal structure is body-centred cubic, calculate the percentage of vacancies in the pure iron.

Avogadro's number $= 6.023 \times 10^{26}$/kmol, atomic weight of iron $= 55.85$ kg/kmol.

Solution 3.6

Calculate the theoretical density of iron (refer to chapter 2).

$$\text{Lattice parameter} = \frac{4r}{\sqrt{3}} = \frac{4 \times 1.24 \times 10^{-10}}{\sqrt{3}} = 2.864 \times 10^{-10} \text{ m.}$$

$$\rho = \frac{\text{mass of two atoms}}{\text{volume of unit cell}} = \frac{2 \times 55.85}{6.023 \times 10^{26} \times (2.864 \times 10^{-10})^3} = 7894 \text{ kg/m}^3$$

$$\text{Percentage difference in density is} = \frac{7894 - 7875}{7894} \times 100 = 0.23 \text{ per cent}$$

This is equivalent to the percentage vacancies in the lattice.

Example 3.7

The largest sites for interstitial atoms in face-centred cubic and body-centred cubic iron are at positions whose coordinates in the unit cell are of the type $(a/2,a/2,a/2)$ and $(a2/,a/4,0)$ respectively, where a is the lattice parameter. Assuming that the atoms are hard spheres and that the radius of the iron atom is 0.124 nm, show that the radii of the largest interstitial atoms which can occupy these sites without straining the lattice are 0.051 nm and 0.036 nm respectively.

Assuming that the radius of the carbon atom is 0.077 nm, explain the differences in solid solubility of interstitial carbon in body centred cubic and face centred cubic iron.

(Southampton University)

Solution 3.7

FCC. The $(a/2,a/2,a/2)$ site is the mid-point of the unit cell. Sketch a (200) plane. The diameter of the available space is seen to be $(a - 2r)$.

The lattice parameter, a, for FCC $= 2r\sqrt{2} = 2 \times 0.124 \times \sqrt{2} = 0.351$ nm.

Diameter of maximum space $= 0.351 - 0.248 = 0.103$ nm, so radius $= 0.0515$ nm.

BCC. Sketch a (100) plane and mark in the $(a/2,a/4,0)$ site. It will be seen that the radius of the available space is $\sqrt{\{(a/2)^2 + (a/4)^2\}} - r$.

The lattice parameter, a, for BCC $= 4r \div \sqrt{3} = (4 \times 0.124) \div \sqrt{3} = 0.286$ nm.

Radius of maximum space is $\sqrt{\{(0.143^2 + 0.0715^2)\}} - 0.124 = 0.036$ nm.

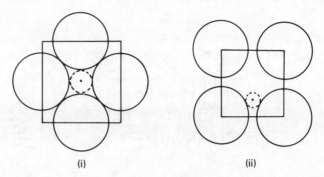

Figure 3.6 *(i) (200) plane in FCC showing (a/2,a/2,a/2) site, (ii) (100) plane in BCC showing (a/2,a/4,0) site*

The diameter of a carbon atom, at 0.077 nm, is about 50 per cent larger than the size of space available in the FCC lattice and more than 110 per cent larger than the size space available in the BCC lattice. The amount of lattice strain caused by a carbon atom entering an interstitial site in the BCC structure will be very great and solid solubility will be very restricted. The amount of strain caused by carbon entering the FCC structure, though large, will be very much less than for BCC and solubility of carbon, although restricted, will be greater than in BCC iron.

Example 3.8

A simple model for the yielding of steel suggests that this should occur at stresses of about 15 GPa. In practice the observed value is rarely higher than 0.05 GPa.

Discuss how the presence of dislocations in the lattice allows the metal to yield at the lower stresses.

Give a short description of three mechanisms that can be used to hinder the movement of dislocations and thus strengthen metals and alloys.

(Southampton University)

Solution 3.8

The simple model which suggests a high yield strength for steel (and other metals) is based on the assumption that the lattice is defect free and slip occurs by the movement of blocks of atoms relative to one another. Metal crystals contain defects known as dislocations. Consider an edge dislocation, as in the accompanying diagram. A shear stress, in the direction of the Burger's vector, will cause the dislocation to move through the lattice generating one increment of plastic deformation.

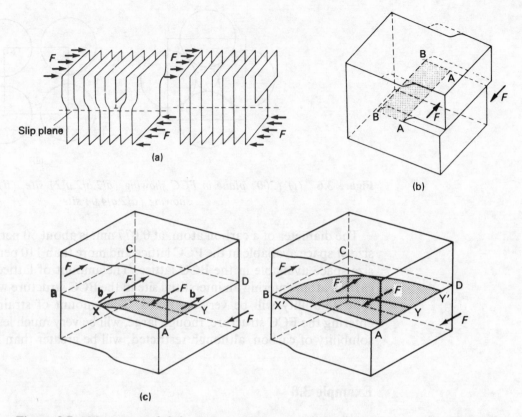

Figure 3.7 *Movement of dislocation under action of shear stress. (a) edge dislocation: application of shear stress F causes the dislocation to move along the slip plane until it leaves this section of lattice causing an increment of plastic deformation; (b) screw dislocation; application of a shear stress F will cause the dislocation to move from AA to BB (slipped area is shaded); (c) slip caused by movement of curved dislocation line across a slip plane ABCD. The dislocation moves from XY to X'Y' (slipped region is shown shaded)*

The stress needed to move a dislocation is a very small fraction of that needed to cause block slip. Similarly, a screw dislocation can move but, in this case, the dislocation moves in a direction normal to the line of stress but the plastic deformation is in the direction of the Burger's vector.

Anything that will hinder the movement of dislocations will increase the shear yield stress, and hence strengthen the metal. The three mechanisms for strengthening metals are strain hardening, solution hardening and dispersion hardening.

Strain hardening. When stressed beyond the elastic limit, dislocations will move across slip planes. This movement will continue until a dislocation reaches some barrier to progress, for example a grain boundary. Continued dislocation movement and further plastic deformation can occur only if the stress is raised so that dislocations may be moved across potential barriers. Additional dislocations are generated during plastic deformation. Slip may be occurring simultaneously in several slip systems. In cubic crystals, with intersecting slip planes, the dislocations may interfere with one another's movement and tangles of dislocations will be created. This, again, will require the imposition of higher stresses to give further dislocation movement. During severe cold working the dislocation density within a metal may be increased from some 10^4–10^6/mm^2 in annealed material to between 10^9 and 10^{10}/mm^2. Severe cold working will increase the tensile yield strength of pure aluminium from about 30 MPa to about 120 MPa but this increase in strength will be accompanied by a major reduction in ductility.

Solution hardening. The presence of substitutional or interstitial solute atoms in a crystal lattice will cause strain and distortion and the value of shear stress required to move dislocations will be increased. Many alloys of commercial importance are solid solution alloys. For example, magnesium can enter into solid solution in aluminium to a limited extent and the tensile yield strengths for alloys containing 2 per cent and 4 per cent magnesium are 75 MPa and 120 MPa respectively, compared with 30 MPa for pure aluminium. Strain hardening can be coupled with solution hardening and the tensile yield strength of an aluminium/2 per cent magnesium alloy can be increased to over 200 MPa by cold working.

Dispersion hardening. Major increases in yield strength can be achieved in some metallic systems by developing a microstructure containing a fine dispersion of very fine second phase or precipitated particles. Such structures may be obtained by one of two means, either by a mechanical dispersion of an insoluble phase such as a refractory oxide throughout the metal, or by a precipitation heat treatment. In some specific alloys, a metastable solid solution can be obtained by very rapid cooling of the alloy from a high temperature. Subsequent reheating at a relatively low temperature, or natural ageing in some cases, will permit diffusion of solute atoms and the formation of extremely fine, but widely dispersed, precipitate particles (see also solution 3.9**(b)**(iii)) giving a large increase in strength. A good example of this is an aluminium/4½ per cent copper alloy. In the annealed condition, with a structure composed of dilute solid solution and coarse precipitate particles, the yield strength is about 250 MPa, but the fully precipitation hardened alloy has a yield strength of about 500 MPa.

Example 3.9

(a) Describe a mechanism for the generation of dislocations under the action of an applied shear stress.
(b) Give a brief account of the following:
  (i) the yield point phenomenon in mild steel,
  (ii) dislocation climb and creep,
  (iii) hindering effect of coherent and non-coherent precipitates.

Solution 3.9

One suggested mechanism for dislocation generation is the Frank–Read source. A dislocation line may be firmly anchored at certain points by obstacles or defects within the lattice. Application of a shear force will cause the length of dislocation line between anchor points to bow. As the stress is increased the bowing increases and a kidney-shaped loop develops. Growth continues and the two sections of the loop moving towards one another cancel out when they meet, as they are of opposing sign. This forms a complete loop and a new length of dislocation line, as shown in the accompanying figures.

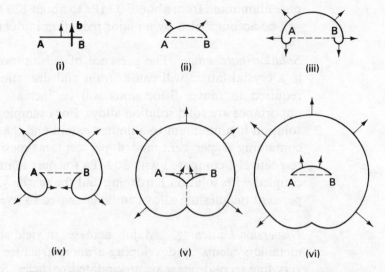

Figure 3.8 *Dislocation generation from a Frank–Read source*

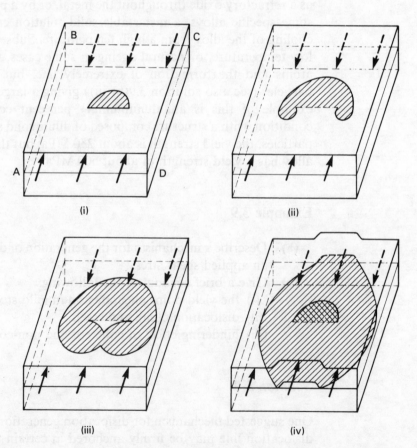

Figure 3.9 *Dislocation loops developing from a Frank–Read source on a slip plane ABCD*

(b) (i) Mild steel, unlike other metals, does not show a gradual transition from elastic to plastic behaviour but yields suddenly when the elastic limit is reached and plastic deformation continues to some extent without the applied stress having to be raised. (See figure below.) If, after yielding, the stress is removed and then reimposed the sudden yield phenomenon will not occur. If, however, after yielding the material is aged for about a week at ordinary temperature (or a shorter period at slightly elevated temperatures) and retested it will be found that the sudden yield behaviour returns. Mild steel contains some carbon in interstitial solid solution. The interstices along a dislocation line are slightly larger than the normal interstitial sites and carbon atoms tend to diffuse to positions on the dislocation lines. This tends to lock the dislocation in position and a high stress is needed to initiate movement. Once the dislocations have been freed from carbon atoms motion can continue at a lower stress. During ageing carbon atoms diffuse through the lattice to points on dislocation lines.

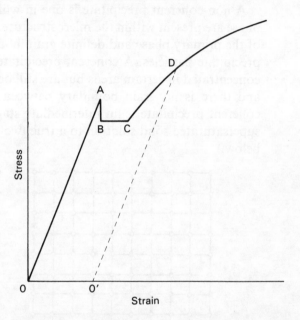

Figure 3.10 *Tensile stress–strain curve for mild steel showing sharp yield point*

(ii) Vacancies can migrate through a crystal lattice. This movement is a diffusion type effect and is a thermally activated process (see chapter 5). When a vacancy reaches a point at a dislocation line, the vacancy will collapse and the dislocation will move up to the next lattice plane at that point. This is termed a *jog*, but if many vacancies diffuse to the same area then a large portion of a dislocation line will climb to the next plane. This effect is shown in the diagram below.

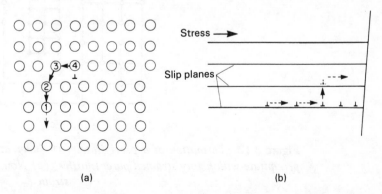

(a)   (b)

Figure 3.11 *Dislocation climb. (a) Lattice containing vacancy and dislocation. If numbered atoms diffuse into vacancy, the vacancy will move to position 4 causing dislocation to climb, (b) Dislocation pile-up at barrier. Climb will permit further dislocation movement*

If, under stress, a series of dislocations have moved until they pile up at a barrier, no further movement and plastic strain can occur unless the stress is increased. However, if thermally activated diffusion and the climb of dislocations occur then a small amount of further dislocation movement can occur without the stress having to be raised. This is a possible mechanism of metallic creep.

(iii) Under some circumstances precipitates within a microstructure can hinder the movement of dislocations and have a major strengthening effect. This is one aspect of dispersion strengthening.

A non-coherent precipitate is one in which separate small crystals of a second phase are present within the microstructure. The crystal lattice is distinct from that of the primary phase and definite grain boundaries exist between the primary and precipitate particles. A coherent precipitate is where solute atoms in a lattice are concentrated in certain areas but are still occupying sites in the parent metal lattice and there is no grain boundary between the main lattice and 'precipitate'. A coherent precipitate is an intermediate stage in the transition from a metastable supersaturated solid solution to a true two-phase structure. (Refer to the diagram below.)

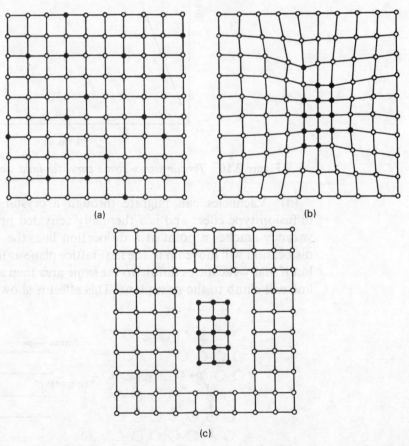

(a)   (b)

(c)

Figure 3.12 *Formation of a precipitate. (a) Supersaturated solid solution, (b) Coherent precipitate with highly strained parent lattice, (c) Non-coherent precipitate relieving lattice strain*

In the formation of a coherent precipitate, areas of very high strain are created within the lattice and these high strain areas will offer great resistance to the movement of dislocations, producing a major strengthening effect. When a non-coherent precipitate begins to form some of the strain in the parent lattice is released and the strength decreases. Non-coherent precipitate particles will offer resistance to the movement of dislocations but the extent of this resistance and, hence, the strength of the material will be related to the size and distribution of the particles with widely dispersed small precipitate particles offering greater resistance than a smaller number of large and widely separated particles.

During precipitation hardening, the strength of the alloy increases as diffusion of solute atoms occurs forming coherent precipitate areas, reaching a maximum immediately prior to the separation of non-coherent crystals. As the amount of non-coherent precipitate increases so the strength reduces. This effect is termed over-ageing.

Example 3.10

(a) A grain count on a sample of mild steel at a magnification of $\times 100$ gives a value of 160 grains/in^2. Calculate the ASTM grain size for this material.
(b) The Petch equation $\sigma_y = \sigma_0 + K d^{-1/2}$ relates the yield strength of a material to its grain size. A steel sample with an ASTM grain size of 6 has a tensile yield stress of 275 MPa, one with an ASTM grain size of 8 has a yield strength of 318 MPa and one with an ASTM grain size of 10 has a yield strength of 375 MPa. Evaluate the constants K and σ_0 and explain the significance of σ_0.

What would be the expected yield strength of a steel sample with an average grain diameter of 0.03 mm?

Solution 3.10

(a) 160 grains/in^2 at $\times 100$ magnification = $N = 2^{(n-1)}$
$\log 160 = (n - 1) \log 2$ so $(n = 1) = 2.204 \div 0.301 = 7.32$
The ASTM grain size, $n = 8.32$.

(b) For $n = 6$, the number of grains/in^2 at $\times 100$, $N = 2^5 = 32$. The number of grains/mm^2 = $32(100^2/25^2) = 512$. The number of grains/mm = $\sqrt{512} = 22.63$ giving a grain diameter of 0.044 mm. Similarly for $n = 8$ and $n = 10$ the grain diameters are calculated to be 0.022 and 0.011 mm respectively.

A graph plot of σ_y against diameter $d^{-1/2}$ can be drawn and the slope is equal to K. The intercept at the ordinate gives a value for σ_0.
The slope of the graph is 21.05 MPa mm$^{1/2}$ and $\sigma_0 = 175$ MPa.

The significance of σ_0 is that it is the yield stress for a material with no grain boundaries, namely a single crystal.

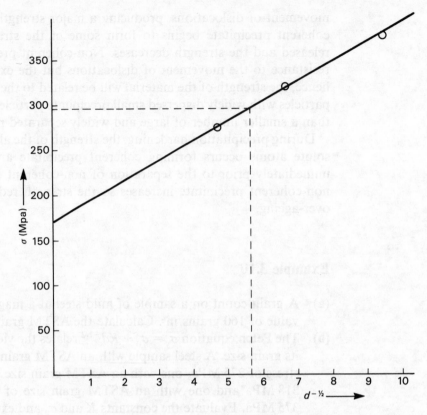

Figure 3.13 *Graph of σ against $d^{-1/2}$*

When $d = 0.03$ mm, $d^{-1/2} = 5.77$. From graph, $\sigma_y = 297$ MPa.

3.3 Questions

Question 3.1

The critical resolved shear stress for slip in a single crystal of pure zinc is 1.8×10^5 Pa. What would be the magnitude of the tensile stress necessary to initiate slip under the following conditions?

(a) Angle between tensile axis and slip direction = 45°,
Angle between tensile axis and normal to slip plane = 45°

(b) Angle between tensile axis and slip direction = 30°,
Angle between tensile axis and normal to slip plane = 60°,

(c) Angle between tensile axis and slip direction = 85°,
Angle between tensile axis and normal to slip plane = 15°.

Question 3.2

The critical resolved shear stress for the {110}⟨111⟩ slip system of a BCC metal is 40 MPa. What would be the stress necessary to initiate slip in the [Ī11] direction on the (110) plane if the stress was applied in the [011] direction?

Question 3.3

Nickel atoms and copper atoms have radii of 1.243×10^{-10} m and 1.276×10^{-10} m respectively and both metals crystallise as FCC. Calculate the proportion of nickel atoms in a copper–nickel FCC solid solution if the lattice parameter of the alloy lattice is found to be 3.58×10^{-10} m.

Question 3.4

Calculate the number of vacancies per 10^6 atoms for a sample of niobium, given that the atomic radius of niobium is 1.426×10^{-10} m and the lattice parameter of the BCC crystal sample is determined as 3.294×10^{-10} m.

Question 3.5

The tensile yield strength of a sample of annealed pure aluminium with an ASTM grain size of 6.5 is 36 MPa and that for a single crystal sample of the metal is 25 MPa. Estimate the tensile yield strengths of samples of aluminium with measured average grain diameters of **(a)** 0.01 mm and **(b)** 0.10 mm.

3.4 Answers to Questions

3.1 **(a)** 0.36 MPa, **(b)** 0.42 MPa, **(c)** 2.14 MPa.
3.2 98 MPa.
3.3 31.2% of the atoms are of nickel.
3.4 690 vacancies/10^6 atoms.
3.5 **(a)** 46.2 MPa, **(b)** 31.7 MPa.

4 Phase Diagrams

4.1 Fact Sheet

(a)

A phase diagram is a map of a system and it shows the phases which should exist under equilibrium conditions for any particular combination of composition and temperature. It consists of lines which divide the diagram into a number of areas or fields. In a binary diagram, the fields may be either single phase or two-phased. Single phase fields are always separated by a two-phase field and three phases can only coexist at a unique point, for example, a eutectic point.

Where a vertical line representing some particular composition crosses a phase diagram line it indicates that some phase change will take place on moving through this temperature.

For any point within a two-phase field, the composition of the two phases in equilibrium with one another can be determined. The positions at which a horizontal tie-line through the point intercept the phase boundary lines denote the compositions of the respective phases.

(b) Lever Rule

The relative proportions of phases present in a two-phase region can be determined using the lever rule. The quantities of phases present are in proportion to the lengths of the lever lines. As an example, consider point U in the accompanying diagram. The phases present are solid A and liquid solution.

$$\frac{\text{quantity of solid A}}{\text{quantity of liquid (composition y)}} = \frac{\text{Uy}}{\text{Ux}}$$

Similarly at V the phases are solid A and B in the ratio

$$\frac{\text{quantity A}}{\text{quantity B}} = \frac{\text{Vr}}{\text{Vp}}$$

Alternatively it could be considered that the phases present are solid A and eutectic mixture in the ratio

$$\frac{\text{quantity of A}}{\text{quantity of eutectic}} = \frac{\text{Vq}}{\text{Vp}}$$

or the percentage of eutectic mixture in the alloy of composition V is

$$\frac{Vp}{pq} \times 100$$

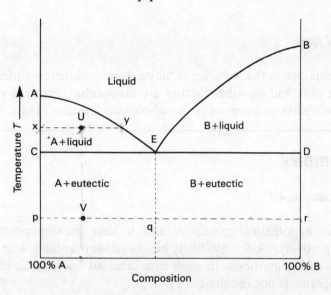

Figure 4.1 *Application of lever rule*

(c) Alloy Formation

Many alloy additions to a metal are taken into solid solution but, depending on the nature of the elements, the extent of solubility may be large or very restricted. The effects of some of the major factors are:

(i) Size

If the relative sizes of the metal atoms lie within 14 per cent of one another, some solid solubility will occur. If relative sizes differ by more than 14 per cent solid solubility, if it occurs at all, will be severely restricted. If the solute atom size is very small in comparison with that of the solvent atoms then an interstitial solid solution may be formed.

(ii) Electro-negativity

When there is a large difference in the degree of electro-negativity of the two elements, the tendency is for solid solubility to be severely restricted and for intermetallic compounds to be formed.

(iii) Valence

Crystal structures are sensitive to a decrease in electron ratio, that is, the ratio of valence electrons to atoms. Consequently a metal of high valence can dissolve little of a metal of lower valence although a metal of low valence may be able to dissolve a large amount of a metal of higher valence.

(iv) Crystal Type

If two metals crystallise in the same form, have atomic diameters differing by not more than 7 per cent and all other factors are favourable then it is possible for complete solid solubility to occur over the whole composition range.

4.2 Worked Examples

Example 4.1

Two hypothetical metals A and B have melting points of 600°C and 850°C respectively. Sketch five likely binary phase diagrams, one for each of the following sets of assumptions. In each case label all features clearly. Interpretation of the diagrams is not required.

(a) Both metals are soluble in one another in all proportions in the solid state.

(b) Both metals are partially soluble in one another in the solid state and a peritectic reaction occurs.

(c) The metals form an intermetallic compound with the formula AB_2.

(d) Both metals are partially soluble in one another in the solid state and an eutectic occurs.

(e) The metals are insoluble in one another in the liquid state.

Solution 4.1

(a) The statement that the two metals are soluble in one another in the solid state presupposes that they must be fully miscible in the liquid state. *(Note that this supposition also applies to (b), (c) and (d).)* The phase diagram must show a single liquid phase at high temperatures and a single solid phase at low temperatures, the two being separated by liquidus and solidus lines. As there is a difference of 250°C between the melting points of A and B, smooth curves without a minimum would be expected.

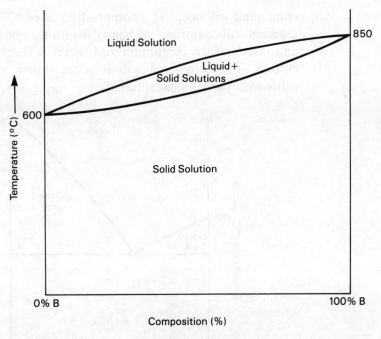

Figure 4.2

(b) Partial solid solubility indicates that there will be two types of solid solution formed, α and β. A peritectic reaction occurs at an unique temperature and is, for cooling, liquid + first solid phase → second solid phase. The phase diagram which shows this relationship is given below.

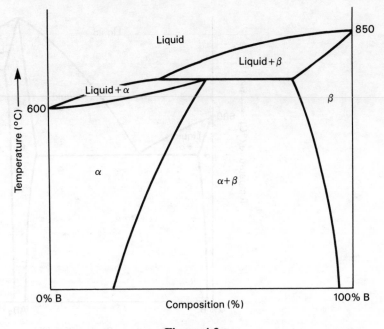

Figure 4.3

(c) Generally an intermetallic compound possesses a different crystal structure from either constituent metal and has a higher melting point. If solid solubility occurs it cannot, therefore, be other than partial. The formula AB_2 shows that the compound will occur at a composition of 66.67 atomic per cent of B. The phase diagram will comprise two binary diagrams, one between metal A and compound and one between compound and metal B. Each section is likely to contain an eutectic. Two alternative solutions are shown, one with no solid solubility, the other with partial solid solubility.

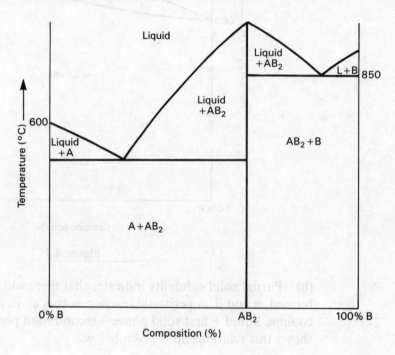

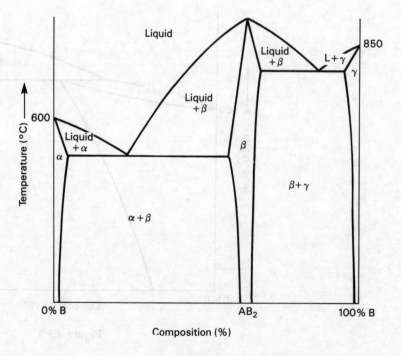

Figure 4.4

(d) As for (b) above there will be two solid phases, α and β, with a eutectic reaction at a temperature below the melting points of the two pure metals.

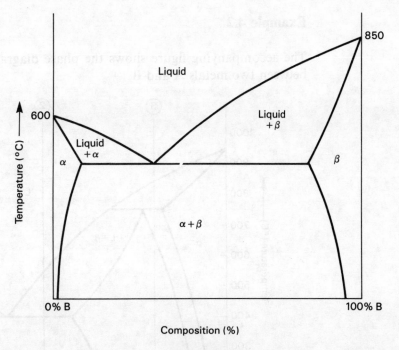

Figure 4.5

(e) Two liquids insoluble in one another will separate into two layers, the less dense floating on top of the more dense. Each metal will solidify at its respective freezing point.

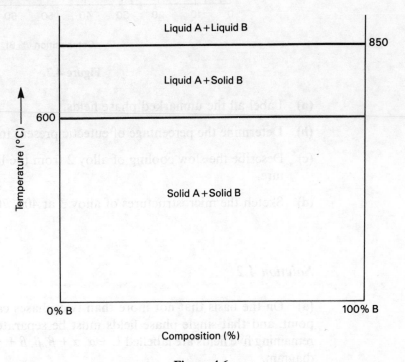

Figure 4.6

Example 4.2

The accompanying figure shows the phase diagram for the binary alloy system between two metals A and B.

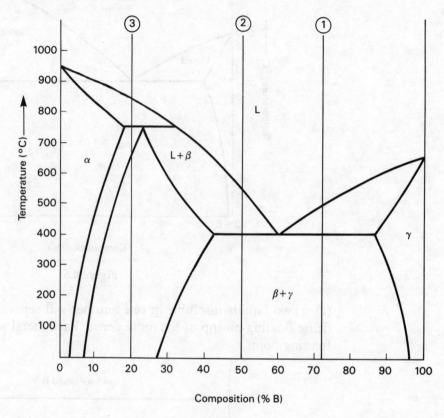

Figure 4.7

(a) Label all the unmarked phase fields.

(b) Determine the percentage of eutectic present in alloy 1 at room temperature.

(c) Describe the slow cooling of alloy 2 from the liquid phase to room temperature.

(d) Sketch the microstructures of alloy 3 at 400, 700 and 800°c.

Solution 4.2

(a) On the basis that not more than two phases can coexist, except at a unique point, and that single phase fields must be separated by a two-phase region the remaining five fields are labelled L + α, α + β, β, β + γ, and L + γ, as in the solution diagram.

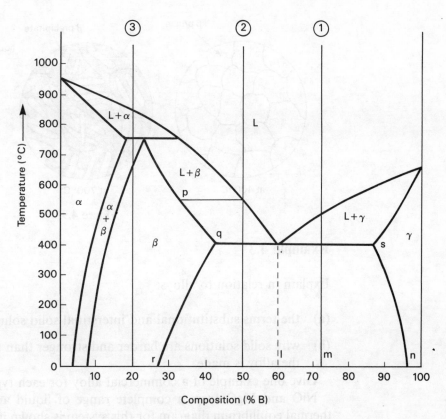

Figure 4.8

(b) The structure of alloy 1 at room temperature is γ and (β + γ) eutectic. Using the lever rule the percentage eutectic in this alloy at room temperature is given by (mn ÷ ln) × 100 = 66 per cent.

(c) A liquid solution with the composition of alloy 2 will begin to solidify at a temperature of about 550°C and the first crystals to form will be of β solid solution with a composition corresponding to p in the accompaning diagram. As the temperature falls the composition of the β phase varies according to the solidus, towards point q while the composition of remaining liquid phase approaches the eutectic composition. When the eutectic temperature (400°C) is reached all remaining liquid solidifies as a fine-graded eutectic mixture of β and γ. As the alloy cools below the eutectic temperature, the compositions of the β and γ phases will vary according to the solvus lines qr and sn.

(d) According to the phase diagram, alloy 3 will be composed entirely of β phase at 400°C, be (α + β) at 700°C, with a high proportion of β phase, and will consist of approximately equal proportions of liquid and α phase at 800°C. These structures are shown below.

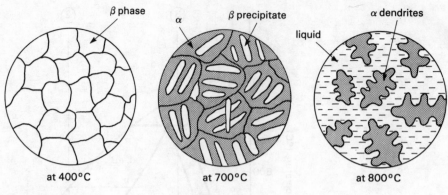

β phase

α

β precipitate

α dendrites

liquid

at 400°C

at 700°C

at 800°C

Figure 4.9

Example 4.3

Explain in relation to alloys:

(a) the terms substitutional and interstitial solid solution, and

(b) why solid solutions are harder and stronger than the base metals from which the alloy is made.

Give one example of a commercial alloy for each type of solid solution.

NiO and MgO form a complete range of liquid and solid solutions and the thermal equilibrium diagram for this system is shown in the accompanying figure.

Identify the phases present for a mixture of 40 per cent NiO/60 per cent MgO at (i) 2600°C, (ii) 2400°C, and (iii) 2100°C.

A 40 per cent NiO/60 per cent MgO ceramic is first melted at 2750°C and then cooled. Determine the composition of the first solid to form and the composition of the last liquid to solidify. (Assume thermal equilibrium obtains.)

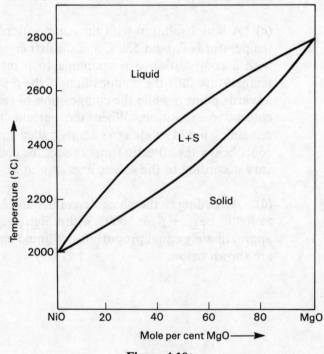

Figure 4.10

If Ni^{++} and Mg^{++} do not readily diffuse in the solidifying crystals during cooling, what effect will this have on the composition of the crystals?

(City University)

Solution 4.3

(a) Solid solutions are single phase structures in which two or more atomic species form a common crystal space lattice. A substitutional solid solution can form when the atomic diameters of the species are of similar size. When the size of a solute atom is very small in comparison with the diameter of solvent metal atoms, an interstitial solid solution may form.

(b) Atoms of differing size in a substitutional solid solution cause the crystal lattice to be distorted. Crystal planes are not perfectly plane, as in pure metals, and the force necessary to cause dislocation movement is increased. Hence, solid solution alloys have higher yield strengths and are harder than the pure metals they are derived from. Interstitial solute atoms are somewhat larger than the maximum size interstitial spaces in the lattice and, again, cause lattice distortion, hence strengthening.

Copper and nickel when alloyed together in any proportion form a FCC structured solid solution. Carbon can enter both α and γ iron, to a limited extent, to give interstitial solid solutions.

The phases present for a 40 per cent NiO/60 per cent MgO mixture are: (i) at 2600°C liquid solution; at 2400°C liquid plus solid solutions; and at 2100°C solid solution. According to the phase diagram, a 40 per cent NiO/60 per cent MgO composition should begin to solidify at about 2570°C. Construction of the tie-line ab shows that the solid in equilibrium with the liquid at this temperature should contain 80 per cent MgO. Similarly, construction of the tie-line cd shows that the last liquid to solidify should have a composition containing 35 per cent MgO.

67

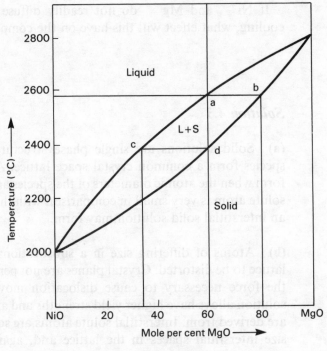

Figure 4.11

If Ni^{++} and Mg^{++} ions do not readily diffuse in the solidifying crystals then a cored structure will result with the centres of crystals being rich in MgO and the outer portions of crystals being rich in NiO.

Example 4.4

Two metals show partial solid solubility in each other. Metal A, of melting point 1000°C, can dissolve 30 per cent of B at 500°C and 20 per cent of B at 0°C. Metal B, of melting point 800°C, can dissolve 20 per cent of A at 500°C and 10 per cent of A at 0°C. An eutectic occurs at 500°C and a composition of 60 per cent B.

Draw and label the phase equilibrium diagram, and assume all lines are straight.

For an alloy containing 50 per cent B, give the compositions of the phases present and their relative proportions at **(a)** 550°C, **(b)** 500°C, and **(c)** 200°C.

Describe the room temperature microstructure of the alloy containing 15 per cent B after solidification by chill casting.

Solution 4.4

From the given data, the phase diagram can be drawn. The complete labelled diagram is shown below. Tie-lines are drawn at 550°C, 500°C and 200°C and the lever rule used to determine the relative proportions of phases present at these temperatures for an alloy containing 50 per cent B.

(a) At 550°C, the phases present are α solid solution containing 27 per cent of metal B and liquid containing 54 per cent of B (given by points a and c). The amount of α phase present is in proportion to the length of line bc while the amount of liquid is in proportion to the length of line ab. So, the ratio amount of α to amount of liquid = 4 to 23.

(b) Similarly, at a temperature fractionally above 500°C the phases will be α phase (30 per cent of B) and liquid (60 per cent of B) present in the ratio 10/20. On cooling to just below 500°C the liquid will solidify as eutectic mixture of α and β.

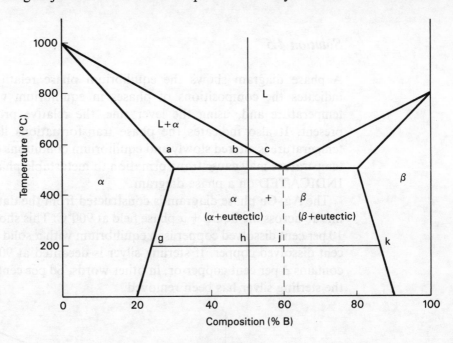

Figure 4.12

(c) At 200°C the phases present can be regarded as either α phase (24 per cent of B) and β phase (86 per cent of B) present in the ratio α/β = hk/gh = 36/26 or as α phase (24 per cent of B) and eutectic mixture (60 per cent of B) present in the ratio α/eutectic = hj/gh = 10/26.

According to the phase diagram, an alloy containing 15 per cent of B should consist of a single phase, α solid solution. Chill casting, a rapid solidification process, may not permit equilibrium conditions to be attained and the structure will consist of cored α crystals, the centres of the crystals being richer in metal A than the outer edges.

Example 4.5

What information can be obtained from a thermal equilibrium phase diagram?

Assuming that the phase boundaries are straight lines, construct a thermal equilibrium diagram for the silver–copper eutectic system from the given data:

  melting temperature of silver is 960°C
  melting temperature of copper is 1083°C
  maximum solid solubility of copper in silver is 8.8 per cent at 780°C
  maximum solid solubility of silver in copper is 8.0 per cent at 780°C
  solid solubility at room temperature is assumed to be zero in each case the
  eutectic composition is 28 per cent Cu/72 per cent Ag.

69

Sterling silver contains 7.5 per cent copper. Such an alloy, when at equilibrium at 900°C, is decanted. What fraction of copper has been removed from the remaining solid?

For what commercial process does the above procedure form a basis?

(Kingston Polytechnic)

Solution 4.5

A phase diagram shows the equilibrium phase relationships for a system. It indicates the compositions of phases in equilibrium with one another at any temperature and, using the lever rule, the relative proportions of each phase present. It also indicates the phase transformations likely to occur when the temperature is altered slowly and equilibrium conditions obtain. Rapid changes of temperature may cause transformation to metastable phases and these ARE NOT INDICATED on a phase diagram.

The Ag–Cu phase diagram is constructed from the data given. Draw in the tie-line ab across the liquid + α phase field at 900°C. This shows that liquid containing 10 per cent dissolved copper is in equilibrium with α solid solution containing 3 per cent dissolved copper. If sterling silver is decanted at 900°C, the remaining solid contains 3 per cent copper or, in other words, 60 per cent of the copper present in the sterling silver has been removed.

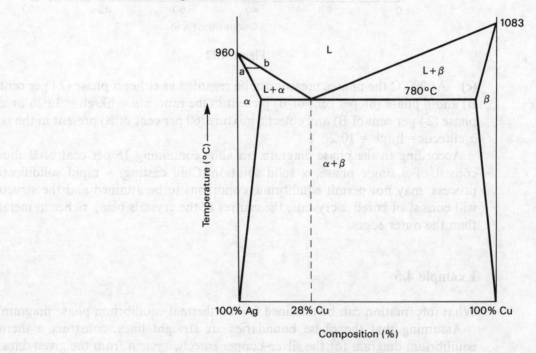

Figure 4.13

This procedure could form the basis for a commercial refining operation.

Example 4.6

A portion of the Cu–Al (aluminium bronze) equilibrium diagram is shown in the accompanying diagram.

Using this diagram:

(a) label the unmarked phase fields and identify the eutectic and eutectoid points,

(b) calculate the relative amounts of the phases present (i) in a 10 per cent Al alloy at 700°C, and (ii) in a 13 per cent Al alloy at 25°C.

(c) Sketch the microstructure of a 12 per cent Al alloy at room temperature after (i) slow cooling from 800°C, and (ii) rapid cooling from 800°C.

(d) Sketch the microstructure of a 5 per cent Al alloy at room temperature after (i) slow cooling from 1200°C, and (ii) rapid cooling from 1200°C.

(e) Explain briefly any differences between your diagrams in the answer to part **(d)**.

(f) Suggest the alloy composition you would choose for the manufacture of (i) cold formed tube, and (ii) a high strength cast component, and give a brief justification for your choice.

(Trent Polytechnic)

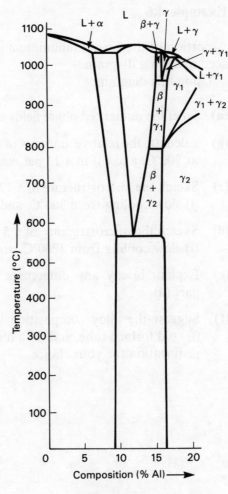

Figure 4.14

Solution 4.6

(a) The unmarked phase fields are labelled α, $\alpha + \beta$, β, $L + \beta$ and $\alpha + \gamma_2$, as shown in the solution diagram below. The eutectic occurs at 8.5 per cent Al and 1037°C; the eutectoid occurs at 11.8 per cent Al and 565°C.

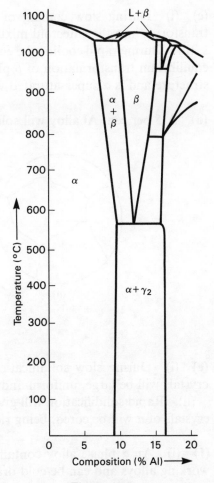

Figure 4.15

(i) The phases present in a 10 per cent Al alloy at 700°C are α and β, their compositions being 8.8 per cent and 11.1 per cent Al respectively. By the lever rule the ratio of amount α/amount $\beta = 1.1/1.2 = 1/1.1$

(ii) The phases present in a 13 per cent Al alloy at 250°C are α and γ_2, their compositions being 9.4 per cent and 16.2 per cent Al respectively. The ratio of amount α/amount $\gamma_2 = 3.2/3.6 = 1/1.13$.

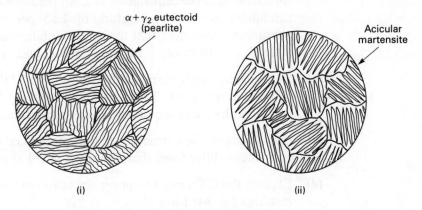

Figure 4.16

73

(c) (i) During slow cooling of a 12 per cent Al alloy from 800°C β phase transforms into the eutectoid mixture of $\alpha + \gamma_2$ according to the phase diagram.

(ii) During rapid cooling the eutectoid transformation is suppressed and a non-equilibrium transformation of β phase into martensite occurs. This is an acicular structure and is α supersaturated with dissolved aluminium (see figure 4.16).

(d) A 5 per cent Al alloy will solidify as α phase.

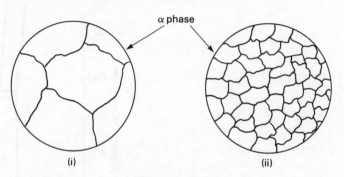

α phase

(i)   (ii)

Figure 4.17

(e) (i) During slow solidification and cooling diffusion can occur and the α crystals will be large, uniform and homogeneous.

(ii) Rapid solidification will give a smaller crystal grain size than in (i) and the crystals of α will be cored, being richer in copper at their centres (see figure 4.17).

(f) (i) An α phase alloy containing 5–7 per cent Al. α phase alloys are cold-working alloys and can be cold drawn into tubing.

(ii) An $\alpha + \gamma_2$ alloy containing 10–12 per cent Al. The increased aluminium content gives increased strength. These alloys cannot be readily cold worked but can be cast.

Example 4.7

(a) Aluminium and silicon melt at 660°C and 1430°C respectively. An eutectic is formed at 11.6 per cent silicon at a temperature of 577°C, with terminal solid solubilities at this temperature of 1.65 per cent silicon and 1 per cent aluminium. Assuming that the solid solubility for each element drops to zero at 25°C, construct and label the thermal equilibrium diagram for the system.

(b) Describe the equilibrium solidification from 1430°C to room temperature for alloys containing: (i) 13 per cent silicon and (ii) 3 per cent silicon, and sketch and label the room temperature microstructures of these alloys.

(c) How does the microstructure of the commercial alloy LM6 containing 13 per cent silicon differ from that described in (b) above and explain why?

(d) Explain the differences in grain structure and tensile strength between sand cast and die cast LM6 alloy.

(Trent Polytechnic)

74

Solution 4.7

(a) The phase diagram drawn on the basis of the data given is shown below.

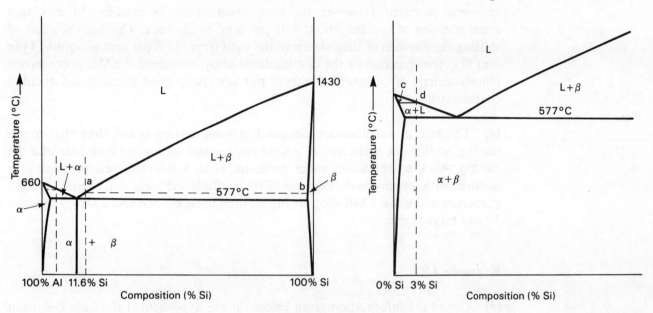

Figure 4.18

(b) (i) When the temperature of the liquid reaches the liquidus value (point a) solidification commences with the formation of primary β phase of composition b. As freezing continues the composition of the remaining liquid varies according to the liquidus line towards the eutectic point. Solidification is completed at 570°C when the remaining liquid freezes as an $\alpha + \beta$ eutectic mixture. As the temperature falls further, aluminium is rejected from solution in silicon, and vice versa, according to the solvus lines. The final structure of the alloy is of primary silicon crystals in a matrix of aluminium/silicon eutectic mixture.

(ii) In this case, solidification begins when the temperature reaches the liquidus line (point d) and the first material to solidify will be primary α crystals of composition c. The composition of remaining liquid varies towards the eutectic composition as the temperature falls. Solidification is completed when the remaining liquid freezes to give the eutectic mixture of α and β at 570°C. As for (i) above silicon is rejected from solution in aluminium, and vice versa, as the temperature of the solid alloy reduces. The final alloy structure will be primary dendritic crystals of aluminium in a matrix of Al/Si eutectic mixture.

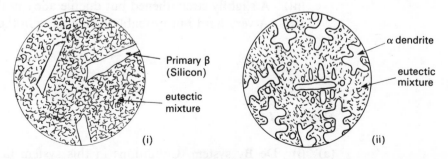

Figure 4.19

(c)   The structure of the commercial alloy LM6 (13 per cent Si) differs from that quoted in (b) (i) above. An alloy structure containing large primary crystals of silicon would possess low strength and ductility and the alloy would not have great economic potential. However, the alloy structure can be modified by making a small addition of sodium, about 0.01 per cent, to the melt. This has the effect of shifting the position of the eutectic to the right (from 11.6 per cent to about 14 per cent Si). The structure of the cast modified alloy, commercial LM6, is composed almost entirely of fine grained eutectic mixture giving good strength and ductility characteristics.

(d)   The rate of solidification obtained in sand casting is less than that in die casting, so that the grain size of a sand casting will be coarser than that of a die casting. Also, solidification under pressure, as in pressure die casting, will give castings with less porosity. Because of these effects the yield and tensile strength properties of die cast LM6 alloy are higher than those of sand cast LM6 by between 30 and 60 per cent.

Example 4.8

(a)   Use of the information given below for the hypothetical elements Delarium (De), Pseudonium (Ps), Luthium (Lu) and Byrium (By) to sketch the probable form of the equilibrium diagrams formed between the following pairs of elements: (i) De–By, (ii) Lu–By, (iii) De–Ps, and (iv) De–Lu. Clearly label all the phase regions on the diagrams.

Element	M.Pt. (°C)	Atomic radius (nm)	Crystal structure	Electro-negativity
De	530	0.124	FCC	1.7
Ps	1400	0.130	HCP	1.9
Lu	400	0.143	BCC	1.3
By	320	0.128	FCC	1.5

(b)   Show on your sketch diagrams a suitable alloy composition (C_1–C_4) for the following requirements and, in each case, justify your choice.
   (i)   The maximum strength alloy in the De–By system (C_1)
   (ii)   A 'plumber's' solder in the Lu–By system (C_2)
   (iii)   A slightly strengthened but ductile alloy in the De–Ps system (C_3)
   (iv)   A very hard but probably brittle alloy in the De–Lu system (C_4).

(Trent Polytechnic)

Solution 4.8

(a)   (i) De–By system. Conditions in this system favour complete solid solubility: both metals are of same crystal type, their atomic radii are within 3 per cent of one another, and they are of similar electronegativity. The difference of 210°C in their melting points indicates a phase diagram without a minimum melting point.

(ii) Lu–By system. The two metals differ in crystal structure and their atomic radii differ by 12 per cent. Partial solid solubility may occur but the extent of this is likely to be restricted. The likely phase diagram is partial solid solubility with a eutectic.

(iii) De–Ps system. Similar to (ii) above, the likely phase diagram will be partial solid solubility with a eutectic, but with a difference in atomic radii of only 5 per cent the extent of solid solubility of one metal in another could be fairly large.

(iv) De–Lu system. The large difference in electronegativity indicates that one or more intermetallic compounds will be formed. The 15 per cent difference in atomic radii means that solid solubility, if it occurs at all, will be very restricted. (For the solution it is assumed that one compound with the formula De_xLu_y is formed.)

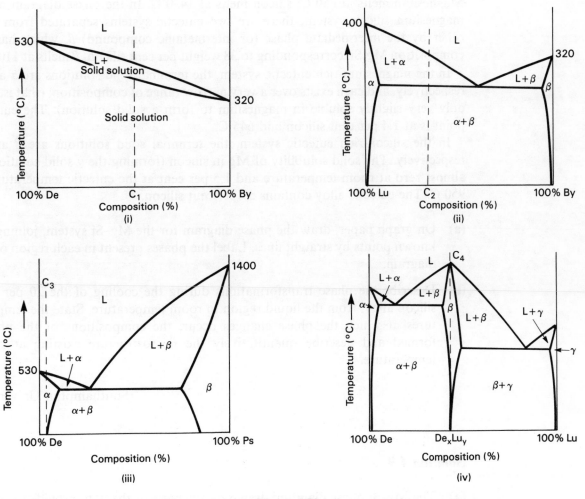

Figure 4.20

(b) (i) De–By system. Solute atoms entering solid solution cause distortion of the parent metal lattice and produce strengthening. For a complete range of solid solutions, maximum distortion of both the De and By lattices and, hence maximum strength, will occur at a composition of about 50 atomic per cent, that is, equal numbers of De and By atoms. This is alloy C_1.

(ii)   Lu-By system. A 'plumber's' solder is one which freezes over a wide range of temperatures. Composition C_2 shown on the solution diagram is one such alloy.

(iii)   De–Ps system. The requirement for a slightly strengthened but ductile alloy can be met by a small addition of Ps to De giving composition C_2. The solid solution effect will give some strengthening. FCC structured metals such as De are ductile while HCP metals such as Ps have low ductility.

(iv)   De–Lu system. Intermetallic compounds generally are harder than either constituent element and are brittle. Composition C_4, the compound De_xLu_y, is likely to be a very hard and brittle material.

Example 4.9

Magnesium melts at 650°C; silicon melts at 1430°C. In the phase diagram of the magnesium–silicon system, there are two eutectic systems separated from each other by the intermediate phase (or intermetallic compound) β, which has the composition Mg_2Si, corresponding to 38 weight per cent silicon. β melts at 1102°C.

In the magnesium-rich eutectic system, the terminal solid solutions are α and β respectively, and each exists over a very narrow range of composition; (that is, Si is only very slightly soluble in magnesium to form a solid solution). The eutectic point is at 1.4 per cent silicon and 645°C.

In the silicon-rich eutectic system, the terminal solid solutions are β and γ respectively. The solid solubility of Mg in silicon (forming the γ solid solution) is almost zero at room temperature and 1.5 per cent at the eutectic temperature of 950°C. The eutectic alloy contains 57 per cent silicon.

(a)   On graph paper, draw the phase diagram for the Mg–Si system, joining the known points by straight lines. Label the phases present in each region of the diagram.

(b)   Describe the phase transformations during the cooling of the 20 per cent silicon alloy, from the liquid region to room temperature. State the temperatures at which the phase changes occur, the compositions of the phases formed and describe quantitatively the microstructure existing at room temperature.

(Southampton University)

Solution 4.9

(a)   The Mg–Si phase diagram, drawn on the basis of the data provided is given below. Note that no quantitative information is given for composition limits of β phase other than that it exists over a very narrow range of composition.

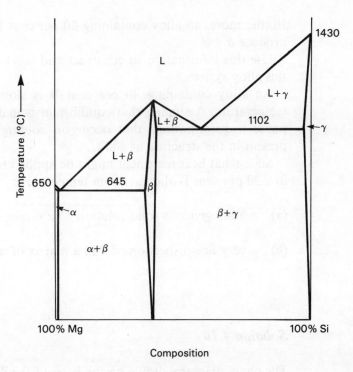

Figure 4.21

(b) During cooling from the liquid region the 20 per cent Si alloy begins to solidify at a temperature of about 880°C, when crystals of β phase (Mg$_2$Si) begin to form. As cooling continues, more β phase is formed and the composition of the liquid varies towards the α/β eutectic composition, according to the liquidus. Solidification is completed at 645°C when the remaining liquid transforms into the eutectic mixture of α and β. During further cooling, the very small amount of dissolved silicon in α phase is rejected from solution and the composition of the β phase alters to 38 per cent Si. The room temperature microstructure consists of primary β (Mg$_2$Si) in a matrix of $(\alpha + \beta)$ eutectic. By the lever rule, the ratio of the amount of β to amount of eutectic is 18.6 to 18, or 1.03 to 1. The ratio of Mg to Mg$_2$Si in the eutectic mixture is 36.6 to 1.4, or 26.1 to 1.

Example 4.10

Two metals, A (melting point 1300°C) and B (melting point 1000°C), are partially soluble in each other to form solid solutions α and β; the following table gives the values for the maximum solubility under equilibrium conditions:

Temperature (°C)	0	200	400	600	800	900	950
Max solubility of B in A (% wt)	3	10	20	32	50	40	35
Max solubility of A in B (% wt)	2	2	3	5	10	5	3

Furthermore, an alloy containing 80 per cent B undergoes a eutectic reaction to produce $\alpha + \beta$.

Use this information to construct and label an appropriate phase diagram for this alloy system.

An alloy containing 40 per cent B is slowly cooled from 1300°C to room temperature. Assuming that equilibrium is maintained, describe the sequence of phase transformations that occur on cooling, and calculate the percentage β present in the structure at 400°C.

State what heat treatment might be applied to produce the following structures in a 30 per cent B alloy at room temperature:

(a) a homogeneous solid solution of α phase,

(b) a very fine dispersion of β in a matrix of α phase.

(Southampton University)

Solution 4.10

The phase diagram, drawn on the basis of the data given is shown below. Draw a vertical line at a composition of 40 per cent B and note where this cuts liquidus, solidus and solvus lines. Construct a tie-line abc at 400°C.

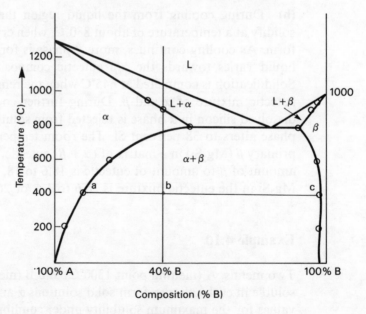

Figure 4.22

Cooling the liquid alloy from 1300°C, solidification will begin when the liquidus temperature is reached at about 1100°C. The first solid to form will be α crystals containing about 20 per cent dissolved B. As cooling proceeds more α phase will solidify and its composition will vary, following the solidus line, while the composition of the remaining liquid will become more rich in metal B, following the liquidus line. Solidification should be completed at a temperature of about 900°C, when the structure should be composed solely of α phase. (*Note*: During slow cooling equilibrium conditions prevail and the α crystals should be homogeneous, but rapid cooling will not permit the attainment of equilibrium and cored crystals will result.) On cooling further, the solvus line will be crossed at 700°C. At this temperature, α phase is fully saturated with dissolved β. Cooling below this temperature will cause β phase to precipitate within the α crystals and at crystal boundaries. Cooling to room temperature will give a final structure of α phase crystals (containing 3 per cent dissolved metal B) with a precipitate of β phase (containing 2 per cent dissolved metal A).

At 400°C the structure will be α and β present in the ratio bc to ac. The percentage β in the structure is (ab ÷ ac) × 100 = (20 ÷ 77) × 100 = 26 per cent.

For an alloy containing 30 per cent B:

(a) An homogeneous α solid solution can be obtained by solution treating the alloy at a temperature just below the solidus, say 900°C, followed by rapid quenching to prevent precipitation of β and give a supersaturated α solid solution.

(b) A finely dispersed β precipitate within α can be obtained by a two-stage treatment. Firstly, a solution heat treatment, as in **(a)** above, followed by either natural ageing or a precipitation heat treatment at a temperature below the solvus line, say at a temperature of about 200°C.

Example 4.11

Two pure metals, A and B, are partially soluble in one another in the solid state. Metal A, of melting point 1000°C, dissolves 20 per cent of B at 500°C and 10 per cent of B at 0°C. Metal B, of melting point 800°C, dissolves 15 per cent of A at 500°C and 5 per cent of A at 0°C. There is a eutectic point at 500°C and 60 per cent of B.

Draw and label the binary phase diagram for the alloy system of metals A and B (assume all lines to be straight).

(a) Describe the solidification of an alloy containing 15 per cent of B when:
   (i)   slowly cooled,
   (ii) rapidly cooled.

(b) For the slowly cooled sample, deduce the relative proportions of phases present in the structures at 0°C.

(c) For the rapidly cooled structure, describe the likely effects that reheating the alloy at 500°C will have on the microstructure.

(d) Will the rate of cooling following treatment **(c)** have any effect on the structure and properties of the alloy and, if so, what will this be?

(Polytechnic of Central London)

Solution 4.11

The phase diagram, drawn according to the data provided, is shown below.

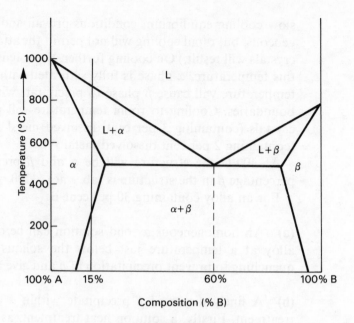

Figure 4.23

(a) This part of the question is similar in principle to example 4.10.

(i) During slow solidification, freezing will begin at about 870°C with the formation of α solid solution crystals and end at about 620°C. Equilibrium conditions will be achieved and homogeneous α phase will result. During further cooling, where the composition line crosses the solvus at about 240°C, a precipitate of β phase will begin to precipitate within the α structure.

(ii) During rapid cooling, equilibrium will not be attained and the α crystals will be cored. Because there is a very great separation between liquidus and solidus in this diagram and, from the diagram, the liquid composition in equilibrium with solid α at 620°C is about 46 per cent B, there is a major likelihood that there will be some β phase present in the structure of the rapidly solidified alloy.

(b) The structure of a slow cooled 15 per cent B alloy at 0°C will be of α crystals containing 10 per cent dissolved B and a β precipitate (containing 5 per cent dissolved A). Using the lever rule, the percentage of β in the structure is given by $5/85 \times 100 = 5.9$ per cent.

(c) When the rapidly cooled alloy is reheated at 500°C, below the solidus, solid state diffusion will occur giving homogeneous α crystals.

(d) The rate of cooling after treatment **(c)** is important and has a major effect. Slow cooling will permit the equilibrium structure to be formed, namely, β phase will begin to precipitate, as in **(a)** (i) above. This is the softest condition for the alloy and is termed the annealed state. Rapid cooling of the alloy from 500°C may prevent the β phase from precipitating and retain a supersaturated solid solution at 0°C. This will be harder and stronger than the annealed state. Such a metastable condition may respond to dispersion strengthening by ageing or a precipitation heat treatment.

Example 4.12

A range of alloys made from two pure metals, A and B, is allowed to cool from the molten state to room temperature. During the cooling process, thermal arrest points are noted for each alloy. These are given in the table below.

Per cent B in alloy	8	30	45	55	78	90
1st arrest point temperature (°C)	810	910	980	1010	1060	1090
2nd arrest point temperature (°C)	760	830	910	910	940	1030
3rd arrest point temperature (°C)	—	720	—	—	800	—

The melting point of pure A is 750°C, the melting point of pure B is 1110°C. Draw, on squared paper, the phase diagram for the binary alloy system of metals A and B and label the diagram fully.

Describe the room temperature microstructure of an alloy containing 78 per cent B in the following conditions:

(a) sand cast,

(b) cast, reheated to 900°C and quenched in water.

(Polytechnic of Central London)

Solution 4.12

Draw the phase diagram axes and plot all the arrest points. The first and second arrest points must refer to the liquidus and solidus temperatures respectively. The third arrest points indicate a solid state change, for example, a solvus line. The phase diagram can now be drawn. It shows partial solid solubility with a peritectic. The solvus lines are drawn dotted as there is insufficient data to show them with exactitude.

(a) According to the phase diagram, an alloy containing 78 per cent of B will begin to solidify at 1060°C and be completely solid at 940°C. When sand cast, β phase crystals will solidify when the temperature falls to the liquidus value. Whether full equilibrium is attained or not will depend on the actual rate of cooling during sand casting and some peritectic α may appear in the microstructure. On further cooling, α phase will be precipitated from the β when the solvus line is crossed at 800°C.

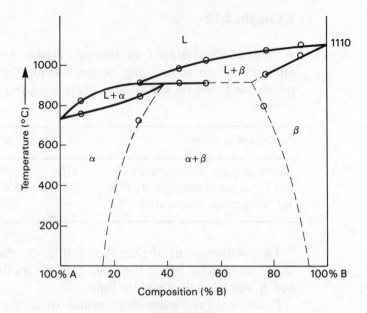

Figure 4.24

(b) The sand cast alloy will have an $\alpha + \beta$ structure but when reheated to 900°C, in the β region of the phase diagram, all α will be taken into solution and the structure will be homogeneous β phase. Water quenching from 900°C should prevent the precipitation of α during cooling, resulting in a supersaturated β solid solution at room temperature.

Example 4.13

Thermal analysis of a number of alloys of copper and silver give the following results:

Per cent copper	5	20	28	50	65	90
Per cent silver	95	80	72	50	35	10
1st arrest (°C)	945	860	780	900	950	1045
2nd arrest (°C)	860	780	—	780	780	780
3rd arrest (°C)	570	—	—	—	—	—

The melting temperature of pure copper is 1083°C and the melting temperature of pure silver is 960°C.

Plot the phase diagram for the copper–silver alloy system, using the above data.

Describe the changes which occur when the following alloy compositions are allowed to cool slowly from the liquid state to room temperature.

(a) 5 per cent copper/95 per cent silver,

(b) 50 per cent copper/50 per cent silver.

Give sketches of the room temperature microstructure in each case.

What differences, if any, would there be in the structure of the 5 per cent copper alloy if the material were rapidly cooled from the liquid state to room temperature?

Solution 4.13

The phase diagram, plotted from the thermal analysis data, is shown below.

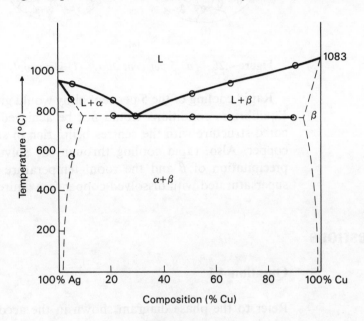

Figure 4.25

(a) The liquid alloy would begin to freeze when the liquidus temperature is reached at 945°C and a solid solution rich in silver, α, separates out. Solidification will be completed when the temperature reaches 860°C, the solidus temperature for this alloy. At this stage the structure will consist entirely of uniform crystals of α silver/copper solid solution. On cooling to 570°C, the solvus temperature, the saturation limit for copper in silver is reached and precipitation of a copper-rich solid solution, β, will occur when the temperature falls below this value. At room temperature the structure will consist of primary α crystals with precipitated β particles (see figure 4.26(a)(i)).

(b) Freezing of the 50 per cent copper alloy will begin at 900°C, the liquidus temperature, and the first crystals to form will be of a copper rich solid solution, β. The composition of remaining liquid will be enriched in silver and its freezing point will reduce, following the liquidus line to the eutectic point. At 780°C the alloy will consist of primary β crystals and liquid of the eutectic composition (28 per cent copper) and at this temperature all remaining liquid freezes to give a fine grained eutectic mixture of α and β crystals. At room temperature the final alloy structure will be of primary β crystals and $(\alpha + \beta)$ eutectic (see figure 4.26(b)).

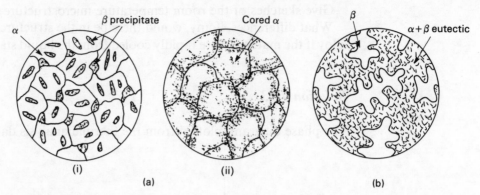

Figure 4.26 (a) 5 per cent alloy: (i) slow cool, (ii) rapid cool (b) 50 per cent alloy.

Rapid cooling of the 5 per cent alloy would give rise to the following differences. Equilibrium conditions would not be achieved and the α crystals would have a cored structure with the centres being rich in silver and the outer edges richer in copper. Also, rapid cooling through the solvus temperature could prevent the precipitation of β and the room temperature structure would be of α crystals supersaturated with dissolved copper (see figure 4.26(a)(ii).

4.3 Questions

Question 4.1

Refer to the phase diagram shown in the accompanying figure. List the phases which exist in each of the six fields of the diagram.

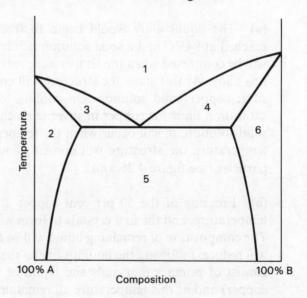

Figure 4.27

Question 4.2

Two pure metals, A and B, and a series of alloys of these two metals were cooled from the liquid state and the following information was obtained:

Composition (per cent of A)	100	95	85	60	30	10	5	0
1st arrest point (°C)	600	575	535	425	300	400	425	450
2nd arrest point (°C)	—	500	300	300	—	300	350	—
3rd arrest point (°C)	—	40	—	—	—	—	200	—

(a) Using these data, plot and fully label the thermal equilibrium diagram for the alloy system of metals A and B.

(b) For the alloy containing 75 per cent of A what phases exist at the following temperatures: (i) 525°C, (ii) 425°C, (iii) 250°C?

(c) Explain how the properties of hardness and tensile strength of slowly cooled alloys would vary with composition from 100 per cent A to 100 per cent B.

Question 4.3

The cooling curves obtained when two pure metals and several of their alloys were cooled from the liquid phase are shown below. Construct and label a phase diagram for the alloy system.

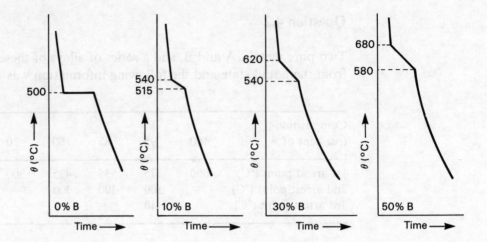

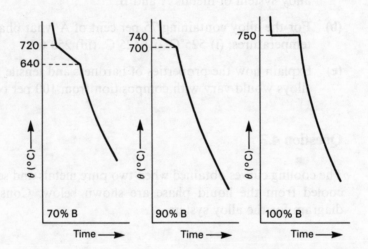

Figure 4.28

Question 4.4

Label all the phase fields in the figure below.

For an alloy containing 30 per cent of... state the phases present, their composition and relative proportions, at the following temperatures (a) 300°C (b) 246°C (c) 200°C (iv) 183°C (v) 150°C

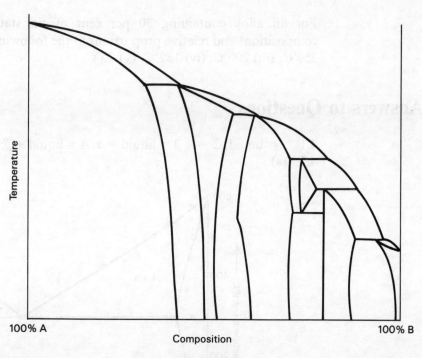

Figure 4.29

Question 4.5

The phase diagram for the lead–tin system is shown below.

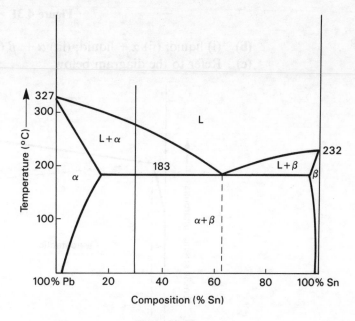

Figure 4.30

For an alloy containing 30 per cent of tin state the phases present, their compositions and relative proportions at the following temperatures: (i) 300°C, (ii) 250°C, (iii) 200°C, (iv) 182°C, (v) 25°C.

4.4 Answers to Questions

4.1 1 = liquid; 2 = α; 3 = liquid + α; 4 = liquid + β; 5 = α + β; 6 = β.
4.2 **(a)**

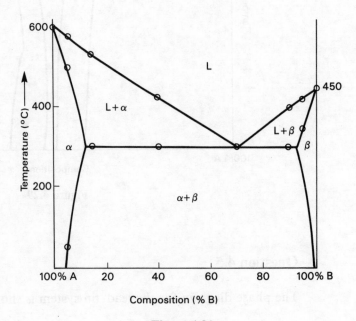

Figure 4.31

(b) (i) liquid; (ii) α + liquid; (iii) α + β (or α + eutectic).
(c) Refer to the diagram below.

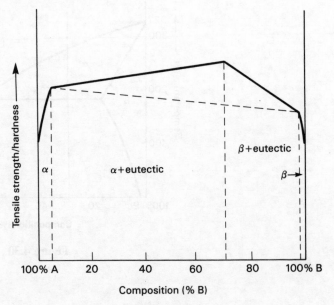

Figure 4.32

4.3 Refer to the diagram below.

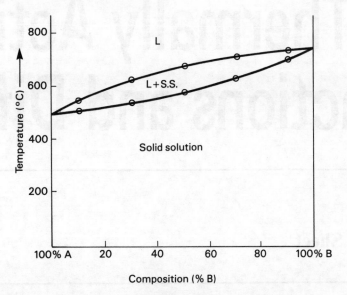

Figure 4.33

4.4 Refer to the solution diagram. Note that any two single-phase fields must be separated by a two-phase region. (The diagram is that for copper and zinc.)

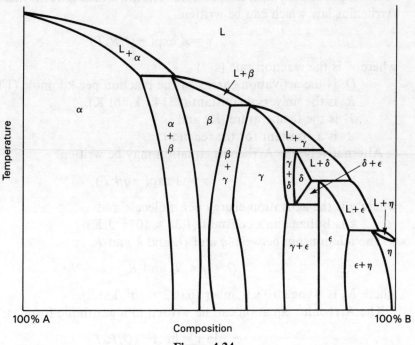

Figure 4.34

4.5 (i) liquid phase (70 per cent Pb/30 per cent Sn. (ii) α phase (containing 9 per cent Sn) and liquid (containing 40 per cent Sn). Ratio of amount α/amount liquid = 10/21. (iii) α phase (15 per cent Sn) and liquid (58 per cent Sn). Ratio amount α/amount liquid = 28/15. (iv) Primary α (17 per cent Sn) and (α + β) eutectic (62 per cent Sn) in the ratio amount primary α/eutectic mixture = 32/13. (v) α (3 per cent Sn) and (α + β) eutectic in ratio amount α/amount eutectic = 32/27.

5 Thermally Activated Reactions and Diffusion

5.1 Fact Sheet

(a) Rate of Reaction

Many processes are thermally activated and the rate at which the process occurs varies exponentially with temperature. The law which governs these processes is the Arrhenius law which can be written:

$$v = A \exp(-Q/R_0 T)$$

where v is the reaction rate (s^{-1})

Q is the activation energy of the reaction per kilomole (J/kmol),

R_0 is the universal constant (8314 J/kmol K),

T is the temperature (K) and

A is a constant for the reaction.

Alternatively, the Arrhenius equation may be written

$$v = A \exp(-q/kT)$$

where q is the activation energy per molecule and

k is Boltzmann's constant (1.38×10^{-23} J/K).

The relationship between q and Q, and k and R_0 is:

$$Q = q \times N_0 \quad \text{and} \quad R_0 = k \times N_0$$

where N_0 is Avogadro's number (6.023×10^{26}/kmol).

The Arrhenius equation can be written in logarithmic form as:

$$\ln v = \ln A - (Q/R_0 T)$$

This is a linear equation of the form $y = c + mx$, the two variables being $\ln v$ and $1/T$. A graph plot of $\ln v$ against $1/T$ will be a straight line with a slope equal to $-Q/R_0$. $\ln A$ is given by the intercept with the ordinate.

If preferred, the logarithmic equation can be written:

$$\log_{10} v = \log_{10} A - (Q/2.3026 R_0 T)$$

The Arrhenius law applies to many reactions, both chemical and physical.

Examples of physical reactions which are thermally activated are diffusion and diffusion-controlled reactions, such as creep, recrystallisation and solid-state phase transformations. For many chemical reactions, activation energies are of the order of 40 MJ/kmol while, for many physical reactions in alloy systems, activation energies are higher than this, many being in the range 150 to 200 MJ/kmol.

(b) Diffusion

Steady state diffusion

In steady state diffusion the concentration gradient is constant and Fick's law of diffusion applies.

Fick's first law of diffusion can be written:

$$J_x = -D \frac{dC}{dx}$$

where J_x is the flux ($kg\,m^{-2}\,s^{-1}$) (the quantity of material crossing a unit area normal to the flux direction in unit time), D is the diffusion coefficient ($m^2\,s^{-1}$) and dC/dx is the concentration gradient ($kg\,m^{-4}$).

Transient state diffusion

A more common case in practice is where the concentration of the diffusing substance changes with time. This means that both the flux and the concentration gradient also change with time. Fick's second law of diffusion covers transient diffusion and it can be written:

$$\frac{dC_x}{dt} = D \frac{d^2C_x}{dx^2}$$

where C_x is the concentration of the diffusing species at distance x from a surface and t is the time (s).

In cases of solid state diffusion where the concentration of the diffusing species at the surface of a material, C_s, remains constant the solution to this differential equation can be written as:

$$\frac{C_s - C_x}{C_s - C_0} = \text{erf}\left(\frac{x}{2\sqrt{(Dt)}}\right)$$

where C_0 is the concentration at the start of the process ($t = 0$) and erf is the Gaussian error function or normalised probability.

For values, up to 0.5, the Gaussian error function can be approximated as erf $y \simeq y$ so that

$$\frac{C_s - C_x}{C_s - C_0} \simeq \frac{x}{2\sqrt{(Dt)}}$$

5.2 Worked Examples

Example 5.1

For a thermally activated reaction with an activation energy of 150 MJ/kmol, calculate by what factor the rate of reaction will be increased if the temperature is raised from 300 K to 900 K. If the reaction is completed in a time of 1 s at 900 K, how long would it take to reach completion at 300 K?

Solution 5.1

This example illustrates the major effect that a change in temperature can have on the rate of a reaction.

$$\text{At } 900 \text{ K, } \exp(-Q/R_0T) = \exp\left(-\frac{150 \times 10^6}{8314 \times 900}\right) = e^{-20} \simeq 10^{-8.5}$$

$$\text{At } 300 \text{ K, } \exp(-Q/R_0T) = \exp\left(-\frac{150 \times 10^6}{8314 \times 300}\right) = e^{-60} \simeq 10^{-25.5}$$

From above, the factor by which the reaction rate changes when the temperature is raised from 300 to 900 K is $10^{-8.5}/10^{-25.5} = 10^{17}$.

The reaction, if completed in 1 s at 900 K would require 10^{17} s at 300 K. This is more than 10^9 years. This is, in effect, a reaction rate of zero at 300 K (room temperature). It means that non-equilibrium states can be retained indefinitely provided that the temperature is low enough and this principle forms the basis for many metallurgical heat treatments.

Example 5.2

The rate of a process varies with temperature and the following table gives experimentally determined values.

Temperature (°C)	175	250	355	500
Rate (mm/s)	1.13×10^{-5}	5.93×10^{-5}	3.10×10^{-4}	1.46×10^{-3}

Show graphically that these data are consistent with the Arrhenius law and calculate the activation energy for the process. Also determine the temperature at which the process rate will be 1.5×10^{-2} mm/s. (Assume $R_0 = 8314$ J/kmol K)

Solution 5.2

The Arrhenius equation can be written in the linear form as:

$$\ln v = \ln A - Q/R_0T$$

from which a graph of $\ln v$ against $1/T$ will be a straight line. The data should first be put into a form suitable for plotting as a graph. This is best done by producing a new table.

$T(°C)$	$T(K)$	$1/T$	$v(mm/s)$	$\ln v$
175	448	2.23×10^{-3}	1.13×10^{-5}	-11.39
250	523	1.91×10^{-3}	5.93×10^{-5}	-9.73
355	628	1.59×10^{-3}	3.10×10^{-4}	-8.08
500	773	1.29×10^{-3}	1.46×10^{-3}	-6.53
?	?	?	1.50×10^{-2}	-4.20

$\ln v$ can now be plotted against $1/T$, as in the figure below. A straight line shows that the data are consistent with the Arrhenius law.

The slope of the line is measured as $-5170 = -Q/R_0$. Therefore the activation energy $Q = 5170 \times 8314 = 43 \times 10^6$ J/kmol.

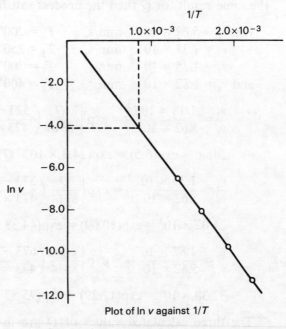

Figure 5.1

From the graph a value of $\ln v = -4.20$ corresponds to $1/T = 0.83 \times 10^{-3}$. Therefore the temperature at which $v = 1.50 \times 10^{-2}$ mm/s is 1205 K or 932°C.

Example 5.3

The rates of linear growth of aluminium crystals during the recrystallisation of cold worked aluminium are as follows:

Temperature (°C)	200	250	300	400
Rate (mm/s)	5.62×10^{-10}	1.38×10^{-7}	1.35×10^{-5}	1.82×10^{-2}

Show, graphically or otherwise, that these results are consistent with the Arrhenius law and, if so, calculate the activation energy of the process.

Solution 5.3

The problem can be solved graphically as in example 1. Alternatively, a numerical method can be used, as follows.

If the reaction rates at temperatures T_1 and T_2 are v_1 and v_2 respectively, then $v_1 = A \exp(-Q/R_0 T_1)$ and $v_2 = A \exp(-Q/R_0 T_2)$.

Dividing

$$\frac{v_2}{v_1} = \exp\left(-\frac{Q}{R_0 T_2} + \frac{Q}{R_0 T_1}\right) = \exp\frac{Q}{R_0}\left(\frac{T_2 - T_1}{T_1 T_2}\right)$$

from which Q can be evaluated.

If this calculation is completed for several pairs of values and each result gives the same result for Q then the process satisfies the Arrhenius law.

Let $v_1 = 5.62 \times 10^{-10}$ mm/s, $\qquad T_1 = 200°C = 473$ K
$\qquad v_2 = 1.38 \times 10^{-7}$ mm/s, $\qquad T_2 = 250°C = 523$ K
$\qquad v_3 = 1.35 \times 10^{-5}$ mm/s, $\qquad T_3 = 300°C = 573$ K
and $v_4 = 1.82 \times 10^{-2}$ mm/s, $\qquad T_4 = 400°C = 673$ K

$$\frac{v_2}{v_1} = \frac{1.38 \times 10^{-7}}{5.62 \times 10^{-10}} = \exp\left[\frac{Q}{8314}\left(\frac{523 - 473}{473 \times 523}\right)\right]$$

$$245.6 = \exp(5.5) = \exp(24.3 \times 10^{-9} Q) \qquad\qquad Q = 226.2 \text{ MJ/kmol}$$

$$\frac{v_3}{v_1} = \frac{1.35 \times 10^{-5}}{5.62 \times 10^{-10}} = \exp\left\{\frac{Q}{8314}\left(\frac{573 - 473}{473 \times 573}\right)\right\}$$

$$24.02 \times 10^3 = \exp(10.09) = \exp(44.38 \times 10^{-9} Q) \qquad Q = 227.4 \text{ MJ/kmol}$$

$$\frac{v_4}{v_1} = \frac{1.82 \times 10^{-2}}{5.62 \times 10^{-10}} = \exp\left\{\frac{Q}{8314}\left(\frac{673 - 473}{473 \times 673}\right)\right\}$$

$$32.38 \times 10^6 = \exp(17.29) = \exp(75.57 \times 10^{-9} Q) \qquad Q = 228.2 \text{ MJ/kmol}$$

The three calculated values of Q are in close agreement indicating that the process obeys the Arrhenius law. The average value of activation energy is $Q = 227.5$ MJ/kmol.

Example 5.4

A thermally activated reaction is completed in 5 seconds at 600°C but requires 15 minutes for completion at 290°C. Calculate the time necessary for the reaction to be completed at 50°C and determine the value of the activation energy for the process.

Solution 5.4

If the reaction requires 5 s for completion at 600°C then the reaction rate is proportional to $1/5 \text{ s}^{-1}$. Therefore, at 600°C (873 K) $v = k/5 \text{ s}^{-1}$ and at 290°C (563 K) $v = k/(15 \times 60) \text{ s}^{-1}$.

Using the expression

$$\frac{v_2}{v_1} = \exp\left\{\frac{Q}{R_0}\left(\frac{T_2 - T_1}{T_1 \times T_2}\right)\right\}$$

$$\frac{v_{873}}{v_{563}} = \frac{15 \times 60}{5} = \exp\left\{\frac{Q}{8314}\left(\frac{873 - 563}{563 \times 873}\right)\right\}$$

$$180 = \exp(5.19) = \exp(75.86 \times 10^{-9} Q) \quad \text{so } Q = 68.4 \text{ MJ/kmol}$$

The activation energy of the process is 68.4 MJ/kmol.

$$V_{563} = \frac{1}{5} = A \exp\left(-\frac{68.4 \times 10^6}{8314 \times 563}\right)$$

$$0.2 = A \exp(-14.62) = 4.49 \times 10^{-7} A \quad \text{so } A = 445 \times 10^3$$

Let the time for the reaction at 50°C (323 K) be t s.

$$\frac{1}{t} = 445 \times 10^3 \exp\left(-\frac{68.4 \times 10^6}{8314 \times 323}\right) = 3.86 \times 10^{-6} \text{ s}^{-1}$$

$$t = 259 \times 10^3 \text{ s} = 71.94 \text{ hours}$$

Example 5.5

The times for a 50 per cent recrystallisation of pure copper are 1 minute at 162°C and 1000 minutes at 72°C. Estimate the time for 50 per cent recrystallisation at 20°C. Discuss what changes you would expect to occur in the mechanical properties of a cold worked copper cable over a period of 10 years.

(Southampton University)

Solution 5.5

As the question does not ask for the activation energy to be evaluated a modified form of the Arrhenius equation can be used: $t = A \exp(B/T)$ where t is the time (any consistent units), T is temperature (K) and A and B are constants.

At 162°C (435 K), $t = \quad$ 1 min so $\quad 1 \quad = A \exp(B/435)$ (1)

At   72°C (345 K), $t = 1000$ min so $\quad 1000 = A \exp(B/345)$ (2)

Equation (2) ÷ (1) gives

$$1000 = \exp\left\{B\left(\frac{435 - 345}{345 \times 435}\right)\right\} = \exp(5.997 \times 10^{-4} B)$$

which gives $B = 11519$

Substituting in (2) $1000 = A \exp(11519 \times 5.997 \times 10^{-4})$

$$A = 3.162 \times 10^{-12}$$

For 20°C (293 K) $t = 3.162 \times 10^{-12} \exp(11519/293) = 374463$ min $= 260$ days. This result indicates that, at 20°C, cold worked pure copper will recrystallise and anneal well within a 10 year period. Recrystallisation will be accompanied by the following changes in mechanical properties: the hardness, yield stress, tensile, compressive and shear strengths will be reduced and the ductility and impact strengths will be increased.

Example 5.6

In a series of age hardening experiments, the first signs of precipitation from a supersaturated solid solution of copper in aluminium were detected after 3 minutes at 102°C, whereas at a temperature of 22°C the time for initiation of precipitation was 3 hours. It is desired to maintain the alloy without the occurrence of precipitation for 3 days. To what temperature should the alloy be cooled to obtain this effect?

(Southampton University)

Solution 5.6

The modified Arrhenius equation, as given in example 5.5 can be used.

At 102°C (375 K), $t = 3$ min   so $3 = A \exp(B/375)$ (1)

At 22°C (295 K), $t = 3$ h $= 180$ min so $180 = A \exp(B/295)$ (2)

Equation (2) ÷ (1) gives

$$\frac{180}{3} = \exp\left\{ B \left(\frac{375 - 295}{295 \times 375} \right) \right\} = \exp(7.232 \times 10^{-4} B)$$

So $B = 5662$

Substituting in (1), $3 = A \exp(5662/375)$, $A = 8.32 \times 10^{-7}$

Let T be temperature for initiation in 3 days (3 days = 4320 min)

$$4320 = 8.32 \times 10^{-7} \exp(5662/T)$$

$$\ln 4320 = \ln(8.32 \times 10^{-7}) + (5662/T)$$

$$8.371 = -14.00 + (5662/T)$$

$$T = 5662 (8.371 + 14.00) = 253 \text{ K} = -20°C$$

The aluminium will have to be maintained at a temperature not exceeding $-20°C$ if precipitation is not to occur within 3 days.

Example 5.7

The maximum hardness of aged aluminium alloy 2014 occurs after 30 hours at 150°C and after 3 minutes at 260°C. Assuming that the rate of reaction as a function of temperature is given by the Arrhenius relationship, calculate the time to achieve maximum hardness at 180°C and 220°C.

Use the above information to plot that part of a TTT diagram for the transformation of 2014 aluminium alloy on the assumption that the precipitate θ'' gives maximum hardness.

(Kingston Polytechnic)

Solution 5.7

At 150°C (423 K), $t = 30$ hours $= 1800$ min; at 260°C (533 K), $t = 3$ min.

$$\frac{1800}{3} = 600 = \exp\left\{\frac{Q}{8314}\left(\frac{533 - 423}{423 \times 523}\right)\right\} = 5.98 \times 10^{-8}\, Q$$

Hence $Q = 109 \times 10^6$ J/kmol.

Let time taken for maximum hardness at 180°C (453 K) and 220°C (493 K) be t_1 and t_2 respectively:

$$\frac{t_1}{3} = \exp\left(\frac{109 \times 10^6 (533 - 453)}{8314 \times 453 \times 533}\right) = 77 \text{ therefore } t_1 = 77 \times 3 = 231 \text{ min}$$

and

$$\frac{t_2}{3} = \exp\left(\frac{109 \times 10^6 (533 - 493)}{8314 \times 493 \times 533}\right) = 7.35 \text{ therefore } t_2 = 22 \text{ min}$$

Maximum hardness will be achieved after 231 min (3.85 hours) at 180°C and after 22 minutes at 220°C.

A portion of the TTT diagram can be obtained by plotting the data using temperature and time as the axes. (It is customary to plot time on a logarithmic scale.) See the diagram below.

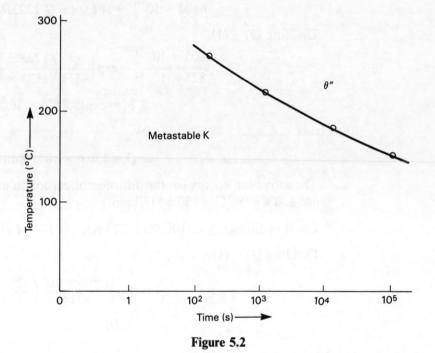

Figure 5.2

Example 5.8

The diffusivity of carbon in mild steel has been measured at two temperatures:

Temperature (°C)	850	950
Diffusivity (m² s⁻¹)	4.826×10^{-12}	1.805×10^{-11}

Using these data calculate:

(a) the activation energy for diffusion of carbon in mild steel for the temperature range 850°–950°C, and

(b) the diffusivity at 1000°C, assuming that the activation energy is unchanged at this higher temperature.

(Sheffield City Polytechnic)

Solution 5.8

At 850°C (1123 K), $D = 4.826 \times 10^{-12}$ m² s⁻¹ and
at 950°C (1223 K), $D = 1.805 \times 10^{-11}$ m² s⁻¹.

Using the Arrhenius equation:

$$4.826 \times 10^{-12} = A \exp(-Q/1123R_0) \qquad (1)$$

$$1.805 \times 10^{-11} = A \exp(-Q/1223R_0) \qquad (2)$$

Dividing (2) ÷ (1),

$$\frac{1.805 \times 10^{-11}}{4.826 \times 10^{-12}} = \exp\left\{\frac{Q}{8314}\left(\frac{1223 - 1123}{1123 \times 1223}\right)\right\}$$

$$3.74 = \exp(8.7575 \times 10^{-6}Q)$$

Hence

$$Q = 150.6 \times 10^6 \text{ J/kmol}$$

The activation energy for the diffusion of carbon in mild steel in the temperature range 850°C–950°C is 150.6 MJ/kmol.

Let D = diffusivity at 1000°C (1273 K), $\quad D = A \exp(-Q/1273R_0) \qquad (3)$

Dividing (3) ÷ (1),

$$\frac{D}{4.826 \times 10^{-12}} = \exp\left\{\frac{150.6 \times 10^6}{8314}\left(\frac{1273 - 1123}{1123 \times 1273}\right)\right\}$$

$$= 6.69$$

So

$$D = 3.229 \times 10^{-11} \text{ m}^2 \text{ s}^{-1}$$

Example 5.9

A case carburising operation for mild steel (0.15 per cent C) is conducted at 1000°C and gives a surface carbon content of 0.85 per cent C and a carbon concentration of

100

0.75 per cent at a depth of 0.25 mm below the surface. It is suggested that economies can be effected if the temperature of the process is reduced to 950°C as furnace fuel costs per hour of furnace operation are 20 per cent less at the lower temperature. Is this suggestion practical if the same quality carburised product is to be obtained?

Assume that the diffusivity of carbon in mild steel varies with temperature according to the Arrhenius law and that the activation energy is 150 MJ/kmol.

Solution 5.9

Let the diffusivities of carbon in mild steel at 1000°C (1273 K) and 950°C (1223 K) be D_1 and D_2 respectively.

$$\frac{D_2}{D_1} = \exp\left\{\frac{Q}{R_0}\left(\frac{T_2 - T_1}{T - T_2}\right)\right\} = \exp\left(\frac{150 \times 10^6 \times -50}{8314 \times 1273 \times 1223}\right) = 0.56$$

Therefore the diffusivity at 950°C (1223 K) is 0.56 of the diffusivity at 1000°C. From Fick's second law, in its approximate form:

$$\frac{C_s - C_x}{C_s - C_0} \simeq \frac{x}{2\sqrt{(Dt)}}$$

where C_s, C_0 and C_x are carbon concentrations at the surface, core and at depth x mm below the surface respectively at time t, and D is the diffusivity. For the same quality to be achieved C_s must remain at 0.85 per cent C and C_x must remain at 0.75 per cent C when $x = 0.25$ mm.

Therefore

$$\frac{C_s - C_x}{C_s - C_0} = \frac{x}{2\sqrt{(D_1 t_1)}} = \frac{x}{2\sqrt{(D_2 t_2)}}$$

and so t_1/t_2 must equal $D_2/D_1 = 0.56$, or $t_2/t_1 = 1/0.56 = 1.79$.

Therefore it would be necessary to increase the length of carburising treatment by 79 per cent to achieve the same quality as at 1000°C. This would be uneconomic as the furnace fuel bills for treatment at 950°C would be $0.8 \times 1.79 = 1.43$ namely increased by 43 per cent.

Example 5.10

A mild steel boiler plate (0.16 per cent C) was exposed to a very strongly oxidising atmosphere at 1000°C due to the failure of a heat exchanger. Estimate the depth below the surface of a 10 mm thick plate at which the concentration of carbon decreases to one-half of its original value after exposure for (a) 1 hour, and (b) 1 day.

Take the diffusivity of carbon in iron at 1000°C as 3.11×10^{-11} m^2/s and discuss any assumptions made in the calculations.

(Southampton University)

101

Solution 5.10

Fick's second law of diffusion is used to solve this problem. The law may be expressed as

$$\frac{C_s - C_x}{C_s - C_0} \simeq \frac{x}{2\sqrt{Dt}}$$

where C_s, C_0 and C_x are concentrations at time t at the surface, in the core and at distance x below the surface respectively and D is the diffusivity. $C_0 = 0.16$ per cent C, $C_x = 0.08$ per cent C, and assume $C_s = 0$ per cent C. For **(a)** $t = 1$ hour $= 3600$ s and for **(b)** $t = 1$ day $= 86400$ s.

(a) $\quad \dfrac{0 - 0.08}{0 - 0.16} = \dfrac{x}{2\sqrt{(3.11 \times 10^{-11} \times 3600)}} \qquad x = 0.335 \times 10^{-3}\,\text{m} = 0.335\,\text{mm}$

(b) $\quad \dfrac{0 - 0.08}{0 - 0.16} = \dfrac{x}{2\sqrt{(3.11 \times 10^{-11} \times 86400)}} \qquad x = 1.64 \times 10^{-3}\,\text{m} = 1.64\,\text{mm}$

The depth below the surface at which the carbon content decreases to one-half of its original value is **(a)** 0.335 mm after 1 hour and **(b)** 1.64 mm after 1 day. The assumptions made were: (i) that the concentration of carbon at the surface of the steel was zero and (ii) that an approximation to Fick's equation was valid.

Example 5.11

The following expression represents the solution to Fick's second law:

$$\frac{C_s - C_x}{C_s - C_i} = \text{erf}\left\{\frac{x}{2\sqrt{(Dt)}}\right\}$$

A gear made from steel of nominal carbon content $C_i = 0.20$ per cent is to be gas carburised at 927°C, when $D = 1.28 \times 10^{-11}\,\text{m}^2\,\text{s}^{-1}$. Calculate the time in minutes necessary to increase the carbon content C_x to 0.40 per cent at a distance $x = 0.55$ mm below the surface, if the carbon concentration at the surface is maintained at 0.90 per cent.

Use the following values of erf y vs y to assist the calculation.

erf y	y	erf y	y
0.6420	0.65	0.7707	0.85
0.6778	0.70	0.7970	0.90
0.7112	0.75	0.8209	0.95
0.7421	0.80	0.8427	1.00

Solution 5.11

Substituting in Fick's second equation:

$$\frac{0.9 - 0.4}{0.9 - 0.2} = \text{erf}\left\{\frac{0.5 \times 10^{-3}}{2\sqrt{(1.28 \times 10^{-11}t)}}\right\}$$

but when erf $y = 0.7143$, $y = 0.756$

so

$$\frac{0.5 \times 10^{-3}}{2\sqrt{(1.28 \times 10^{-11}t)}} = 0.756$$

from which $t = 8543$ s $\equiv 2$ hours 22 minutes.

5.3 Questions

Question 5.1

The time required to recrystallise aluminium varies with temperature and can be expressed by the relationship $t = A \exp(B/T)$ where A and B are constants, t is the recrystallisation time and T is the temperature (K).

Derive the values of A and B if $t = 100$ hours at 260°C and $t = 6$ min at 330°C.

(Kingston Polytechnic)

Question 5.2

The time required to soften a deformed metal by 50 per cent at 400 K is 1.5 min and at 430 K is 0.5 min. Calculate the activation energy of this softening process.

(Sheffield City Polytechnic)

Question 5.3

The strength of a given steel component designed for use at high temperature is reduced below its working limit after 50 per cent recrystallisation has occurred by an activated energy process. This limit is reached after 4250 s at 851 K and after 3.6 s at 1023 K. Assuming that the Arrhenius law applies, calculate the maximum temperature at which a working life of 10^4 hours is attainable.

(Polytechnic of Central London)

Question 5.4

The variation in thermionic emission from a tungsten filament with temperature is given below.

Temperature (K)	Current density (mA/mm²)
1470	7.63×10^{-7}
1543	4.84×10^{-6}
1761	4.62×10^{-4}
1897	4.31×10^{-3}

Show graphically that the above data are consistent with the Arrhenius law and calculate the activation energy (work function) for tungsten.

Determine the thermionic current density for a tungsten filament temperature of 2000 K.

(Hint: Current is a rate, $1A = 1Cs^{-1}$. Use Boltzmann's constant.)

Question 5.5

If the creep strain rate of a metal is $3 \times 10^{-9} \text{ s}^{-1}$ at 560°C, determine the creep strain rate at 650°C, assuming that the applied stress remains constant. Assume that the creep process has an activation energy of 65 MJ/kmol and the universal constant is 8.314 kJ/kmol K.

(Polytechnic of Central London)

Question 5.6

The diffusion rates for carbon in titanium were determined at the following temperatures:

Temperature (°C)	736	782	835
Diffusion coefficient, D (m² s⁻¹)	2×10^{-13}	5×10^{-13}	1.3×10^{-12}

(a) Determine whether the equation $D = A \exp(-Q/RT)$ applies and, if so, evaluate the frequency constant, A, and the activation energy for diffusion, Q.

(b) Calculate the rate of diffusion at 500°C and comment on the value for 1000°C.

(Salford)

Question 5.7

Calculate the percentage of carbon 0.3 mm below the surface of a 0.15 per cent C mild steel component which has been case carburised for 10 hours at 850°C.

Assume the surface carbon concentration has been maintained at 1 per cent C during the process and the diffusivity of carbon in mild steel at 850°C is $4.5 \times 10^{-12} \text{ m}^2 \text{ s}^{-1}$.

Question 5.8

A steel containing 1.2 per cent C is heated at 1000°C in a strongly oxidising atmosphere. Estimate the depth below the surface at which the carbon concentration is reduced to 0.6 per cent after 1 hour's exposure.

Take D for carbon in steel at 1000°C as $3.1 \times 10^{-11} \text{ m}^2 \text{ s}^{-1}$. Assume that the concentration of carbon at the surface during oxidation is zero.

Question 5.9

In a case carburisation process, the surface of a 0.2 per cent carbon steel sheet is maintained at 1.2 per cent carbon for 100 minutes at 800°C. Calculate the depth at which the carbon content is 0.6 per cent carbon after this process. The diffusion coefficient of carbon in steel at 800°C is $2.4 \times 10^{-12}\,\mathrm{m^2\,s^{-1}}$.

(Southampton University)

5.4 Answers to Questions

5.1 $A = 8.564 \times 10^{-23}$; $B = 31.72 \times 10^3$.

5.2 52.37 MJ/kmol.

5.3 700 K.

5.4 7.79×10^{-19} J/atom; 2.0×10^{-2} mA/mm².

5.5 7.5×10^{-9} s⁻¹.

5.6 **(a)** $A = 2.586 \times 10^{-4}$; $Q = 176$ MJ/kmol.

 (b) D at 500°C $= 1.55 \times 10^{-11}\,\mathrm{m^2 s^{-1}}$; A value for D at 1000°C can be calculated but is unlikely to be correct as there is an allotropic change and α-Ti transforms to β-Ti on heating through 880°C.

5.7 0.68 per cent C.

5.8 0.33 mm.

5.9 0.144 mm.

6 Iron and Steel

6.1 Fact Sheet

(a)

The iron–carbon phase diagram is the key to an understanding of steels and cast irons. This diagram is shown below.

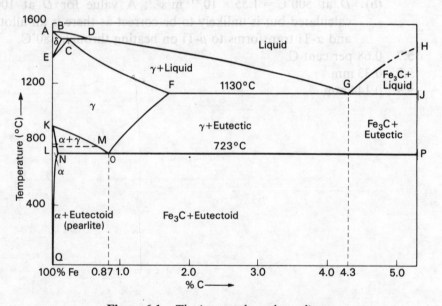

Figure 6.1 *The iron–carbon phase diagram*

(b) Steels

Steels are, essentially, alloys of iron and carbon containing up to 1.5 per cent carbon. The $\alpha \rightarrow \gamma$ transition in iron is responsible for giving a phase diagram containing a eutectoid. This permits the modification of alloy structures and properties through heat-treatment.

Slow cooling through the critical temperature range will allow the α/Fe_3C eutectoid pearlite to form. Rapid cooling will give formation of α' (martensite), an extremely hard but brittle phase. Low temperature heat treatment of martensite, tempering, will cause a reduction of hardness and an improvement in toughness.

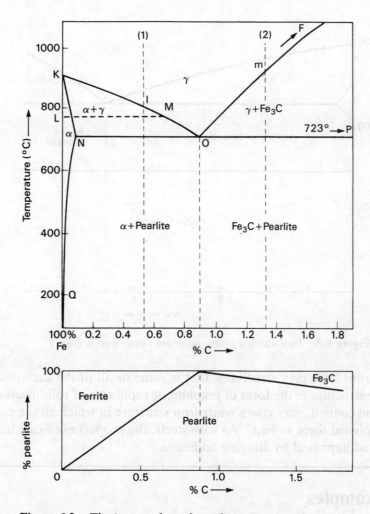

Figure 6.2 *The iron–carbon phase diagram—(steel portion)*

The addition of alloying elements to steels will give improved strength, through solid solution strengthening, and increase hardenability. For small alloy additions, steel microstructures will be similar to those of plain carbon steels and similar heat treatments can be given. Large alloy additions may give materials whose structures and heat treatments differ considerably from those of plain carbon steels, for example, stainless steels.

(c) Cast Irons

Cast irons contain between 2 and 5 per cent carbon. The high carbon section of the iron–carbon phase diagram (see below) covers this range of compositions but does not give a true prediction of the phases which can appear in an iron structure. The structures of cast irons are affected by several factors, namely composition, rate of solidification and subsequent heat treatment.

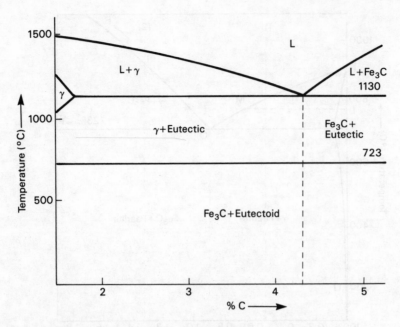

Figure 6.3 *Iron–carbon phase diagram (cast iron section)*

Most cast irons have grey structures, that is some or all of the carbon content appears in the structure in the form of graphite. A rapid rate of solidification, or a very low silicon content, may give a white iron structure in which all the carbon is present in combined form as Fe_3C. As with steels, the properties of cast irons can be modified and improved by alloying additions.

6.2 Worked Examples

Example 6.1

(a) Give definitions of the following: (i) ferrite, (ii) martensite, (iii) austenite, (iv) pearlite, (v) bainite.

(b) How would the following heat treatments be conducted, quoting approximate temperatures and cooling rates:
  (i)   normalising of a plain carbon steel containing 0.4 per cent C,
  (ii) hardening of a plain carbon steel containing 0.8 per cent,
  (iii) process annealing of a cold rolled mild steel?

Solution 6.1

(a) (i)   Ferrite is the body-centred cubic allotrope of iron, α and δ forms, and body-centred cubic solid solutions.

(ii)   Martensite, or α', is the non-equilibrium phase formed by rapid cooling of austenite. It is a supersaturated solution of carbon in α-Fe, has a body-centred tetragonal structure, and is hard and brittle.

(iii)   Austenite is the face-centred allotrope of iron, δ-Fe, and face-centred cubic solid solutions. It is non-magnetic.

(iv)   Pearlite is the eutectoid mixture of ferrite and cementite, Fe_3C, formed by the transformation of austenite during cooling. Generally it has a lamellar structure.

(v) Bainite is one of the transformation products of austenite formed by isothermal transformation after an interrupted quench or, in some alloy steels, during the direct cooling of austenite. Its characteristics are intermediate between pearlite and martensite.

(b) The following diagram can be used as a guide for heat treatment temperatures for plain carbon steels.

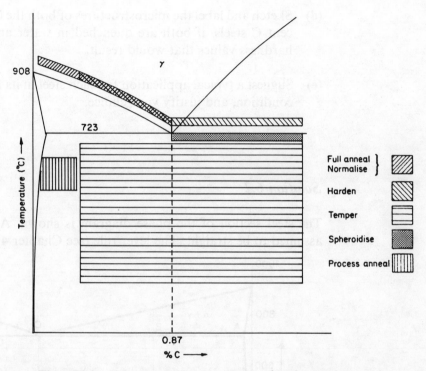

Figure 6.4 *Heat treatment temperatures for plain carbon steels*

(i) Normalising is cooling in still air from a temperature of about 30°C above the upper critical temperature. For a plain carbon steel of 0.4 per cent carbon content this would be about 850°C.

(ii) A plain carbon steel containing 0.8 per cent C would be hardened by water quenching from a temperature of about 30°C above the upper critical temperature, namely about 770°C.

(iii) A process anneal, or sub-critical anneal, can be used for softening a cold worked mild steel and involves heating the steel at about 550–600°C. Cold worked ferrite (some 80–85 per cent of the structure) is recrystallised while the pearlite is largely unaffected.

Example 6.2

With reference to the iron–iron carbide phase diagram, for two plain carbon steels, namely 0.4 per cent and 1.0 per cent C:

(a) Calculate the amount of austenite present in each of these steels at a temperature of 724°C.

(b) Calculate the amount of pearlite present in each of these steels at 25°C, assuming slow cooling.

(c) Estimate the proportion of cementite existing at the grain boundaries as free cementite and the proportion present with ferrite in pearlite in the hypereutectoid steel at room temperature (Fe_3C contains 6.67 per cent C).

(d) Sketch and label the microstructures of both the 0.4 per cent C and the 1.0 per cent C steels, if both are quenched in water and indicate the approximate hardness values that would result.

(e) Suggest a typical application for each steel in its fully hardened and tempered condition, and justify your choice.

(Trent Polytechnic)

Solution 6.2

The steel section of the phase diagram is shown. All phase boundary lines are assumed to be straight. The lever rule (see Chapter 4) is used.

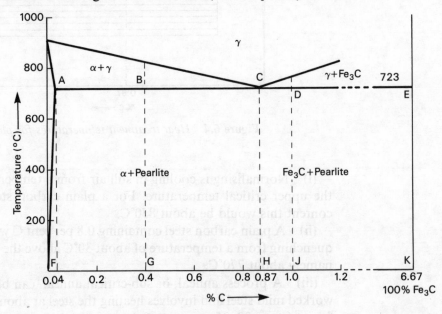

Figure 6.5

(a) (i) for 0.4 per cent C steel, the percentage of γ in structure is given by:

$$(AB/AC) \times 100 = (0.36/0.83) \times 100 = 43 \text{ per cent}$$

(ii) for 1.0 per cent C steel, the percentage of γ in structure is given by:

$$(DE/CE) \times 100 = (5.67/5.80) \times 100 = 98 \text{ per cent}$$

110

(b)   (i)   for 0.4 per cent C steel, the percentage of pearlite in structure is given by:

$$(FG/FH) \times 100 = (0.40/0.87) \times 100 = 46 \text{ per cent}$$

    (ii)   for 1.0 per cent C steel, the percentage of pearlite in structure is given by:

$$(JK/HK) \times 100 = (5.67/5.80) \times 100 = 98 \text{ per cent}$$

(c)   It is valid to use the tie-line FK for room temperature proportions as F is, to all extents, at 0 per cent C.

    From **(b)**(ii), 98 per cent of the structure is pearlite and 2 per cent is grain boundary cementite. Within pearlite the percentage is given by

$$(FH/FK) \times 100 = (0.87/6.67) \times 100 = 13\%$$

So in a 1.0 per cent C steel, 13 per cent of 98 per cent of the structure, namely 12.8 per cent, is the cementite within pearlite. The amount of cementite existing as grain boundary cementite is, therefore $(2/14.8) \times 100$ or 13.5 per cent and the remaining 86.5 per cent of the cementite is present with ferrite in the pearlite areas.

(d)   The type of microstructures expected after water quenching are shown below. For the 0.4 per cent C steel, the structure is martensite. For the 1.0 per cent C steel, about 2 per cent of the structure is spheroidised cementite and the remainder is martensite.

    The hardness values which would be achieved are $H_D = 700$–800 for the 0.4 per cent C steel and $H_D = 1000$–1100 for the 1.0 per cent C steel.

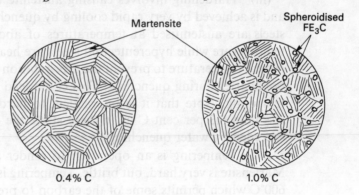

Figure 6.6

Note: In the absence of full information it is assumed for part (d) that water quenching was from the correct austenitising temperatures, namely 30°C above the upper critical temperature for the 0.4 per cent C steel and 30°C above the lower critical temperature for the 1.0 per cent C steel.

(e)   0.4 per cent C steel is suitable for the manufacture of shafts. Correctly heat treated it will have a high surface hardness to withstand wear and possess good strength and toughness to transmit power.

    1.0 per cent C steel is a tool steel. The high surface hardness obtainable would make it suitable for use as, for example, a milling cutter.

Example 6.3

(a) Explain what is meant by the following heat treatment terms as applied to plain carbon steels: (i) full annealing, (ii) normalising, (iii) hardening, (iv) tempering, (v) spheroidising.

(b) State, giving reasons, the type of steel which should be selected for each of the following applications, and the nature of the heat treatment which should be given: (i) a hacksaw blade, (ii) steel sheet for making car body pressings.

(Polytechnic of Central London)

Solution 6.3

(a) (i) Full annealing is a treatment to put a hypoeutectoid steel into its softest condition and involves heating the steel at about 30°C above the upper critical temperature followed by slow cooling in a furnace. Austenite transforms into ferrite and coarse pearlite.

(ii) Normalising is a softening treatment for hypoeutectoid steels similar to full annealing but involving cooling in still air rather than in a furnace. The somewhat faster rate of cooling gives a finer grain structure than full annealing and a product that is somewhat harder and stronger.

(iii) Hardening involves causing austenite to transform into α' or martensite and is achieved by very rapid cooling by quenching in water or oil. Hypoeutectoid steels are austenitised at temperatures of about 30°C above the upper critical temperature while hypereutectoid steels are heated at about 30°C above the lower critical temperature to prevent the precipitation of pro-eutectoid cementite at grain boundaries during quenching. This could lead to the steel remaining brittle after tempering. Note that it is impractical to harden plain carbon steels containing less than 0.3 per cent C as in these steels the critical cooling velocity cannot be exceeded by water quenching.

(iv) Tempering is an operation to render a hardened steel suitable for use. Martensite is very hard, but brittle. Tempering is a heat treatment in the range 200–600°C which permits some of the carbon to precipitate from supersaturated solid solution giving a reduced hardness and improved toughness.

(v) If a hypoeutectoid steel is cooled slowly from above the upper critical temperature a network of brittle pro-eutectoid Fe_3C will be formed. Spheroidising is the preferred softening treatment for these steels and involves heating the steel for a lengthy period at about the lower critical temperature. During the treatment the Fe_3C reforms into spheroidal shaped particles to give a structure of great toughness.

(b) (i) A hacksaw blade. A hacksaw blade needs to have a very high hardness and would be a high carbon steel containing 1.2–1.3 per cent C. The heat treatment would be hardening followed by tempering. A relatively low tempering temperature, about 220°C would be used, to give some increased toughness with little loss of hardness.

(ii) Steel for car body pressings needs to have high ductility and be readily formable by rolling to give sheet with a good surface finish. A mild steel with a low carbon content (about 0.05 per cent C) would be used. After cold rolling it would need to be annealed to make it suitable for presswork and deep drawing and would be fully annealed in a controlled atmosphere to prevent surface scaling.

Example 6.4

(a) A plain carbon steel containing approximately 0.6 per cent C is heat treated as follows:
    (i)   heated to 800°C and quenched in cold water,
    (ii) heated to 800°C and slowly cooled in the furnace,
    (iii) heated to 800°C, quenched in water and reheated at 250°C,
    (iv) heated to 800°C, quenched in water and reheated at 600°C.
Describe with the aid of diagrams the structures obtained by these treatments.

(b) Indicate, in a general way, what sort of physical properties you would expect the different treatments to produce.

(c) Which heat treatment would you consider best for (i) cutting tools and (ii) dynamically stressed engineering components?

Solution 6.4

(a) 800°C is about 25°C above the upper critical temperature for a 0.6 per cent C steel and the structure would be austenitised on heating to this temperature.

(i) Rapid quenching will produce martensite in the outer layers of the steel. Martensite has an acicular structure and the appearance of the microstructure is of small, ill-defined needles. The core material, cooling more slowly, will have a fine ferrite + pearlite structure.

(ii) Furnace cooling is the full annealing process. Slow transformation of austenite will give a structure comprising ferrite and coarse lamellar pearlite. Approximately 70 per cent of the structure will be pearlite in a steel of this composition.

(iii) The microstructure will be similar to sample (i) but may etch more rapidly to a darker appearance. Tempering at 250°C will not permit much precipitation of carbon from α'.

(iv) Tempering at 600°C will allow most of the carbon to precipitate from supersaturated solid solution in the form of roughly spheroidal particles of Fe_3C in an α matrix.

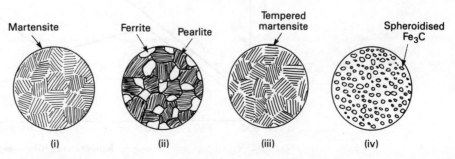

Figure 6.7

113

(b) (i) The martensitic structure will be very hard and also very brittle.

(ii) The ferrite + coarse pearlite structure is the softest condition for this steel. The coarse nature of the pearlite will mean that, although of reasonable ductility, the notch impact strength will be comparatively low (lower than that of a normalised steel).

(iii) Tempering at 250°C will cause a small reduction in hardness from the fully hardened state and a small increase in the impact strength.

(iv) Tempering at 600°C will reduce the hardness considerably and it will approach the hardness of the annealed or normalised state. The structure containing spheroidal Fe_3C is, however, extremely tough and this state will have an impact strength very much higher than that of normalised material.

(c) (i) For cutting tools, hardening and tempering at 250°C would be appropriate. (Most cutting tools would have much higher carbon contents than 0.6 per cent but some wood-working tools are of 0.6–0.7 per cent C steel.)

(ii) Hardening and tempering at 600°C would be appropriate because of the high toughness giving good resistance to shock loading.

Example 6.5

The graph plots of change in length against temperature obtained from a dilatometer test on a hypoeutectoid steel sample are shown in the accompanying diagram. The rates of heating and cooling during the test were maintained at 15°C per minute.

(a) Determine the equilibrium values of the critical temperatures for this steel and explain any differences from values expected from consideration of the iron–carbon phase diagram.

(b) Estimate the percentage carbon in the steel.

(Polytechnic of Central London)

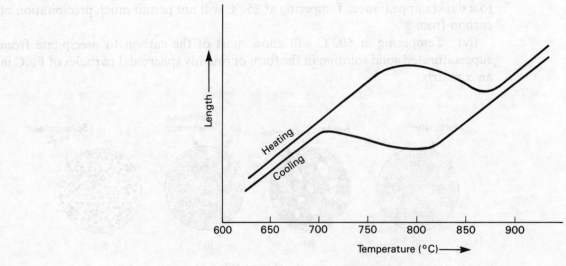

Figure 6.8

114

Solution 6.5

The critical temperatures, A_1 and A_3, are the temperatures at which phase changes begin and end. They occur at the points on the curves where linear expansion ceases and recommences and not at the points of inflexion.

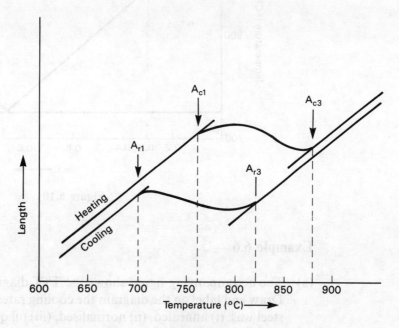

Figure 6.9

(a) From the solution diagram it will be seen that the critical temperatures are: $A_{c1} = 760°C$, $A_{c3} = 880°C$, $A_{r1} = 700°C$, $A_{r3} = 820°C$. A_{c1} and A_{c3} mean A_1 and A_3 temperatures as determined during heating, while A_{r1} and A_{r3} mean temperatures determined during cooling, from the French *chauffage* (heating) and *refroidissement* (cooling). As the rates of heating and cooling are the same, the equilibrium values for A_1 and A_3 will be the mean of the A_c and A_r temperatures, namely $A_1 = (760 + 700) \div 2 = 730°C$ and $A_3 = (880 + 820) \div 2 = 850°C$.

From the iron–carbon diagram the lower critical temperature, the A_1, should be 723°C. Plain carbon steels invariably contain some manganese, an element which lowers the critical temperatures but this steel has an A_1 value above 723°C and this would be consistent with a low alloy steel containing some chromium, an element which raises the critical temperatures.

(b) Sketch a portion of the iron–carbon diagram (see below) and mark the critical temperatures of the unknown steel on this. It will be necessary to make a correction to the figures to do this, by subtracting 7 from each value giving 723°C and 843°C. An A_3 value of 843°C corresponds to a carbon content of 0.30 per cent.

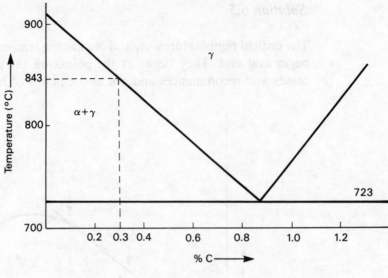

Figure 6.10

Example 6.6

(a) The accompanying figure shows the TTT diagram for a 0.6 per cent C steel. Draw and label on the diagram the cooling rates that would be expected if this steel was: (i) annealed, (ii) normalised, (iii) oil quenched, (iv) water quenched.

Sketch the microstructures that would be obtained at 25°C for each of (i), (ii) and (iv).

(b) Using the diagram, calculate the critical cooling rate. Also estimate the time for 50 per cent transformation of a sample quenched to 400°C and held there.

(c) What effect does (i) the addition of carbon, (ii) the addition of alloying elements have on the hardenability of a steel? Why is hardenability important in the industrial application of a steel?

(Trent Polytechnic)

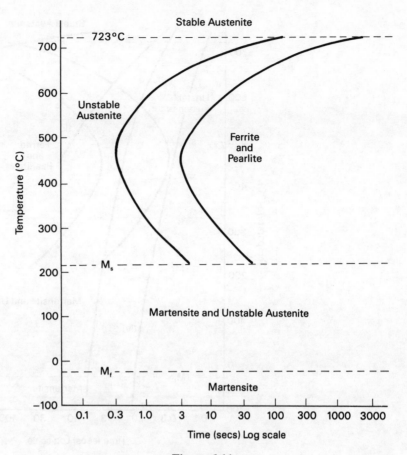

Stable Austenite

723°C

Unstable
Austenite

Ferrite
and
Pearlite

M$_s$

Martensite and Unstable Austenite

M$_f$

Martensite

Temperature (°C)

Time (secs) Log scale

Figure 6.11

Solution 6.6

(a) The rates of cooling which are achieved are approximately as follows: (i) slow furnace cool, 0.01–0.05°C/s; (ii) air cool, 5–10°C/s; (iii) oil quench, 100–200°C/s; (iv) water quench, 500–1000°C/s.

See the solution diagram.

It will be seen that during annealing transformation of austenite occurs at a high temperature, only just below the critical temperatures, giving coarse pearlite, but during normalising the transformation into pearlite occurs between about 670°C and 600°C and a finer pearlite will be formed. With oil quenching, transformation into a very fine pearlite will commence at about 570°C and some 70 per cent of the austenite will have transformed by the time the temperature has fallen to 450°C. The remaining austenite will transform into martensite when the M_s temperature is reached. Water quenching will keep to the left of the nose of the curve and austenite will transform into martensite.

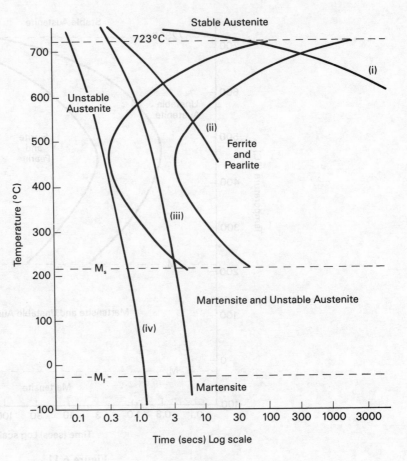

Figure 6.12

The microstructures expected at 25°C for (i), (ii) and (iv) are shown below. In (i) and (ii) transformation will have been completed giving coarse pearlite + ferrite and fine pearlite + ferrite respectively. In (iv) transformation into martensite begins at the M_s temperature of about 220°C. At 25°C the structure is of martensite with some retained austenite.

Figure 6.13

(b) The cooling rate curve which just grazes the nose of the TTT diagram is the critical cooling rate and it is about 900–1000°C/s.

For a sample quenched rapidly to 400°C and maintained at that temperature, 50 per cent transformation is achieved in about 1.5 s.

(c) Both the addition of carbon and the addition of other alloying elements have the effect of moving the TTT diagram toward the right, in other words, reducing the critical cooling velocity and increasing hardenability. The effect of alloying

118

elements, such as manganese, nickel and chromium, is much greater than that of carbon in this respect.

Hardenability is an important property of a steel. A steel of high hardenability will harden to a greater depth below the surface than one of lesser hardenability for the same rate of cooling. Also, a martensitic structure can be achieved with a slower rate of cooling in a steel of high hardenability than is the case for a low hardenability steel, in some alloy steels even cooling in air is sufficiently rapid. The less drastic quenching techniques that are needed lessens the risk of cracking and distortion occurring in heat treated components.

Example 6.7

(a) Explain the concept of TTT curves. How are they obtained and how do they help in understanding the various transformation products observed in steels?

(b) What is meant by the term 'hardenability'? Use this concept to account for the differences in properties you would expect from air quenched and tempered samples of (i) 0.4 per cent C, 0.8 per cent Mn steel (080M40) and (ii) 0.4 per cent C, 0.8 per cent Mn, 1.5 per cent Ni, 1.0 per cent Cr, 0.2 per cent Mo steel (817M40). Give examples of the use of these steels in engineering applications.

(Southampton University)

Solution 6.7

(a) Phase diagrams show only equilibrium states and give no indication of non-equilibrium phases such as martensite and bainite. Solid state transformations into both equilibrium and non-equilibrium phases can be shown on TTT diagrams. Such diagrams show the effects of differing rates of cooling on the temperature at which change occurs, the rate of change and the nature of the product. The data to construct TTT diagrams are obtained from observation of structural changes using a variety of techniques involving cooling at differing rates, interrupted quenching, thermal analysis and microscopy.

(b) Hardenability refers to the ease with which martensite is formed during quenching from the austenitic state and the depth of hardening which can be achieved in steels.

(i) Steel 080M40 is a plain carbon steel of low hardenability. An air quench is not likely to cause hardening and the structure would be of fine ferrite and pearlite in approximately equal proportions. Tempering would have no effect on this structure. The steel would be of moderate hardness (about $H_D = 240$), a tensile strength of about 850 MPa and good toughness (Charpy notch impact strength about 350 kJ/m^2). A medium carbon steel of this composition could be used for making shafts, connecting rods and high tensile tubing, but should be used in the hardened and tempered condition.

(ii) Steel 817M40 is a low alloy steel of high hardenability. Although this steel is generally oil quenched, air quenching of a small section would give a martensitic/bainitic structure. The final properties would depend on the tempering temperature. Tempering at 200°C would give a hardness of about $H_D = 600$, a tensile

119

strength of about 2000 MPa and Charpy impact strength of about 260 kJ/m^2. In this condition, it is suitable for gear manufacture. If tempered at 600°C the hardness is reduced to about $H_D = 250$, but the tensile strength is about 1000 MPa and the Charpy value is about 650 kJ/m^2.

Example 6.8

(a) (i) Name two types of steel capable of being hardened.
(ii) Briefly distinguish between the effects of annealing and normalising on a steel.

(b) (i) State a quenching medium that will produce (1) a rapid quench and (2) a slow quench.
(ii) What is the significance of the rate of quenching?
(iii) Define the term ruling section.

(c) (i) Briefly describe the nitriding hardening process.
(ii) What condition must the steel be in before nitriding?
(iii) What are the advantages of nitriding?

(Sheffield University)

Solution 6.8

(a) (i) Many steels can be hardened; these include both medium carbon and tool steels, in the plain carbon range, and most low alloy steels.

(ii) Both are softening processes but, because of the slower rate of cooling, an annealed steel is softer than a normalised steel. The grain size of a normalised steel is finer and this gives greater hardness, static strength and impact strength.

(b) (i) (1) Water or brine; brine gives a more drastic quench than water. (2) Oil, or for some alloy steels, an air quench.

(ii) The quench rate must exceed the critical cooling velocity for hardening to occur. For a steel of a given hardenability, an increase in the quench rate will increase the depth of hardening. For a steel of high hardenability, a slow quench rate will cause hardening with less risk of distortion and cracking.

(iii) Ruling section is the maximum diameter of section that can be hardened to give uniformity of properties across the section.

(c) (i) Nitriding is a surface hardening process in which nitrogen is diffused into the steel surface. Hard nitrides are formed giving an extremely hard surface (hardness of $H_D = 1100$). The steel is heated for 50–100 hours at 500–540°C in a cracked ammonia atmosphere.

(ii) The steel is hardened by oil quenching and tempered at 600–700°C before nitriding. No subsequent heat treatment is needed because of the low nitriding temperature.

(iii) Advantages are that an extremely hard surface is produced and the steel has improved corrosion resistance, components can be finish machined in the soft condition before heat treatment and nitriding. The disadvantages are that the process is fairly costly and it is necessary to use special nitriding quality steels.

Example 6.9

(a) Describe how the hardenability of a steel may be determined experimentally.
(b) Sketch the types of hardenability curves which would be obtained from tests on the following steels:
  (i) steel 080M40 (0.4 per cent C; 0.8 per cent Mn)
  (ii) steel 817M40 (0.4 per cent C; 0.8 per cent Mn; 1.5 per cent Ni; 1.0 per cent Cr; 0.2 per cent Mo)
  (iii) steel 835M30 (0.3 per cent C; 0.5 per cent Mn; 4.0 per cent Ni; 1.25 per cent Cr)

Solution 6.9

(a) An experimental test for determining hardenability is the Jominy end quench test in which a bar of steel, nominal dimensions 100 mm × 25 mm diameter, is fully austenitised in a furnace and then placed in a quenching rig such that a water jet plays on the end surface of the bar (see diagram below) and the bar cools slowly through heat conduction to the quenched face. When the bar has fully cooled, two small diametrically opposed flats are ground on the bar surface and a series of diamond hardness tests are made along these flats from the quenched end. The variation of hardness with distance from the quenched end approximates to the variation in hardness with depth below the surface for the steel.

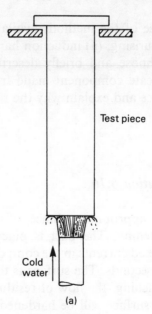

(a)

Figure 6.14

(b) See the Jominy hardenability curves in the diagram below.

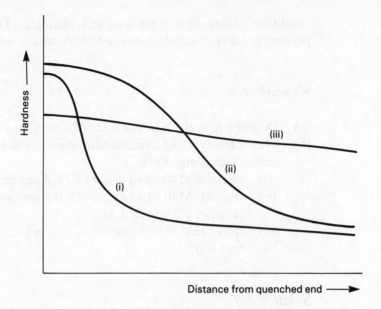

Figure 6.15

(i) Steel 080M40 is a plain carbon steel of low hardenability.

(ii) Steel 817M40 is a low alloy steel. The presence of 1.5 per cent Ni and 1.0 per cent Cr will give increased hardenability.

(iii) Steel 835M30 with 4.0 per cent Ni and 1.25 per cent Cr has a very high hardenability and the Jominy curve is almost flat. This type of steel is an air hardening steel.

Example 6.10

Three of the methods available for surface hardening steel components are: (i) carburising, (ii) induction hardening, and (iii) nitriding.

Choose and briefly describe the appropriate method for case hardening an intricate component made from 0.4 per cent C plain carbon steel. Justify your choice and explain why the remaining two methods would be unsuitable.

(Trent Polytechnic)

Solution 6.10

The appropriate choice of a surface hardening method would be induction hardening. The part is placed inside a high-frequency induction coil and the induced currents in the component heats the surface to a high temperature within a few seconds. The surface is then quench hardened by cooling water sprays. After quenching, the flow of residual heat from the centre will self-temper the surface. The surface will be hardened to about $H_D = 600$ to a depth of about 3 mm and minimal distortion occurs. This method can be used for hardening gears and shaft journal areas.

Carburising is a process suitable for mild steels (0.15 per cent C) to give a hard surface with a soft and tough core. Nitriding is a process for putting a very hard surface on a steel of 0.3–0.4 per cent C, but is used in connection with special alloy steels—Nitralloy steels containing aluminium. If a plain carbon steel is nitrided, some nitrogen could diffuse into the core forming brittle nitrides in what should be a tough core.

Example 6.11

Summarise the effects of the following elements as alloying additions to steels: nickel, chromium, manganese, molybdenum, vanadium.

Indicate some types of commercial alloy steels which make use of the effects you have referred to in the answer above.

(City University)

Solution 6.11

Nickel.   Nickel has a strengthening effect, lowers the critical temperature range, increases hardenability and improves resistance to fatigue. Up to 5 per cent nickel may be added to 0.3–0.4 per cent C steels used for shafts and other parts subject to fatique.

Chromium.   Chromium increases strength and hardness, raises the critical temperatures, increases hardenability and forms hard and stable carbides. Quantities greater than 12 per cent make the steel stainless. 1–1.5 per cent chromium in medium and high carbon steels is used for gears, springs, tools and ball bearings.

Manganese.   Manganese is always present to some extent in steels as it is used as a deoxidising agent. It increases strength and hardness, lowers the critical temperatures, increases hardenability and forms a carbide. More than 12 per cent Mn will give an austenitic steel. Hadfield's steel (13 per cent Mn; 1 per cent C) is a very hard, non-magnetic, austenitic steel used in applications where extreme resistance to abrasion is needed, for example excavator bucket teeth, jaws for rock crushers.

Molybdenum.   Molybdenum is a strong carbide forming element. It also reduces temper-brittleness in pearlitic Ni/Cr steels and improves high temperature creep resistance. It is not used on its own, but up to 0.5 per cent Mo is often added to Ni/Cr steels to reduce temper-brittleness.

Vanadium.   Vanadium is a strong carbide forming element and it has a strong scavenging action producing very clean, inclusion-free steels. It is not used on its own but is added to high speed steels and to some pearlitic chromium steels to give inclusion free tool steels with a high impact strength.

Example 6.12

(a)   Describe the structures of the main types of grey and white cast irons and account for their continued use as engineering materials.

(b) In what way does the silicon content and section thickness affect the structure of cast iron?

(c) What is meant by the term carbon equivalent?

(d) Why was the discovery of a method of manufacturing nodular iron so important and what are the advantages of nodular iron over malleable iron?

Solution 6.12

(a) Cast iron structures can be classified as either *white, mottled* or *grey*. Grey irons may be sub-divided further into *pearlitic grey, ferritic grey* and *nodular* or *spheroidal graphite* cast irons.

In a white iron, the total carbon content is present in combined form and the microstructure is composed or primary cementite and pearlite. The material is hard, non-machinable and brittle.

The structure of a mottled iron contains a small quantity of free carbon and the microstructure comprises cementite, graphite and pearlite. Mottled iron is difficult to machine.

In grey irons, a considerable amount of the carbon is present as graphite flakes and microstructures may be graphite + pearlite, graphite + pearlite + ferrite or graphite + ferrite. All these types have good machinability and the type with the highest strength is the graphite + pearlite variety. In nodular irons, the graphite appears in the structure as spheroidal nodules rather than as flakes and this structure gives higher strength and toughness than that of flake irons.

Cast irons are used widely as engineering materials for a number of valid reasons:

  (i)   they are relatively low cost materials,
  (ii)   they have relatively low melting temperatures (1100–1200°C) and are readily cast into simple or complex shapes,
  (iii) all grey irons possess excellent machinability,
  (iv)   they have reasonable tensile strength (180–350 MPa, up to 600 MPa for nodular irons) and very high compressive strength,
  (v)   they have a high damping capacity.

(b) The silicon content has a major effect on the structure of a cast iron. A high silicon content promotes the formation of graphite and a low silicon content is necessary for production of a white iron. The structure is also affected by the solidification rate, increased cooling rate promoting a white iron structure. The sectional thickness affects the rate of solidification within a sand mould, with thin sections tending to solidify white. (See the illustrations below.)

124

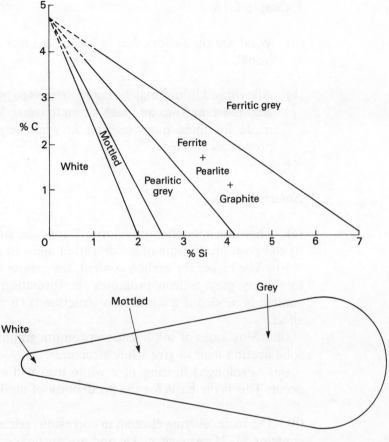

Figure 6.16

(c) The position of the eutectic point is affected by composition. The eutectic in the iron–carbon diagram occurs at a composition of 4.3 per cent carbon but the presence of other elements, notably silicon and phosphorus, reduces the carbon content of the eutectic. The effects of these elements on the phase diagram can be quantified and a carbon equivalent value quoted. The carbon equivalent = total per cent C + $\frac{1}{3}$ (per cent Si + per cent P). For example an iron containing 3.3 per cent C, 3 per cent Si, 1.2 per cent P has a C.E. = 3.3 + $\frac{1}{3}$ (3 + 1.2) = 4.7 per cent C. In other words this iron with 3.3 per cent C would possess a hypereutectic structure because of the effects of the silicon and phosphorus contents on the position of the eutectic.

(d) Graphite flakes act as points of stress concentration within a structure and flake graphite cast irons are brittle. Irons of high ductility, known as malleable irons, can be made by giving irons a prolonged heat treatment (up to 120 hours at 900°C). This heat treatment produces a structure containing spheroidal nodules of graphite but is an expensive process. The discovery of a process for producing nodular irons by a direct casting process gave a more economic method of obtaining high strength, high ductility castings. Generally, nodular irons produced by direct casting have similar ductilities and impact strengths to malleable irons but have higher tensile strengths.

Example 6.13

(a) What are the factors that influence the form that carbon takes up in a cast iron?

(b) Alloying additions may be made to irons to produce corrosion resistant irons, heat resistant irons and high strength irons. What are the principal additions made for these purposes and in what ways are the microstructures and properties affected?

Solution 6.13

(a) There are a number of factors affecting the structure of cast irons, these being (i) composition, (ii) rate of solidification and (iii) effect of heat treatment.

(i) The higher the carbon content, the greater will be the tendency for the iron to solidify grey. Silicon promotes the formation of graphite and a low silicon content is needed if a white iron structure is to be formed. Nickel has a similar effect.

(ii) Slow rates of solidification promote graphite formation, while more rapid solidification tend to give white structures.

(iii) Prolonged heating of a white iron will cause graphitisation of Fe_3C to occur. This is the basis for the production of malleable irons.

(b) The main alloying element in corrosion resistant cast irons is nickel. This type contains 11–25 per cent nickel and are austenitic in structure. They may contain some chromium and up to 6 per cent copper to give increased corrosion resistance.

A heat resistant iron needs to have a ferrite + graphite structure, otherwise growth could occur consequent upon graphitisation of cementite during prolonged high temperature service. Heat resistant irons have more than 2.5 per cent C plus about 5 per cent of silicon or silicon and nickel to give a fully graphitic structure. Small additions of alloying elements, principally chromium, nickel and molybdenum are made to give improved strength characteristics.

Example 6.14

(a) Show how a variation in the cooling rate of an iron–carbon–silicon alloy of suitable composition can lead to the formation of white, pearlitic grey or ferritic grey cast iron.

(b) What heat treatments would be required to convert the white iron into a malleable form with higher ductility and fracture strength?

(c) Explain how the addition of rare-earth elements allow the direct production of nodular iron and indicate the practical advantages of nodular irons over simple grey irons.

(Southampton University)

126

Solution 6.14

(a) As stated in solution 6.13, a rapid rate of solidification will tend to cause an iron to solidify white, whereas slow solidification will promote formation of graphite. This effect can be seen if a casting with variable sectional thickness is sand cast (see also diagram in solution 6.12).

(b) There are two major types of malleable iron which may be made from white cast irons by heat treatment, these being the whiteheart process and the blackheart process. In the former process, a white iron casting is heated in contact with an oxidising material, such as hematite ore, at about 900°C for a prolonged period. During the treatment, carbon is lost from the surface layers by oxidation. In the central parts of the section, cementite decomposes into rosettes or nodules of graphite, known as temper carbon, giving a structure of pearlite and graphite nodules. For thin sections, the amount of decarburisation may be such that the section may be wholly ferritic. The process for producing a blackheart malleable iron involves heating a white iron casting in a neutral atmosphere at about 900°C for a prolonged period. During the process, all cementite decomposes into rosettes or nodules of temper carbon and the final structure is of ferrite and graphite nodules.

(c) The innoculation of a molten iron with a small amount of a rare-earth element, such as cerium, will cause spheroidal graphite nodules to form during the direct solidification of a casting, giving a strong iron of high ductility. Innoculation of the melt with a small amount of magnesium, usually added in the form of a magnesium-nickel alloy, will have the same effect. This is a more economic method of producing a ductile cast iron than making a white iron casting and subjecting it to an expensive heat treatment.

6.3 Questions

Question 6.1

Microexamination of two plain carbon steels shows that steel 1 contains about 60 per cent ferrite and 40 per cent pearlite and steel 2 contains about 5 per cent free cementite and 95 per cent pearlite. Estimate the percentage carbon in each steel.

Question 6.2

The TTT diagram for a steel is shown in the accompanying diagram.

(a) Using this diagram determine:
   (i)   a cooling rate to give a structure containing coarse pearlite,
   (ii) a cooling rate to give a structure containing very fine pearlite, but no bainite or martensite,
   (iii) the minimum rate of cooling at which martensite will be formed.

(b) The minimum hold time, after rapid quenching to 425°C, to produce a fully bainitic structure.

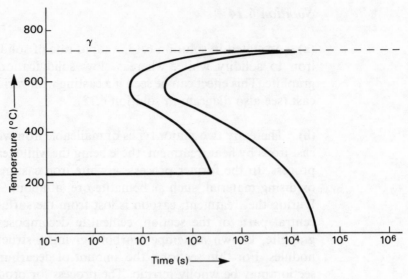

Figure 6.17

Question 6.3

The following results were obtained from a thermal analysis experiment on a hypoeutectoid plain carbon steel sample in which the rates of both heating and cooling were maintained at 15°C/min: $A_{c1} = 725°C$, $A_{c3} = 835°C$, $A_{r1} = 665°C$, $A_{r3} = 775°C$.

(a) Determine the equilibrium values of the critical temperatures for this steel and explain any differences from values expected from consideration of the iron–carbon phase diagram.

(b) Estimate the percentage carbon in the steel.

(c) To what temperature should this steel be heated prior to hardening by quenching?

(Polytechnic of Central London)

Question 6.4

Jominy hardenability curves for three steels are shown in the figure.

(a) Which curve relates to the steel of greatest hardenability?

(b) Which curve relates to the steel of highest carbon content?

(c) Estimate the ruling section of steel B.

(d) What would be the likely microstructure of a 15 mm diameter bar of steel A water quenched from the austenitising temperature?

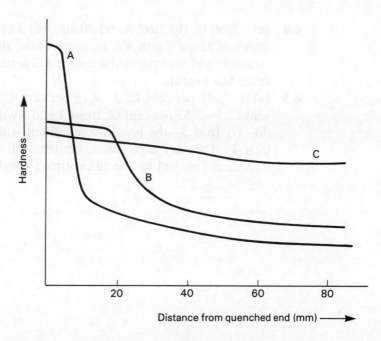

Figure 6.18

Question 6.5

The compositions of several different cast irons are given in the table below.

	C %	Si %	Mn %	P %
1	3.5	1.2	0.8	0.1
2	3.3	2.2	0.5	0.3
3	3.6	1.8	0.5	0.8
4	3.0	5.0	0.3	0.1
5	3.3	0.6	0.5	0.1

(a) Determine the carbon equivalents of these irons and state which will show a hypereutectic structure.

(b) State, giving reasons:
  (i) which iron would be most likely to solidify white when sand cast, and
  (ii) which iron would be most suitable for service at high temperatures.

6.4 Answers to Questions

6.1 Steel 1—0.45 per cent C, Steel 2–1.15 per cent C.
6.2 **(a)** (i) 10–20°C/min, (ii) 10–20°C/s, (iii) 40°C/s, **(b)** 450 s (7.5 min).
6.3 **(a)** $A_1 = 695°C$ and $A_3 = 805°C$. Plain carbon steels contain manganese, an element which lowers critical temperatures. (The corrected values to plot on the Fe–C diagram should be: A_1–723°C, A_3—833°C.) **(b)** 0.36 per cent (refer to worked example 6.5). **(c)** 835–855°C.

6.4 **(a)** Steel C, **(b)** Steel A, **(c)** 40 mm, **(d)** The outer layers of the section, to a depth of about 2 mm will be martensitic, the core will have a fine pearlitic structure and the intermediate zone will contain some martensite, bainite and some fine pearlite.

6.5 **(a)** 1—3.93 per cent C, 2—4.13 per cent C, 3—4.47 per cent C, 4—4.7 per cent C, 5—3.53 per cent C. Irons 3 and 4 will show hypereutectic structures. **(b)** (i) Iron 5—the low silicon content will aid a white iron structure. (ii) Iron 4—The very high silicon content will tend to give a wholly graphitic structure. This will not be susceptible to high temperature growth.

7 Non-ferrous Metals

7.1 Fact Sheet

(a)

Of all the metallic elements, only a comparatively small number are used in quantity as the basis for engineering materials, although many others are used as alloying elements for specific purposes. The metals used in large amounts are aluminium, copper, magnesium, nickel, titanium and zinc.

(b)

Some non-ferrous metals are used in the pure form but in many cases the metals are alloyed. The main reasons for alloying are:
  (i)   to strengthen by forming solid solutions,
  (ii) to create alloys which will respond to strengthening heat treatments.
  (iii) to reduce melting temperatures and increase castability, or
  (iv) to improve some other characteristic such as corrosion resistance.

(c)

Many metals and alloys can be work hardened but will not respond to any heat treatment other than stress relief or annealing.

Some alloys are very difficult to cold work and can only be formed by hot working operations or casting.

Some alloys will respond to precipitation hardening heat treatments.

7.2 Worked Examples

Example 7.1

A portion of the copper–zinc (brass) equilibrium diagram is shown in the figure below. In relation to this diagram:

(a)   Mark the peritectic points and identify the unlabelled phase fields.

(b) Calculate the relative amounts of the phases present: (i) at 25°C for a 40 per cent zinc alloy and (ii) at 950°C for a 30 per cent zinc alloy.

(c) Sketch the expected microstructure at 25°C for (i) a rapidly cooled 30 per cent zinc alloy and (ii) a slowly cooled 40 per cent zinc alloy.

(d) Indicate the approximate relative values of tensile strength and percentage elongation for (i) the 30 per cent zinc alloy and (ii) the 40 per cent zinc alloy, after slow cooling from the melt.

(e) State, giving reasons, which composition should be chosen for (i) hot press stamping and (ii) cold rolled sheet.

(Trent Polytechnic)

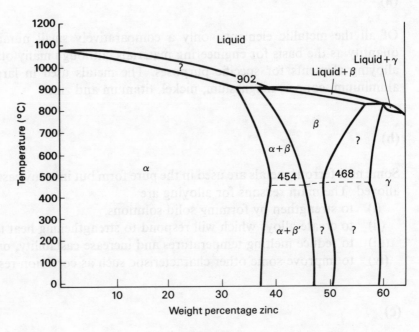

Figure 7.1

Solution 7.1

(a) The two peritectic points are at temperatures of 902°C and 825°C, marked as points X and Y on the solution diagram. The labelling to be inserted in the unmarked phase fields is (Liquid + α), (β + γ), β′, and (β′ + γ), as shown in the solution diagram.

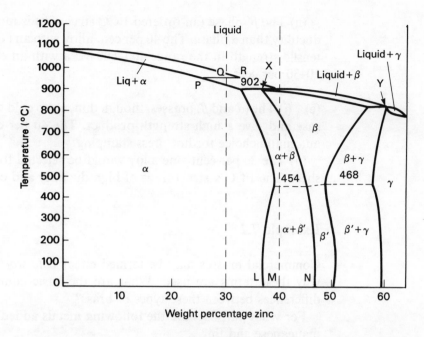

Figure 7.2

(b) (i) The phases present are α and β′. Draw a tie-line LMN. The ratio amount α/ amount β′ = MN/LM = 7.0/3.0 = 2.33/1.

(ii) The phases are liquid and α. Draw a tie-line PQR. The two phases are present in the ratio amount liquid/amount α = PQ/QR = 4/4 = 1/1.

(c) (i) Rapid cooling will not permit the equilibrium structure to be formed. The α crystals will be cored, with the centre zones being richer in copper, and the last liquid to solidify at α boundaries is likely to undergo a peritectic reaction transforming into β phase.

(ii) Slow cooling will allow equilibrium to be attained. The liquid will solidify as β phase with a large grain size. From about 800°C, α phase will start precipitating within the β structure. On further cooling, β will transform into β′, an ordered solid solution.

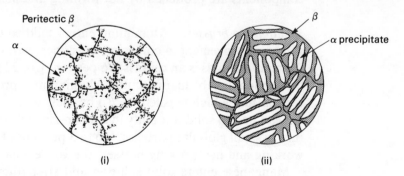

Figure 7.3

(d) (i) α brasses (FCC structure) are relatively soft and ductile and the 30 per cent zinc alloy has a greater ductility than pure copper. Slowly cooled cast material would have a tensile strength in the range 200–270 MPa and a percentage elongation value in the range 15–40 per cent.

(ii) The β' phase (an ordered BCC structure) is much stronger and has a lower ductility than α phase. The 40 per cent alloy with an $(\alpha + \beta')$ structure would have a tensile strength in the range 400–600 MPa with an elongation value in the range 10–30 per cent.

(e) (i) The (α and β) brasses, though difficult to cold work, can be hot worked with ease and give a high strength product. The 40 per cent zinc alloy would be the automatic choice for hot press stamping.

(ii) The 30 per cent zinc alloy would be selected for manufacture of cold rolled sheet. The FCC α structure is of high ductility and can be readily cold worked.

Example 7.2

Commercial brasses may be termed either *cold working* or *hot working*. Explain why these terms are used. What are the basic compositional and metallurgical differences between these types of brass?

For what purposes are the following metals added to brasses: aluminium, lead, manganese and tin?

Solution 7.2

Commercial brasses are copper alloys containing up to 50 per cent of zinc and may possess α, $(\alpha + \beta')$ or β' structures (see Cu–Zn phase diagram in example 7.1). α phase is FCC, is highly ductile, and can be cold worked with ease. The α alloys, containing up to 37 per cent zinc are termed cold working brasses and used for the manufacture of sheet and strip, tubing and wire. Sheet and strip can be further processed by any of the cold sheet forming processes such as deep drawing, spinning and pressing. β' phase, an ordered BCC solid solution, is hard and strong and is difficult to cold work, but can be hot worked by rolling, forging, hot stamping and extrusion. The alloys with zinc contents of between 40 and 50 per cent with $(\alpha + \beta')$ or β' structures are referred to as hot working alloys and components are produced by hot forming and also by sand and die-casting.

Additions to brasses.   Aluminium enters solid solution giving additional strength and an improvement in corrosion resistance, particularly in marine environments. Aluminium brass is an α brass (76 per cent Cu, 22 per cent Zn, 2 per cent Al) used for condenser tube manufacture. Aluminium is present, in amounts of up to 5 per cent, in many high tensile $(\alpha + \beta')$ brasses.

Lead has no solid solubility in copper–zinc alloys and appears in the microstructure as small globular particles. Up to 3 per cent of lead may be added to both cold working and hot working brasses to give free-machining characteristics.

Manganese enters solid solution and strengthens. It is used as an addition to $(\alpha + \beta')$ materials to give high tensile brasses. An early name for high tensile brasses containing manganese was *manganese bronze*.

Tin improves the resistance to marine corrosion and a one per cent addition may be made to cold or hot working brasses. *Admiralty brass* (70 per cent Cu, 29 per cent Zn, 1 per cent Sn) is an α brass and *naval brass* (62 per cent Cu, 37 per cent Zn, 1 per cent Sn) is an $(\alpha + \beta')$ brass.

Example 7.3

(a) Explain why a brass containing 70 per cent copper and 30 per cent zinc is known as a single phase alloy. If an alloy of this composition were cast into bar form describe the typical structural features of (i) a macrosection and (ii) a microsection.

(b) A plate of this alloy in the fully soft condition has the dimensions length = 2 m, width = 50 mm, thickness = 12 mm and is cold rolled to give a 50 per cent reduction of area. What are the length, width and thickness after cold rolling?

(c) Discuss how the mechanical and electrical properties change as a result of cold rolling.

(d) The cold rolled plate may be heated treated to cause the processes of (i) recovery and (ii) recrystallisation. Discuss the changes in structure and properties which these processes cause in the alloy.

(City University)

Solution 7.3

(a) When zinc is added to copper it enters solid solution. More than 30 per cent of zinc can be added before the solubility limit for zinc in the FCC structure (α phase) is reached (refer to the Cu–Zn phase diagram in example 7.1). An alloy containing 30 per cent zinc is, therefore, a single phase alloy. (*Note*: Under some circumstances, for example, rapid solidification, peritectic β phase may appear in the microstructure (refer to solution 7.1 (c)(i)) but if the cast structure is annealed the equilibrium structure of wholly α phase will be produced.)

The macrostructure of a cast bar would show a coarse grain structure with columnar crystals growing from the mould faces and equiaxial crystals in the central portion of the bar, as shown in the sketch below. The microstructure would show some coring of the α crystals and probably a small amount of peritectic β phase at the α grain boundaries.

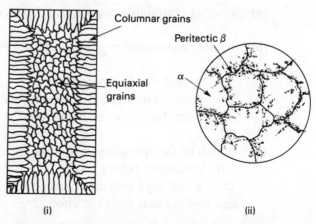

Figure 7.4 *(i) Macrostructure, (ii) Microstructure*

135

(b) Cold rolling is a directional process and gives a reduction in thickness with virtually no lateral spread. A 50 per cent reduction in area refers to cross-sectional area and the final plate dimensions would be length 4 m, width 50 mm, thickness 6 mm.

(c) Cold rolling causes work hardening, the effects of which are to increase the hardness, electrical resistivity, yield strength and tensile strength and reduce the ductility. The 0.1 per cent proof stress of this alloy will be increased from about 75 MPa to about 500 MPa, the tensile strength increased from about 325 MPa to about 700 MPa while the percentage elongation on a 50 mm gauge length will be reduced from about 70 per cent to about 5 per cent.

(d) Full elastic recovery does not occur after cold rolling and the cold worked material will contain residual stress. Heat treatment may be given to remove the effects of cold working.

(i) Heating at a comparatively low temperature, about 200–250°C, for this brass will cause recovery, or stress relief, to occur. At these temperatures, there will be recovery of the locked-in elastic strains and the removal of internal stresses. There is no visible alteration to the microstructure and the values of hardness and strength remain unaltered, but there will be a small decrease in the electrical resistivity.

(ii) Heating to a higher temperature, 250–400°C, will permit recrystallisation to occur. Nucleation of new unstrained crystal grains begins at points of high dislocation density and these grow into crystals with a low dislocation density until all the plastically-deformed grains have been eliminated. This is the process of annealing and the new structure is composed of small equiaxial grains. When recrystallisation is complete, some grains may continue to grow at the expense of others. This process of grain growth will be rapid if the material is heated to a high temperature. As a consequence of recrystallisation and the formation of an unstrained equiaxial structure, the hardness, strength, ductility and resistivity return to their original pre-cold worked values.

Example 7.4

Part of the copper–aluminium phase diagram is shown below.
Describe the room temperature microstructures for:

(a) an alloy containing copper and 5 per cent aluminium,

(b) an alloy containing copper and 10 per cent aluminium treated in the following ways:
  (i) cooled slowly from 900°C,
  (ii) cooled rapidly, but not quenched, from 900°C, and
  (iii) quenched in water from 900°C.

(c) Which of the two alloys would be most suitable for fabrication as:
  (i) condenser tubing, and
  (ii) a cast high pressure pump body,
  and give reasons for your choice?

(Polytechnic of Central London)

136

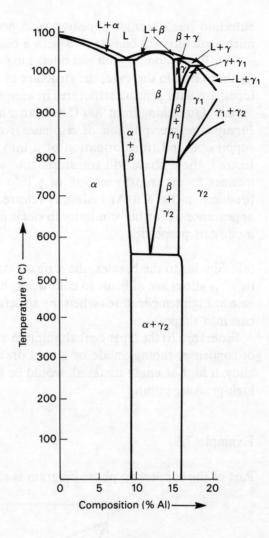

The phase diagram figure shows Temperature (°C) on the vertical axis from 0 to 1100, and Composition (% Al) on the horizontal axis from 0 to 20. Phase regions labelled: L+α, L, L+β, β+γ, L+γ, γ+γ₁, L+γ₁, β, γ, γ₁, γ₁+γ₂, α+β, α, β+γ₁, γ₂, β+γ₂, α+γ₂.

Figure 7.5

Solution 7.4

(a) The phase diagram shows that an alloy containing 5 per cent of aluminium solidifies as α phase and that no structural changes occur as the alloy cools to room temperature. The room temperature microstructure will show uniform crystals of α phase, the FCC solid solution of aluminium in copper.

(b) From the phase diagram, it can be seen that the alloy containing 10 per cent aluminium solidifies as β phase and that at 900°C the alloy structure will be composed entirely of β. Further cooling of this alloy will result in structural change. The exact nature of the phase changes will be determined by the rate of cooling, as follows.

(i) During slow cooling from 900°C, the first changes will be the precipitation of α crystals from β when the phase boundary line is crossed at about 850°C. Precipitation of α continues until the eutectoid temperature, 565°C, is reached, when remaining β phase of eutectoid composition transforms into the α + γ₂ eutectoid mixture. Slow cooling will give a coarse eutectoid structure. (This eutectoid has a similar appearance to pearlite in steels.) The room temperature microstructure will consist of α with a coarse eutectoid.

(ii)   Rapid cooling, but not quenching, will result in a similar microstructure to (i) above but, in this case, the structure of the eutectoid mixture will be much finer (compare with pearlite structures in annealed and normalised steels).

(iii)   Quenching from 900°C will cause a different type of structure to be formed. Firstly, the precipitation of α phase from β between 850° and 565°C may be suppressed and transformation of β into the $\alpha + \gamma_2$ eutectoid will be prevented. Instead, the β phase will transform into a non-equilibrium phase α', in a similar manner to the transformation of γ into martensite in steels. In fact, the phase produced in the Cu–Al system is referred to as martensite and has an acicular appearance. A further similarity to steels is that this martensite can be tempered to modify its properties.

(c)   Similar to the brasses, the α phase is FCC and can be cold-worked while the $(\alpha + \gamma_2)$ alloys are difficult to cold work, but they can be hot worked with relative ease at high temperatures when the structure is $(\alpha + \beta)$ or β phase and can also be cast into shapes.

From this: (i) the 5 per cent aluminium alloy is most suitable for the manufacture of condenser tubing, made by a cold drawing process and (ii) the 10 per cent Al alloy, a high strength material, would be suitable for producing a cast body for a high-pressure pump.

Example 7.5

Part of the copper–tin phase diagram is shown below.

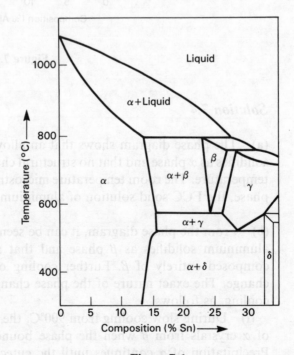

Figure 7.6

Tin bronzes containing 8 per cent of tin show δ phase in their microstructures, in addition to the primary α phase. Why is this?

A small quantity of phosphorus is added to tin bronzes before casting. For what reasons is this addition made? Explain why the phosphorus addition is normally made before the addition of tin.

Phosphor bronzes make good bearing materials. Explain the part played by each of the constituent phases when the material is used in this way.

(Polytechnic of Central London)

Solution 7.5

There is a very wide gap between liquidus and solidus in the copper–tin phase diagram. The solidus temperature for an 8 per cent Sn alloy is about 900°C and at this temperature, according to the phase diagram, α phase is in equilibrium with liquid containing more than 20 per cent Sn. During the casting of an 8 per cent Sn alloy, the last liquid will solidify as β phase and during cooling this will transform first into $(\alpha + \gamma)$ eutectoid and then into $(\alpha + \delta)$ eutectoid.

Phosphorus is used as a deoxidiser and frequently sufficient is added to leave some residual phosphorus in the alloy. The alloys are then termed phosphor-bronzes. α bronzes contain up to 0.3 per cent phosphorus, the limit of solid solubility for phosphorus in copper, and this strengthens the alloy. $(\alpha + \delta)$ bronzes may contain up to 1 per cent phosphorus and the excess, beyond the solubility limit, forms Cu_3P, a very hard constituent. This is usually associated with the $(\alpha + \delta)$ eutectoid in the structure.

If, during the manufacture of a bronze, tin is added to the liquid copper ahead of phosphorus, some tin may oxidise to form tin oxide. This is very difficult to remove and, if it remains in the alloy, can cause serious loss of strength. The copper should be deoxidised by phosphorus before tin is added.

Phosphor bronzes containing between 10 and 13 per cent tin are used widely as bearing materials. They possess a duplex microstructure consisting of the very hard $(\alpha + \delta)$ eutectoid with associated hard Cu_3P in a matrix of more ductile α phase. The very hard constituents give excellent resistance to abrasion and wear while the tough but ductile α phase will withstand mechanical shock.

Example 7.6

What feature is required on the phase diagram for an alloy if it is required to alter its properties by a process of precipitation hardening? Show how this process is applied in the copper–beryllium system, indicating the changes in structure and properties that occur at each stage.

Solution 7.6

If the phase diagram for an alloy system shows partial solid solubility with a relatively wide difference between solubility limits at high and low temperatures, as in the diagram below, then there is a possibility that the alloy compositions in the range marked X may respond to precipitation hardening. The Cu–Be system is a good example of this.

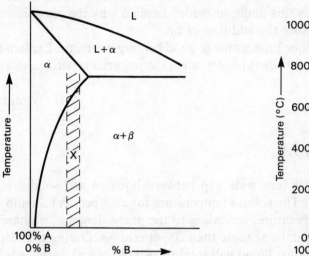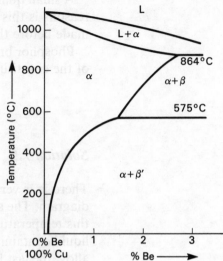

Figure 7.7

Alloy compositions containing between 1.75 per cent and 2.5 per cent Be can be strengthened by means of a two-stage heat treatment. The first stage, solution heat treatment, involves heating the alloy at about 850°C, to ensure that all beryllium is taken into solid solution and the structure is entirely α phase, followed by rapid quenching to retain α phase as a metastable super-saturated solid solution at room temperature. In this condition, the alloy has a tensile strength of between 450 and 520 MPa, an elongation value in the range 40–50 per cent and can be cold-worked, if necessary. The second stage of the treatment involves heating to a temperature of 250–350°C to permit diffusion and formation of coherent precipitate areas of the β' phase (the intermediate phase CuBe). This diffusion and precipitate formation is accompanied by a considerable increase in strength. The tensile strength of the precipitation hardened alloy is 1100–1200 MPa (1200–1400 MPa if the alloy was cold-worked prior to the precipitation treatment) but the elongation value falls to some 2–5 per cent.

Example 7.7

(a) Sketch the aluminium-rich portions (up to the eutectic compositions) of the equilibrium diagrams for:
  (i) the aluminium–copper system, and
  (ii) the aluminium–magnesium–silicon system.

  For each system, describe the procedure required to develop maximum tensile strength. Comment on the structural changes which occur at each stage of the treatment and how they affect the properties.

(b) Outline some of the advantages and disadvantages of each type of alloy and give some typical examples of the engineering applications of these materials.

(Kingston Polytechnic)

Solution 7.7

(a) The aluminium-rich portions of the two phase diagrams are shown in the diagrams below. Note that magnesium and silicon form an inter-metallic compound, Mg$_2$Si, and a binary diagram (Al–Mg$_2$Si) can be drawn for the system.

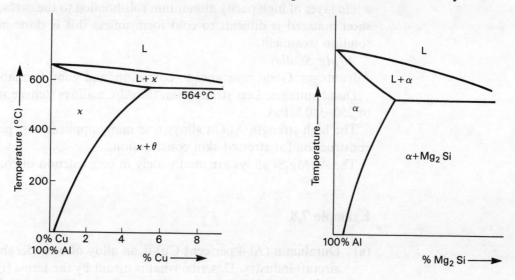

Figure 7.8

Both of these phase diagrams conform to the pattern described in solution 7.6 and certain alloy compositions in each will respond to precipitation hardening. In each case the first stage in the development of maximum strength is solution heat treatment to produce a metastable supersaturated solid solution at room temperature. Alloys containing 3.5–4.5 per cent Cu and alloys containing about 1 per cent Mg and 1 per cent Si are heated to a temperature in the range 500–530°C followed by quenching in water.

After solution heat treatment, an Al–4 per cent Cu alloy will begin to age naturally at room temperature, that is, copper atoms begin to diffuse through the aluminium lattice creating areas rich in copper which build up into coherent precipitate areas of θ' phase accompanied by a significant increase in strength. Maximum strength will be achieved after an ageing period of 5–10 days at room temperature. The process may be accelerated by heating the alloy at a temperature of the order of 160–170°C when maximum strength will be reached in about 10 hours. If heated at too high a temperature, θ phase, CuAl$_2$, will form as non-coherent precipitate particles. If this stage of precipitation begins, the hardness and strength will begin to reduce. This is termed over-ageing. The process with the Mg$_2$Si alloys is similar but these alloys do not age naturally after the solution treatment and have to be precipitation hardened at about 170°C. Some of the heat-treatable aluminium alloys contain both copper and Mg$_2$Si. These need to be precipitation heat treated to develop the maximum properties.

(b) *Al–4% Cu alloys.*

Advantages: Can be heat treated and naturally aged to give strengths of up to 400–450 MPa. The natural ageing process can be halted by keeping the material at about 0°C after the solution treatment. The natural ageing phenomenon is useful in

141

that Al/Cu alloy rivets can be installed in the solution treated condition and they will strengthen *in situ*. An increase in the magnesium content will prevent natural ageing and give increased strength alloys (tensile strengths of 500–550 MPa).

Disadvantages: Poor resistance to corrosion, but this can be improved by surface treatments, or by manufacturing Alclad, sheet or plate material in Al/Cu alloy with a thin layer of high purity aluminium roll-bonded to the surfaces. Naturally ageing sheet material is difficult to cold form unless this is done immediately after the solution treatment.

Al/Mg$_2$Si alloys.

Advantages: Good resistance to corrosion, and good formability.

Disadvantages: Less strong than the Al/Cu alloys (tensile strengths of the order of 250–350 MPa).

The high strength Al/Cu alloys find many applications, particularly in aircraft construction for stressed-skin construction.

The Al/Mg$_2$Si alloys are used widely in construction of road and rail vehicles.

Example 7.8

(a) Duralumin (Al/4 per cent Cu) is an alloy of considerable importance in the aircraft industry. Describe what is meant by the terms (i) ageing, (ii) solution treatment and (iii) precipitation treatment when applied to this material for the promotion of mechanical properties.

(b) Equivalent properties are obtained in such a material when treated at 527°C for 2 minutes or when treated at 327°C for 2 hours. How long would it take such equivalence to be obtained if treated at 127°C?

(Salford)

Solution 7.8

(a) (i) Ageing is the term used for the increase in strength which takes place over a period of 5–10 days at ordinary temperatures following a solution treatment (refer to solutions 7.6 and 7.7 for further details).

(ii) Solution treatment is the production of a metastable supersaturated solid solution of copper in aluminium by heating the alloy at a temperature just below the solidus followed by rapid quenching.

(iii) Precipitation treatment is the low-temperature heat treatment at about 170°C following solution treatment which brings about diffusion of copper and the formation of a coherent precipitate to strengthen the material. Maximum strength can be achieved in about 10 hours in this way, as compared to several days with ageing.

(b) Ageing is a diffusion-controlled process and the Arrhenius law applies (refer to chapter 3).

$$t = A \exp(B/T)$$
$t = 2$ min at 527°C (800 K); $t = 2$ hr (120 min) at 327°C (600 K)

$$2 = A \exp(B/800) \qquad (1)$$
$$120 = A \exp(B/600) \qquad (2)$$

Dividing (2) by (1) gives $\dfrac{120}{2} = \exp B \left(\dfrac{800 - 600}{600 \times 800} \right)$

$$60 = \exp(4.167 \times 10^{-4} B)$$
$$B = 9825.6$$

From this, A can be evaluated as 9.27×10^{-6}.

At 127°C (400 K), $t = 9.27 \times 10^{-6} \exp(9825.6/400) = 431608$ min $= 7193.5$ hr $= 299.7$ days.

Example 7.9

(a) You are provided with small pieces of four materials which are visually indistinguishable from each other but known to comprise (i) commercial purity aluminium, (ii) an aluminium–13 per cent silicon alloy, (iii) an Al–4 per cent Cu alloy and (iv) an Al–4 per cent Cu–2 per cent Ni alloy. How may the four materials be identified if the only equipment available is: a Vickers hardness test machine, a furnace with a protective atmosphere and a working temperature range from 60°C to 600°C, temperature measuring equipment accurate to ± 5°C and a water supply?

(b) Which of the four alloys would be most suitable for the following applications?
   (i) die casting,
   (ii) manufacture of a load bearing aircraft component for use at elevated temperatures.

(Polytechnic of Central London)

Solution 7.9

(a) Heat each sample to a temperature of 500°C and quench in water. This will anneal the pure aluminium and the Al/Si alloy but solution heat treat the others. Determine the hardness of each sample immediately. The commercial purity aluminium will be the softest and have an annealed hardness of about $H_D = 20$. Then determine the hardness of the other three samples at intervals over a period of about 4 hours. The Al/Cu alloy will be ageing naturally and its hardness will show an increase over this period. Having identified two out of the four materials, place the remaining two in the furnace set at a temperature of 170°C. Precipitation hardening of the Al/Cu/Ni alloy will take place but the hardness of the Al/Si alloy will be unchanged by the treatment.

(b) (i) The aluminium–13 per cent silicon alloy is an excellent die-casting material. This composition is close to the eutectic composition and the alloy melts

143

at about 560°C and has very good fluidity and castability. This alloy is usually modified by the addition of a small amount of sodium immediately before casting. Modification prevents the formation of primary silicon crystals, which could have an embrittling effect, and promotes a much finer eutectic structure giving a strong tough material.

(ii) The Al/Cu/Ni alloy would be the material to use for a load bearing aircraft component capable of withstanding elevated temperatures. The presence of nickel raises the temperature at which over-ageing occurs and, unlike the straight Al–4 per cent Cu alloy, this alloy could be used for extended service at temperatures of the order of 150°C without any loss of strength occurring. This type of material is used in the construction of the supersonic airliner Concorde as it withstands the increased temperatures caused by kinetic heating effects at speeds of Mach 2.

Example 7.10

What are the necessary metallurgical characteristics required in a good bearing metal? Compare and contrast lead-base, tin-base, copper-base and aluminium-base bearing alloys.

Solution 7.10

Most metallic bearing materials are based on duplex microstructures in which particles of a very hard phase are distributed throughout a softer but tough matrix. In these systems, the hard particles provide abrasion and wear resistance and the matrix provides toughness. The soft matrix is also capable of yielding to accommodate any localised high pressures which may be caused by slight misalignment. Some bearing metals, on the other hand, operate on a reversed principle and have duplex structures in which particles of a soft phase are distributed within a matrix. In this type, a thin film of the soft phase spreads across the matrix surface as a result of the relative motion between bearing surface and journal and this film acts as a solid lubricant. Lead-base and tin-base bearing metals are referred to as *white metals*. The tin-base materials, known as Babbit metals, are tin–antimony–copper alloys and they may also contain some lead. The structural features are hard cuboids of SbSn compound and needles of Cu_6Sn_5 in a matrix of tin–antimony solution and eutectic. This type of bearing material, on a steel backing, is widely used for plain bearings in internal combustion engines and they can be operated at high speeds and relatively high loads. Lead is added to tin-base alloys to reduce cost but the maximum load at which the bearing can be used is also reduced. The lead-base materials are lead–antimony–tin alloys with a structure of SbSn cuboids in a ternary eutectic matrix and these are suitable for low or medium loads only at relatively low running speeds.

Copper-base bearing metals. The two main alloys used are phosphor bronzes with 10–15 per cent tin and copper–lead. The phosphor bronze structure is $(\alpha + \delta)$ eutectoid and associated Cu_3P in a softer matrix of α phase. These alloys can sustain much higher loads than white metals but generally are used at high loads and relatively low speeds. The harder matrix than in white metals with a higher yield strength means that careful alignment is needed. Lead may be added to phosphor bronzes. These alloys are used for high-load applications. Some lead is squeezed out and spreads over the surface and can act as a lubricant and prevent seizure in the case of an oil lubrication breakdown. Phosphor bronze powder may be compacted and sintered to form porous bushes and bearings. These can be soaked in lubricant before installation and act for long periods without maintenance. Graphite powder may also be part of the mix in the production of sintered bronze bearings. Copper–lead alloys containing 25–30 per cent lead are useful bearing materials and can sustain somewhat heavier loading and run at higher speeds than tin-base materials. They are, in consequence, used for crankshaft bearings in diesel engines.

Aluminium-base bearing metals.   The main aluminium bearing materials are Al–Sn alloys. Tin is insoluble in aluminium and the structure comprises particles of tin in a matrix of aluminium. The alloys are produced as strip which is roll bonded to steel backing strip for the production of plain shell bearings. In this form, they give bearings which can operate at higher loads and speeds than white metals.

Example 7.11

'Nickel is vital for the maintenance of a manufacturing economy.' Discuss this statement and list some of the major applications of nickel and its alloys in engineering.

Solution 7.11

Nickel is a metal which is vital in the context of present-day engineering technology. Pure nickel is applied to metals as an electroplated layer for corrosion protection purposes and finds widespread use as an alloying element in many steels and cast irons where it is used in low alloy steels to improve static strength, fatigue strength, toughness and hardenability, in austenitic stainless steels and in cast irons to strengthen and promote high temperature properties. Also it is an important additive to a number of specialist copper and aluminium alloys. However, in addition to all these applications, many important nickel-based alloys have been developed. The main types of nickel alloys and their principal uses are given below.

Monel.   An alloy containing 30 per cent copper and 2 per cent iron possessing an excellent corrosion resistance and good strength at elevated temperatures which finds use in chemical engineering plant and for the manufacture of steam turbine blades.

Inconel.   An alloy containing 14 per cent chromium and 6 per cent iron with excellent corrosion and high-temperature oxidation resistance. This material is used in chemical engineering applications and also for the manufacture of heating elements and exhaust manifolds. The nickel–20 per cent chromium alloy, known under the trade name Brightray, is another material which finds use in the manufacture of heating elements for furnaces, kettles and so on.

Superalloys.   This is the term used to cover many alloys developed for their high-temperature creep strength and oxidation resistance. Nickel is the basis metal for these. The Hastelloy range of alloys contain around 50 per cent nickel with chromium, iron, molybdenum and tungsten. They are used in chemical engineering and for the manufacture of components for the hot end of gas turbine engines. The Nimonic series of alloys are nickel/chromium and nickel/chromium/cobalt alloys together with small amounts of carbon, titanium, iron, aluminium and other elements developed mainly for gas turbine and high temperature furnace applications. Some of the alloying elements give solid solution strengthening while others form carbides and inter-metallic compounds which can be widely dispersed as stable precipitate particles increasing strength, particularly creep strength at high temperatures.

Many aspects of technology and, in particular, high-temperature engineering and gas turbine development would have been adversely affected in the absence of a metal such as nickel.

Example 7.12

Give an account of the main applications of magnesium and zinc as engineering materials.

Solution 7.12

Both magnesium and zinc have HCP crystal structures. This means that they have a tendency to be brittle.

One very attractive property of magnesium is its low density of 1740 kg/m^3 (65 per cent of the density of aluminium). In addition, it has a relatively low melting temperature at 649°C and a very good corrosion resistance. The unalloyed metal is not used for engineering components and the principal alloying element added to improve strength is aluminium in amounts up to 10 per cent. Small additions of thorium, zirconium or zinc will give precipitation hardening alloys and tensile strengths of up to 300 MPa can be achieved. Magnesium has low ductility and is more difficult to cold work than aluminium but it can be hot worked with ease and is readily castable by sand and die-casting methods. Some of the principal applications of magnesium alloys are in aircraft construction and road vehicles. Wheels for aircraft and other vehicles, and engine crankcases are die-cast from magnesium alloys, airscrew blades are hot forged and aircraft fuel tanks can be fabricated from magnesium alloy sheet. Magnesium possesses a low neutron capture cross-section and is used as a canning material for nuclear fuel elements.

Zinc has a very low melting point at 419°C. One of the major uses of zinc is for die-casting. The die-casting alloys contain about 4 per cent aluminium and, with their low melting temperatures and good fluidity, can be used for the manufacture of precision castings. Applications include automotive components such as carburettors, fuel pumps and door fittings, and casings and housings for small machines and electric motors. Although zinc is quite brittle at ordinary temperatures, it can be plastically deformed quite readily at temperatures of 60°C and above. Sheet zinc, used for the manufacture of cases for dry cells, is produced by rolling at moderately elevated temperatures. Zinc alloyed with 20 per cent aluminium exhibits super-plasticity at temperatures of the order of 250°C and alloy sheet of this composition can be formed into extremely complex shapes without the risk of cracking. A major use for zinc is for galvanising, namely the corrosion protection of steel sheet and sections by a surface coating of zinc.

Example 7.13

Give the main characteristics of the metal titanium. What are the main advantages and disadvantages of titanium and its alloys as engineering materials?

Solution 7.13

The main characteristics of titanium are:

- *structure.* It is an allotropic metal, α-Ti being HCP and β-Ti being BCC (The $\alpha \rightarrow \beta$ transition is at 880°C).
- *density.* At 4540 kg/m^3 it is much less dense than steels.
- *corrosion resistance.* This is excellent and the metal is resistant to most acids and alkalis but, unfortunately, it reacts with oxygen and nitrogen at temperatures above 600°C and this makes processing both difficult and expensive.
- *strength.* It can be alloyed with various elements to give both α and $(\alpha + \beta)$ structures with strengths of up to 1500 MPa.

The major advantages offered by titanium are production of materials with a very high strength/weight ratio and excellent resistance to corrosion. The main disadvantage is the high cost of the material and the high costs of fabricating components. Aluminium, in amounts of up to 6 per cent, is the major alloying element and gives a solid solution strengthening effect. Iron and chromium tend to stabilise the β phase and will give alloys with an $(\alpha + \beta)$ structure. The α phase, being HCP in structure, is difficult to deform plastically at ordinary temperatures and only a limited amount of cold work can be performed. Hot-working, rolling and forging, are performed in the temperature range 700–1100°C and the surface contamination caused by absorption of oxygen and nitrogen at these temperatures is removed by machining or grinding followed by pickling in strong acid solutions. Titanium alloy shapes can be made by casting, but it is necessary to melt and cast *in vacuo* using moulds lined with graphite. Because of the high costs, usage of titanium tends to be restricted to the aerospace and chemical industries. Titanium alloy sheet, forgings and castings are used for aircraft structural components, bulkheads and panelling, for compressor blades and discs in gas turbine engines, and in chemical engineering plant.

There is no list of supplementary questions printed with this chapter as this section of the subject does not lend itself to numerical questions.

8 Polymer Materials

8.1 Fact Sheet

(a)

Polymer materials contain very large molecules, mainly composed of carbon and hydrogen. Polymers are made by reacting together substances with relatively small molecular weights (monomers) to synthesise very large molecules. There are two polymerisation mechanisms: (i) addition polymerisation of unsaturated compounds, for example ethylene (ethene) to polyethylene, $n(CH_2{=}CH_2) \rightarrow ({-}CH_2{-}CH_2{-})_n$ and (ii) condensation polymerisation, for example between phenol, C_6H_5OH, and formaldehyde, HCHO, to give a P-F resin

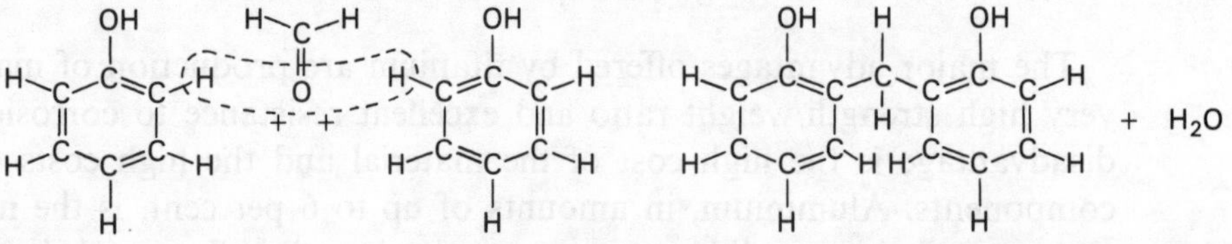

Figure 8.1

(b)

Addition polymerisation produces linear polymers. Condensation polymerisation may produce linear polymers, such as polyamides, or may give hard rigid network structure materials. Linear polymer materials may be converted into non-linear structures, giving modified properties, by branching and cross-linking reactions.

(c)

Polymers may be classified as thermoplastic, thermosets and elastomers. Thermoplastic materials soften when heated and regain their rigidity when cooled. These are polymers with linear, branched or lightly cross-linked structures.

Thermosets soften or melt when first heated but then cure to become permanently hard rigid materials with network structures. Cold-setting polymers are similar but cure at ordinary temperatures after a resin and hardener have been mixed together.

Elastomers (natural and synthetic rubbers) are lightly cross-linked materials with very low elastic moduli which can accommodate large amounts of strain but return to their original dimensions when the load is removed.

(d)

Thermoplastics and elastomers possess a glass transition temperature, T_g, below which molecular movement by bond rotation ceases. The value of T_g is approximately two-thirds of the melting temperature, T_m, in Kelvin. Below T_g the material is a brittle glassy solid, above T_g it is soft, flexible and possesses viscoelastic properties. The value of T_g depends on the molecular structure of the material. It is low in molecules with a simple symmetrical structure, for example $T_g = -120°C$ for polyethylene, but high in a substance where the monomer is non-symmetrical with a large radical group attached, for example $T_g = 95°C$ in polystyrene.

(e)

Some thermoplastics exhibit crystallinity. Some crystallinity is most likely in linear polymers with no large radical groups attached to the chain to prevent close packing. A crystalline polymer, with a closer packing, has a higher density than the amorphous variety of the same material.

(f)

The degree of polymerisation is the average polymer molecular size in terms of the number of monomer units per molecule. An increase in the degree of polymerisation increases the melting temperature (see example 8.5).

(g)

Thermoplastics show viscoelastic behaviour at temperatures above T_g. This type of behaviour can be simulated by combining a Hookean spring, for which strain $\varepsilon = \sigma/E$, and a dashpot for which strain rate $de/dt = \sigma/\eta$, η being viscosity. In the Maxwell model, a spring and dashpot are connected in series while, in the Voigt–Kelvin model, a spring and dashpot are combined in parallel.

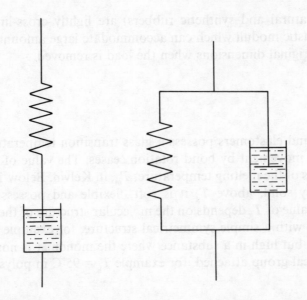

Figure 8.2 *Maxwell element*   *Voigt–Kelvin element*

For a Maxwell element with constant stress,

$$\varepsilon = \sigma \left(\frac{1}{E} + \frac{t}{\eta} \right)$$

For a Voigt–Kelvin element,

$$\varepsilon = \frac{\sigma}{E} \left\{ 1 - \exp \left(\frac{-Et}{\eta} \right) \right\}$$

8.2 Worked Examples

Example 8.1

(a) What is meant by the term *polymerisation*?

(b) The structural formulae of three monomers are shown below. For each of the compounds state the type of reaction involved in the manufacture of a polymer and show, using simple equations, how the polymerisation occurs.

(i)
```
 H   H
  \ /
   C=C
  / \
 H   Cl
```

(ii)
```
 H       H H H H H O
  \      | | | | | ||
   N—C—C—C—C—C—C—OH
  /      | | | | |
 H       H H H H H
```

(iii)
```
 H   H
  \ /
   C=C
  /    \
 H      C
       / \
      H   H

   H—C       C—H
      \\     //
       C     C
      /       \
     H         H
        C
        |
        H
```

Figure 8.3

(c) For the polymer produced from monomer (iii) sketch the types of force–

extension curves which would be obtained in standard tensile tests conducted at: (i) 0°C, (ii) 50°C, (iii) 100°C.

(Polytechnic of Central London)

Solution 8.1

(a) Polymerisation is the term for chemical reactions in which comparatively simple substances react together to give large, complex molecular forms with very high molecular weights. There are two types of polymerisation reaction, namely addition and condensation polymerisation. The reactants in polymerisation reactions are known as *monomers* (meaning single unit) and the product of the reaction is a *polymer* (many units).

(b) (i) The monomer shown is vinyl chloride and this polymerises into a linear polymer, polyvinyl chloride (PVC), by an addition process. The double covalent bond in each monomer molecule splits permitting the molecules to join together forming a long chain of carbon atoms, all with single covalent bonding. This can be shown as: $nCH_2 = CH.Cl \rightarrow (-CH_2 - CH.Cl -)_n$.

It will be seen that, although a long chain molecule can be built up in this manner, there will be an unused covalent bond at each end of the chain. A small quantity of another reactant, termed an initiator, is used in the polymerisation to terminate the molecular chains. The average chain length and mean molecular weight of the polymer is determined by controlling the amount of initiator added.

(ii) This compound is an amino acid (ω-aminocaproic acid) which can polymerise by means of condensation type reactions in which an $-NH_2$ (amine) group reacts with an acid ($-COOH$) group. In this reaction water, as steam, is expelled.

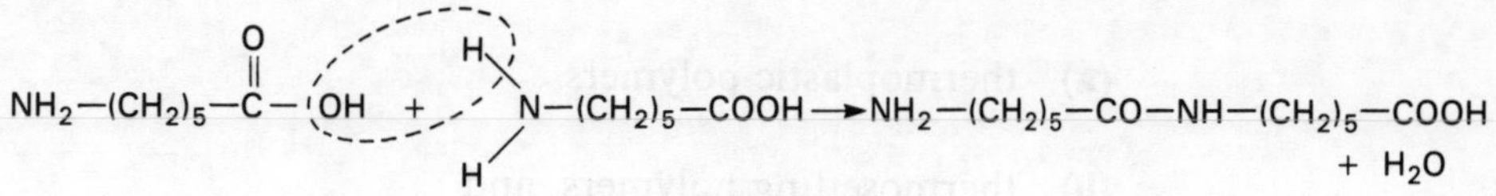

$$NH_2 - (CH_2)_5 - \overset{\overset{\displaystyle O}{\|}}{C} - OH \ + \ \overset{H}{\underset{H}{N}} - (CH_2)_5 - COOH \rightarrow NH_2 - (CH_2)_5 - CO - NH - (CH_2)_5 - COOH + H_2O$$

Figure 8.4

This reaction, repeated many times, produces the linear polyamide known as PA 6 or nylon 6.

$$nNH_2 - (CH_2)_5 - COOH \rightarrow (-NH - (CH_2)_5 - CO -)_n + nH_2O$$

It will be seen that an initiator is not needed for this type of reaction as is the case with addition polymerisation.

(iii) The compound shown is styrene and it can be polymerised in the presence of an initiator by addition polymerisation to give polystyrene.

$$nCH_2 = CH(C_6H_5) \rightarrow (-CH_2 - CH(C_6H_5)-)_n$$

(c) Polystyrene at ordinary temperatures is a brittle glassy substance and it behaves in a purely elastic manner. (This statement does not refer to toughened and high-impact grades of polystyrene.) As the temperature is raised, the elastic modulus of the material reduces slightly and some plasticity is observed but the major change occurs when the glass transition temperature, T_g, is reached. At this temperature, there is a major reduction in the value of E and the material behaves in a viscoelastic manner. T_g for polystyrene is 95°C. The influence of temperature on the type of force–extension curve is shown in the diagram below.

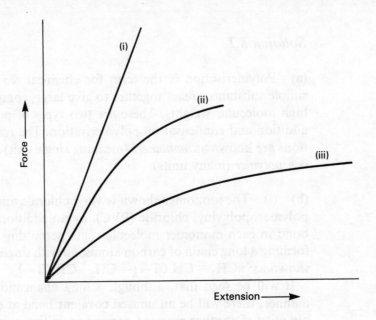

Figure 8.5

Example 8.2

Describe the structure and properties of the three main polymer groups:

(a) thermoplastic polymers,

(b) thermosetting polymers, and

(c) elastomers.

(Sheffield City Polytechnic)

Solution 8.2

(a) In general, thermoplastic polymers are linear polymers, made up of long covalently bonded carbon chains, but some thermoplastic materials may be of the branched type or be lightly cross-linked (see solution 8.4 for a full explanation of these terms). A thermoplastic material softens when heated and sets into a rigid form again on cooling, the changes during heating and cooling being reversible. The properties of thermoplastics are sensitive to temperature, structure and strain rate. Below a certain temperature, the glass transition temperature T_g, a thermoplastic is a brittle elastic solid but above this temperature the value of E reduces greatly and the material becomes visco-elastic. The value of T_g is dependent on the complexity of the molecular structure and is $-120°C$ for polyethylene and $95°C$ for the more complex structured polystyrene.

(b) Thermosets are materials which, on first heating, melt and then set or cure into a hard rigid shape at temperature. During this curing or setting process a full network molecular structure is developed producing a material which is a hard elastic solid. This is a non-reversible process. Cold setting plastics are of the same type but in this case the curing reactions forming a network structure take place at room temperature once resin and a hardener have been mixed together.

(c) Elastomers are a group of thermoplastic materials which have low elastic moduli giving large deformations under relatively low loads and which return to their original dimensions after the loads have been released. They possess linear polymer structures with a small number of cross-links between molecules and, in many cases, the molecules form into coils behaving as minute helical springs. It is the presence of cross-links which causes the materials to return to their original dimensions after load removal.

Example 8.3

Can the compounds whose formulae are given below be polymerised and, if so, what type of polymerisation reactions are involved?

Give, in general terms, the likely properties of any resultant polymer.

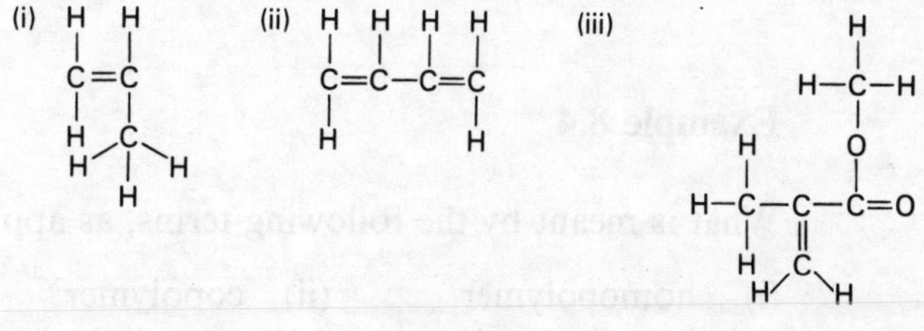

Figure 8.6

Solution 8.3

All three compounds listed are monomers which can be polymerised by an addition mechanism. (i) and (iii) are compounds of the type:

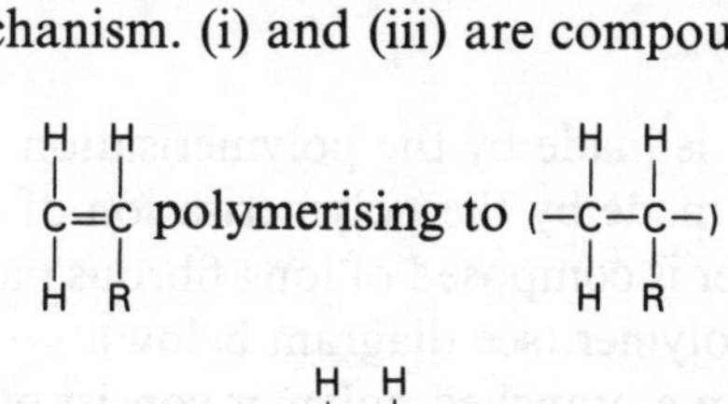

Monomer (i) is $\underset{H\;CH_3}{C=C}$ This is propylene polymerising to polypropylene (PP).

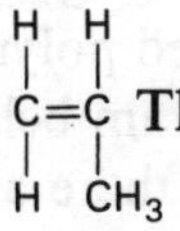

Monomer (iii) is $\underset{H\;COO.CH_3}{\overset{H\;CH_3}{C=C}}$ which is methyl methacrylate polymerising to

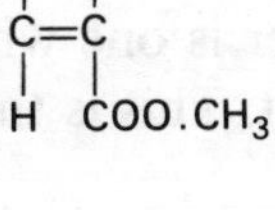

153

polymethyl methacrylate (PMMA), a tradename for which is *perspex*.

Monomer (ii), butadiene, has two double covalent bonds. Both of these split during polymerisation, but forming one double covalent bond between the two centre carbon atoms of the monomer unit, as below:

$$\begin{array}{cccc} H & H & H & H \\ | & | & | & | \\ C=C-C=C \\ | & & & | \\ H & & & H \end{array} \quad \text{polymerising to} \quad (-\begin{array}{cccc} C-C=C-C- \\ \end{array})$$

The double covalent bond in the polymer is reactive and permits cross-links to be made between adjacent molecules.

The polymer produced from (i), polypropylene, is similar to polyethylene but has a higher melting temperature and possesses greater rigidity and strength. The presence of the —CH_3 groups attached to the linear chains tend to restrict relative movement between adjacent molecules.

Polybutadiene, (ii), is an elastomer (refer to solution 8.2(c)). Cross-links can be formed by vulcanising, namely the reaction of sulphur with some of the double covalent bonds in the polymer, Polybutadiene, BR, is an important synthetic rubber with similar properties to natural rubber.

Polymer (iii) polymerises to give polymethyl methacrylate (PMMA), perspex. The relatively complex shape of the repetitive unit suggests that the polymer will be hard and rigid with a high value of T_g. PMMA is a hard, rigid material with a high impact strength and transparent to light. It can be formed into shapes quite readily when heated to temperature above its T_g value of 110°C.

Example 8.4

What is meant by the following terms, as applied to polymer structures?

(i)   homopolymer,   (ii) copolymer,   (iii) linear polymer,
(iv) branched polymer,   (v) cross-linked polymer,   (vi) network polymer.

Describe briefly how branching and cross-linking can occur and how these reactions modify the strength of a polymer.

Solution 8.4

(i)   A homopolymer is made by the polymerisation of a single monomer.

(ii)   A copolymer is made by the polymerisation of two species of monomer.

(iii)   A linear polymer is composed of long fibrous molecular chains and may be a homopolymer or copolymer (see diagram below).

(iv)   The molecules in a branched polymer consist of linear chains with a series of side chains grafted on (see diagram below).

(v)   In a cross-linked polymer, there are short links joining adjacent polymer chains to one another at various points (see diagram below). The hardness and rigidity of the material increases as the number of cross-links increases.

(vi)   A network polymer is one whose molecular structure is in the form of a large three-dimensional net. This is the typical structure of a thermoset material.

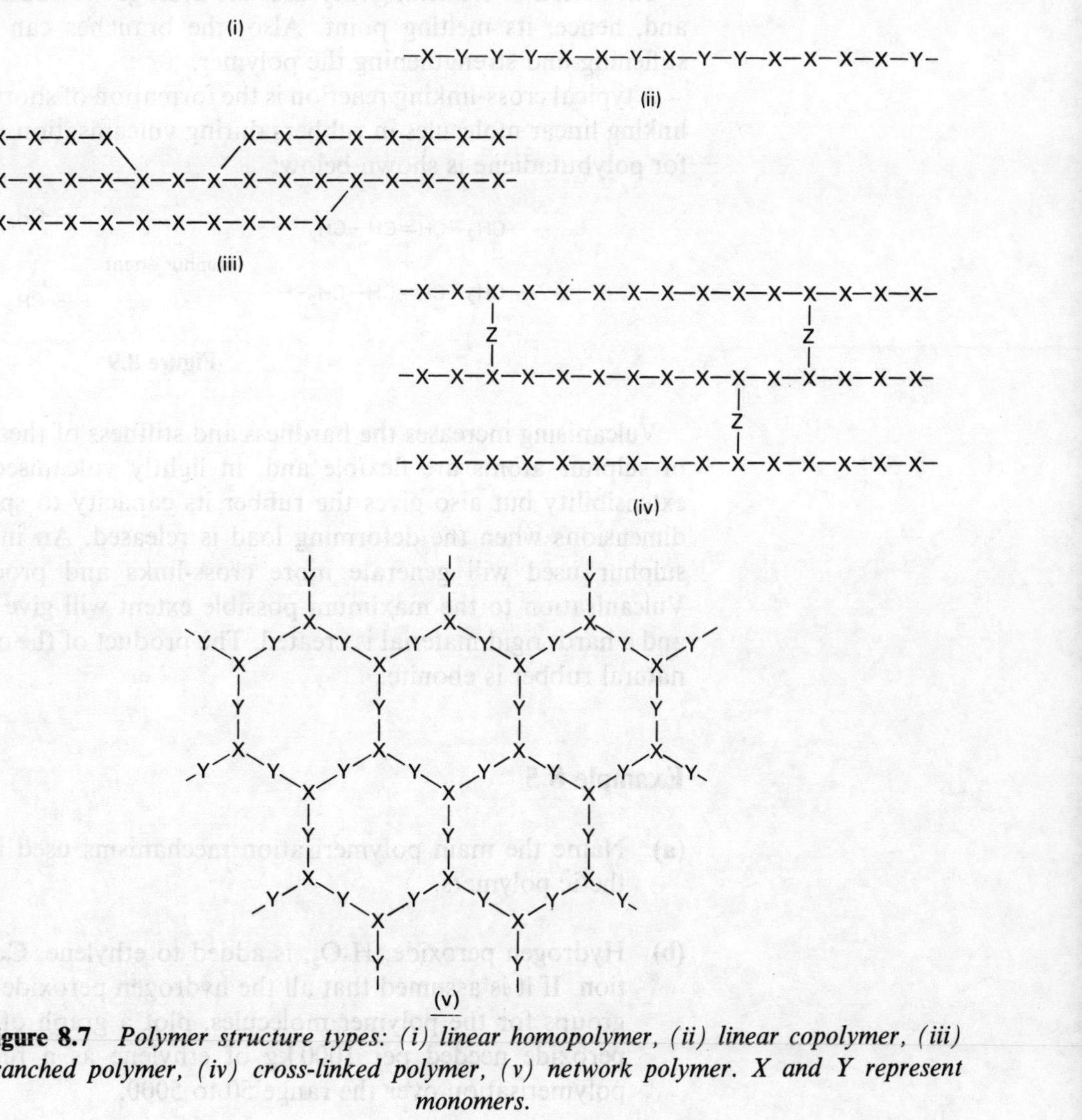

Figure 8.7 *Polymer structure types: (i) linear homopolymer, (ii) linear copolymer, (iii) branched polymer, (iv) cross-linked polymer, (v) network polymer. X and Y represent monomers.*

One method of causing branching reactions in a polymer is to irradiate the material with γ-rays. The incident high-energy photons can stimulate branching reactions. A schematic representation of the branching of polyethylene is given below:

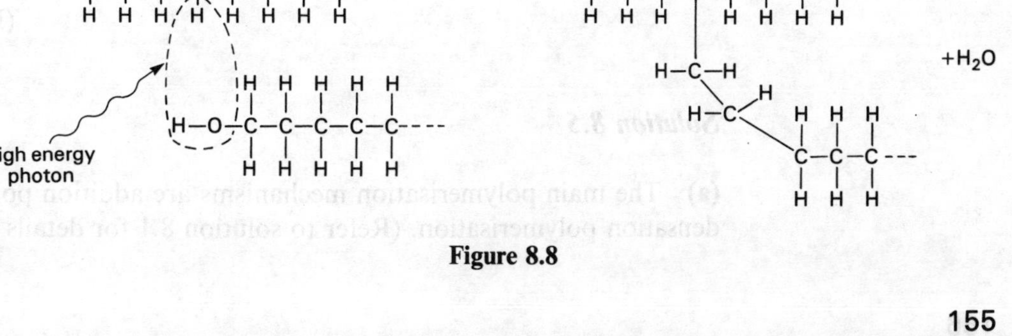

Figure 8.8

155

The action of branching increases the average molecular weight of the substance and, hence, its melting point. Also, the branches can enmesh in one another stiffening and strengthening the polymer.

A typical cross-linking reaction is the formation of short chains of sulphur atoms linking linear molecules in rubbers during vulcanisation. The vulcanising reaction for polybutadiene is shown below:

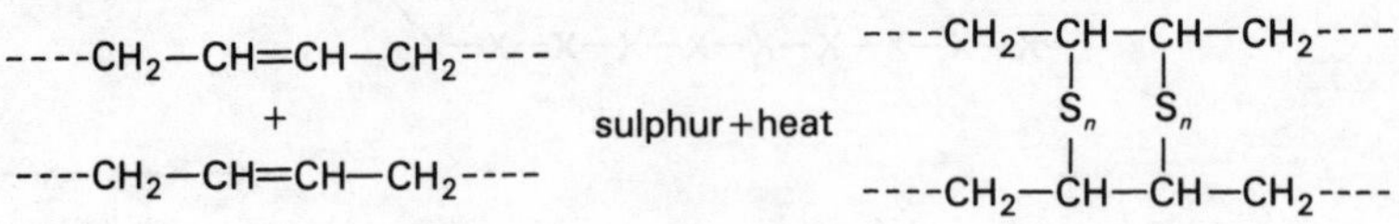

$$----CH_2-CH=CH-CH_2---- \\ + \\ ----CH_2-CH=CH-CH_2---- \qquad \text{sulphur+heat} \qquad \begin{array}{c} ----CH_2-CH-CH-CH_2---- \\ | \quad\;\; | \\ S_n \;\; S_n \\ | \quad\;\; | \\ ----CH_2-CH-CH-CH_2---- \end{array}$$

Figure 8.9

Vulcanising increases the hardness and stiffness of the rubber. The short chains of sulphur atoms are flexible and, in lightly vulcanised material, permit good extensibility but also gives the rubber its capacity to spring back to its original dimensions when the deforming load is released. An increase in the amount of sulphur used will generate more cross-links and produce a harder product. Vulcanisation to the maximum possible extent will give a full network structure and a hard, rigid material is created. The product of the complete vulcanisation of natural rubber is ebonite.

Example 8.5

(a) Name the main polymerisation mechanisms used in the formation of synthetic polymers.

(b) Hydrogen peroxide, H_2O_2, is added to ethylene, C_2H_4, prior to polymerisation. If it is assumed that all the hydrogen peroxide is used to form terminal groups for the polymer molecules, plot a graph of the weight of hydrogen peroxide needed per 1000 kg of ethylene as a function of the degree of polymerisation over the range 50 to 5000.

(c) If the melting temperature (K) of polyethylene is given by:

$$T_m = \{0.0024 + (0.017/n)\}^{-1}$$

where n is the number of carbon atoms in the polymer molecule, plot the melting temperature of polyethylene as a function of the degree of polymerisation over the range 50 to 5000. (Assume atomic mass numbers are: H = 1.008, C = 12.01, O = 15.999.)

(Kingston Polytechnic)

Solution 8.5

(a) The main polymerisation mechanisms are addition polymerisation and condensation polymerisation. (Refer to solution 8.1 for details of these.)

(b) When hydrogen peroxide is used as an initiator, one molecule of H_2O splits and two —OH groups are available to terminate one linear polymer molecule.

Molar mass of $H_2O_2 = 34.014\,kg/kmol$. Molar mass of $C_2H_4 = 28.052\,kg/kmol$. For a degree of polymerisation of 50, $(28.052 \times 50)\,kg\ C_2H_4$ requires $34.014\,kg$ H_2O_2 or $1000\,kg\ C_2H_4$ requires $24.25\,kg\ H_2O_2$.

The masses of hydrogen peroxide required for other degrees of polymerisation can be calculated similarly. Some results are given in the table below:

Degree of polymerisation	Molar mass of polymer (kg)	Mass of H_2O_2 required per 1000 kg ethylene (kg)
50	1402.6	24.25
100	2805.2	12.125
500	14026	2.425
1000	28052	1.213
2000	56104	0.606
3500	98182	0.346
5000	140260	0.243

This data in graphical form is shown below.

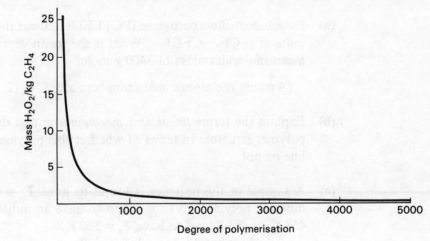

Figure 8.10

(c) In expression $T_m = \{0.0024 + (0.017/n)\}^{-1}$, $n = 2 \times$ degree of polymerisation as each monomer unit contains 2 carbon atoms.

Substituting various values of n in the expression gives a series of values for T_m, as shown in the following table and graph.

Degree of polymerisation	n	T_m (K)
50	100	389.1
100	200	402.4
250	500	410.8
400	800	413.0
500	1000	413.7
5000	10000	416.4

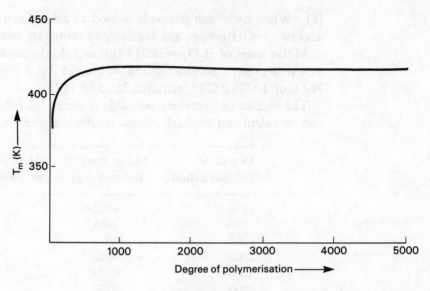

Figure 8.11

Example 8.6

(a) Polychlorotrifluoroethylene (PCTFE) is a linear thermoplastic with repeating units of —CF_2—CFCl—. What is the mean degree of polymerisation for a mean molecular mass of 3400 g/mole?

(Assume the atomic mass numbers are: C = 12, F = 19, Cl = 35.5.)

(b) Explain the terms *linear* and *thermoplastic* and discuss the influence of the polymer structure in terms of whether this polymer may be partially crystalline or not.

(c) A sample of the polymer is found to have T_m = 493 K and T_g = 120 K. A different polymer, PVC, is found to have an indistinct T_m in the range from 458 K to 483 K and to have T_g = 360 K.
   (i)   To what do T_m and T_g refer?
   (ii) Give reasons for the different melting behaviour of the two polymers.
   (iii) Explain the significance of the T_g values on mechanical properties.

(City University)

Solution 8.6

(a) The molar mass of PCTFE = (12 × 2) + (19 × 3) + 35.5 = 116.5 g/mole. The mean degree of polymerisation = 34000 ÷ 116.5 = 291.8.

(b) The term linear polymer means that each molecule is made up of single chains of carbon atoms, with no side branch chains or covalent bonding cross-links to other molecules. A thermoplastic is a material which becomes softer and more flexible when heated, the properties reversing when cooled.

The related polymer PTFE ($—CF_2—CF_2—$) is crystalline. The monomer is symmetrical and fluorine atoms are of roughly similar size to carbon atoms and the molecules can pack closely together to give areas of crystallinity. In PCTFE the monomer is not symmetrical, chlorine atoms are larger than either carbon or fluorine atoms, and the likelihood of the polymer being partially crystalline is less than for PTFE, although a small amount of crystallinity is possible.

(c) (i) T_m refers to the melting point of the substance while T_g is the glass transition temperature.

(ii) A unique melting temperature indicating a sharp transition from the solid phase to liquid phase is a feature characteristic of a crystalline material. This infers that PCTFE is a crystalline polymer. An amorphous material tends not to show a sharp transfer from a definite solid to a completely fluid state. As the temperature rises there is a gradual reduction in viscosity. The indistinct T_m for PVC is an indication that this is an amorphous polymer.

(iii) T_g is an important transition temperature in thermoplastic materials. Below T_g, there is no translational movement of the polymer molecules and the material behaves as a brittle, glassy solid. Above T_g, molecular movement can occur by the process of bond rotation so that, at any instant, portions of a polymer molecule may show translational movement although the complete molecule may not be moving as a single entity. At these temperatures, the material is in the *rubber* state and is viscoelastic. Major property changes occur at T_g. There is a major reduction in the values of E and tensile strength as the temperature rises through T_g. The value of T_g can be determined by observing the changes in dimensions, or density, of a polymer over a range of temperature. There is a marked change in the slope of the expansion curve at T_g (see the diagram below).

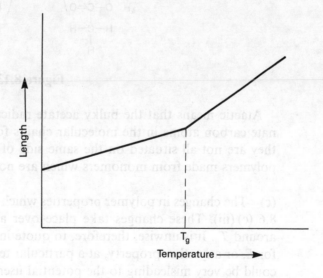

Figure 8.12

Example 8.7

Vinyl acetate, $CH_2\!\!=\!\!CH—COO.CH_3$, polymerises to form a linear or chain type polymer (PVA) which is atactic.

159

(a) If the atomic weights are $C = 12$, $H = 1$ and $O = 16$ and a mean degree of polymerisation is 550, what is the mean molecular weight?

(b) Describe how vinyl acetate polymerises to the chain type polymer and explain why the atactic form is a reasonable product.

(c) A sample of PVA has a glass transition temperature of 298 K. Describe the differences in behaviour when samples are used at 293 K and 303 K.

In a reference book, it is stated that the value for Young's modulus for PVA at 293 K is 700 MPa. Criticise this statement.

(City University)

Solution 8.7

(a) The molecular weight of vinyl acetate is:

$$(12 \times 4) + (1 \times 6) + (16 \times 2) = 86.$$

Average molecular weight for a mean degree of polymerisation of 550 is $86 \times 550 = 47300$.

(b) The polymerisation reaction for vinyl acetate can be written:

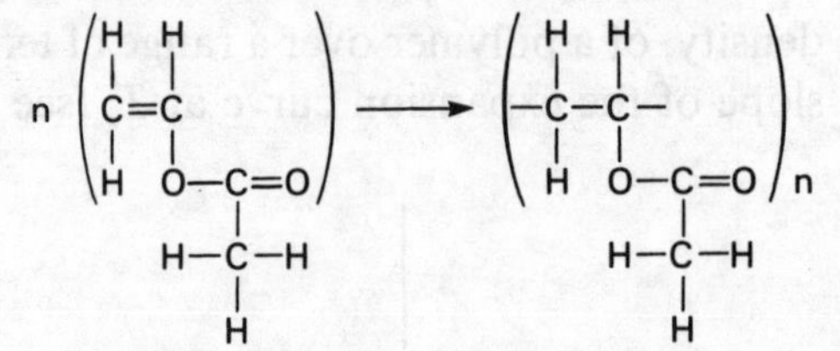

Figure 8.13

Atactic means that the bulky acetate radicals ($—COO.CH_3$) attached to alternate carbon atoms in the molecular chains form a random arrangement, in that they are not all situated on the same side of a chain. This is the usual state for polymers made from monomers which are non-symmetrical in shape.

(c) The changes in polymer properties which occur at T_g are discussed in solution 8.6 (c) (iii). These changes take place over a small temperature range of $\pm 10°$ around T_g. It is unwise, therefore, to quote in a reference work one specific value for E, or any other property, at a particular temperature which is close to T_g. This could be very misleading to the potential user of the material.

Example 8.8

(a) Vinyl chloride, $C_2H_3.Cl$ and vinyl acetate, $C_2H_3.COO.CH_3$, can be copolymerised to form a thermoplastic. With the aid of simple diagrams show how the polymerisation can occur.

(b) Reason whether the copolymer is likely to be partly crystalline or not.

(c) A sample of the copolymer has a mean molecular mass of 59440 g/mole and a degree of polymerisation of 800. Calculate the ratio of vinyl chloride to vinyl acetate monomer. (Assume atomic mass numbers are O = 16.00, H = 1.01, C = 12.01, Cl = 35.45).

(d) The copolymer can be calendered (a form of rolling process) at 335 K to produce 0.5 mm thick sheet. At normal ambient temperature of about 293 K, the sheet can be embossed for such items as flexible identity cards. At 160 K, it shows totally brittle behaviour. Explain why the properties vary with temperature

(City University)

Solution 8.8

(a) The structural formulae of vinyl chloride and vinyl acetate can be written

$$\begin{matrix} H & H \\ | & | \\ C = C \\ | & | \\ H & Cl \end{matrix} \quad \text{and} \quad \begin{matrix} H & H \\ | & | \\ C = C \\ | & | \\ H & COO.CH_3 \end{matrix} \quad \text{which polymerise to produce} \quad \begin{matrix} H & H \\ | & | \\ -C - C - \\ | & | \\ H & Cl \end{matrix} \quad \text{and} \quad \begin{matrix} H & H \\ | & | \\ -C - C - \\ | & | \\ H & COO.CH_3 \end{matrix}$$

These two monomers can be copolymerised by an addition type reaction.

(b) This copolymer is unlikely to be partly crystalline because the presence of large acetate radical groups and relatively large chlorine atoms attached to the carbon chain will prevent close packing of the chains which is necessary if crystallites are to be formed.

(c) The molecular mass of vinyl chloride is $(12.01 \times 2) + (1.01 \times 3) + 35.45 = 62.5$ g/mole and the molecular mass for vinyl acetate is $(12.01 \times 4) + (1.01 \times 6) + (16.00 \times 2) = 86.1$ g/mole. The mean monomer mass in the copolymer is $59440 \div 800 = 74.3$ g.

Let the proportion of vinyl chloride in the copolymer be x. Then, $(62.5 \times x) + (86.1(1 - x)) = 74.3$. From which $x = 0.5$. Therefore the ratio of vinyl chloride to vinyl acetate in the copolymer is 1:1.

(d) The properties of a thermoplastic vary with temperature and T_g, the glass transition temperature, is an important transition for amorphous polymers. Below T_g, van der Waal's forces of attraction exist between the polymer molecules and there is no molecular movement. The material is a brittle glassy solid. At 160 K, the vinyl chloride/vinyl acetate copolymer is well below its T_g and behaves in a totally brittle manner. At T_g, the thermal energy available is sufficient to overcome the van der Waal's bonding forces and some molecular movement can occur. The material loses its brittleness and becomes tough and flexible. The term *leathery* is used to describe this stage. The copolymer is in this state at 293 K, a temperature close to the T_g value. As the temperature rises further and expansion occurs greater molecular movement becomes possible until eventually the secondary van der Waal's bonds cease to exist and the polymer behaves as a highly viscous fluid. In this condition the polymer can be moulded and shaped. At 335 K, this copolymer is sufficiently viscous to be calendered into thin sheet.

Example 8.9

A sample of a thermoplastic material was heated in a dilatometer and the following data recorded.

Temperature (°C)	30	40	45	50	55	60	65	70	75	80	85
Dilatometer reading (mm × 10⁻²)	15.5	24.5	28.5	33.0	37.0	41.0	45.0	51.5	61.0	70.5	79.5

Plot a curve showing the relationship between temperature and change in length and explain its significance.

What structural changes occur within the material and what effects do such changes have on the properties?

Solution 8.9

The graph of change in length against temperature plotted from the given data is shown below:

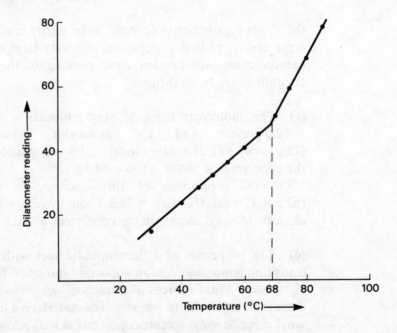

Figure 8.14

There is a change of slope at 68°C and this corresponds to T_g for the material. Below 68°C, the material is in the glass state and is a hard and brittle material while above 68°C the polymer is in the rubber state and is viscoelastic. (Refer to solution 8.6 (c)(iii) for details of property changes.)

Example 8.10

Illustrate the Voigt–Kelvin viscoelastic model and derive from first principles the creep equation:

$$\varepsilon = \frac{\sigma}{E}\left\{1 - \exp\left(\frac{-Et}{\eta}\right)\right\}$$

where ε is creep strain, σ is applied stress, E is modulus of elasticity, η is viscosity and t is time.

What is the significance of η/E?

(Trent Polytechnic)

Solution 8.10

The Voigt–Kelvin viscoelastic model comprises a Hookean spring and a dashpot in parallel, as shown below.

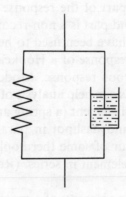

Figure 8.15

For a Hookean spring $\sigma_s = E\varepsilon$ and for a dashpot $\sigma_d = \eta\,\mathrm{d}\varepsilon/\mathrm{d}t$.

For a spring and dashpot in parallel total stress, $\sigma = \sigma_s + \sigma_d$, so $\sigma = E\varepsilon + \eta\,\mathrm{d}\varepsilon/\mathrm{d}t$ which may be rewritten as $\dfrac{\mathrm{d}t}{\eta} = \dfrac{\mathrm{d}\varepsilon}{(\sigma - E\varepsilon)}$

Integration gives

$$\frac{t}{\eta} = -\frac{1}{E}\ln(\sigma - E\varepsilon)\ \text{ or }\ \exp\left(-\frac{Et}{\eta}\right) = \sigma - E\varepsilon$$

From which

$$\varepsilon = \frac{\sigma}{E}\left\{1 - \exp\left(-\frac{Et}{\eta}\right)\right\}$$

The ratio η/E is the retardation time for viscous flow. This time factor reduces with temperature, according to an Arrhenius-type relationship, as the viscosity reduces.

163

Example 8.11

(a) Explain what is meant by *viscoelasticity* in polymeric materials.

(b) Discuss the dependence of the viscoelastic modulus on temperature in an amorphous polymer.

(c) Explain the difference between *creep* and *stress-relaxation* in polymers.

(Southampton University)

Solution 8.11

(a) An elastic body, in response to a stress, σ, will instantaneously strain and the amount of strain, ε, will be related to the stress by: $\varepsilon = \sigma/E$. Removal of stress will cause full instantaneous recovery of strain. For a viscous material, on the other hand, strain will not occur instantaneously but be a function of time so that $\varepsilon = \sigma t/\eta$ where η is the viscosity and t is time. Thermoplastic materials are fully elastic at temperatures below T_g and fully viscous at temperatures above T_m, the melting temperature but, between these temperatures show viscoelastic behaviour in that part of the response to a stress is elastic strain, part is a retarded elastic strain and part is a non-recoverable strain due to viscous flow. Several mechanical models have been used to help understand and explain these phenomena.

The response of a Hookean spring is fully elastic while an oil dashpot shows a full viscous response. Models comprising various combinations of springs and dashpots can help analysis of viscoelastic behaviour. These models are based on the Maxwell element (a spring and dashpot in series) and the Voigt–Kelvin element (a spring and dashpot in parallel). One model which approximates closely to the behaviour of some thermoplastics is the combination of a Maxwell and a Voigt–Kelvin element in series. (Refer to example 8.13.)

(b) The viscosity of a material decreases exponentially with the rise in temperature according to an Arrhenius-type relationship. This means that, for a viscoelastic material, the rate of strain at a constant stress σ will also vary in a similar way such that $\varepsilon/t = A \exp(-B/T)$. But the modulus, E, is σ/ε so $E = \sigma/\varepsilon = \sigma/At \times \exp(B/T)$. From this it can be seen that the viscoelastic modulus for a thermoplastic will reduce exponentially as the temperature rises.

(c) Creep is a continued slow strain with time when subject to a constant load. Stress relaxation is the gradual reduction in stress which occurs with time when a material is subject to a constant strain.

The continued strain due to viscous flow under the influence of a constant stress has been mentioned but the relaxation phenomenon requires some elaboration. Consider a Maxwell element. If an instantaneous strain of ε is imposed on the material, an instantaneous stress $\sigma_0 = E\varepsilon$ will be developed. As viscous flow occurs with time, the stress will reduce. The stress, σ_t, at some time t is given by:

$$\sigma_t = \sigma_0 \exp\left(-\frac{Et}{\eta}\right) = E\varepsilon \exp\left(-\frac{Et}{\eta}\right)$$

It is not possible to consider the imposition of an instantaneous strain on a Voigt–Kelvin element as the characteristic response of this element is retarded strain development.

Example 8.12

The parts of a water pump casing are held together by nylon bolts which are tightened until they are stressed in tension to 50 MPa. It is calculated that the joint will leak if the stress in the bolts falls to 40 MPa. How long will the pump casing survive without leaking given that E for nylon is 1.5 GPa and its viscosity at the operating temperature is 7.5×10^{18} poise? (1 poise = 1×10^{-1} Pa s).

(Nottingham)

Solution 8.12

Substituting in the formulae,

$$\sigma_t = \sigma_0 \, exp \left(-\frac{Et}{\eta} \right) \text{ or } \ln \left(\frac{\sigma_0}{\sigma_t} \right) \frac{Et}{\eta}$$

$$\ln \left(\frac{50 \times 10^6}{40 \times 10^6} \right) = 0.2231 = \frac{1.5 \times 10^9 \ t}{7.5 \times 10^{17}} = 2 \times 10^{-9} t$$

from which $t = 1.116 \times 10^8$ s. The survival time without leaking is 1.116×10^8 s = 31,000 hours = 3.54 years.

Example 8.13

The diagram below shows the full creep curve for a polymeric material

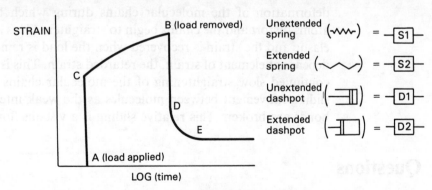

Figure 8.16

Using the notation given in the diagram:

(a) Draw the full Maxwell–Kelvin model to describe the situation initially (at A) and at maximum strain (at B).

(b) Indicate the state of the springs and dashpots to describe the other points on the curve (namely at C, D and E).

(c) Describe briefly what occurs in the polymer structure to give rise to:
 (i) the instantaneous changes,
 (ii) the retarded changes and irrecoverable changes.

(Trent Polytechnic)

Solution 8.13

(a) The Maxwell–Kelvin model is a Maxwell element (a Hookean spring and a dashpot in series) in series with a Kelvin, or Voigt–Kelvin element (a spring and dashpot in parallel). The arrangements at A (no strain) and at B (maximum strain) are shown below:

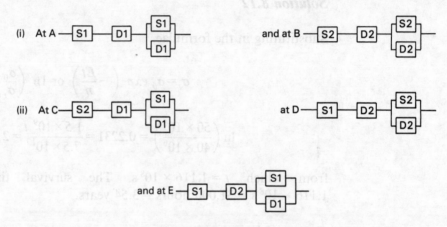

Figure 8.17

(iii) When a tensile load is applied to a thermoplastic polymer at a temperature above T_g, an instantaneous strain is generated. This is the result of elastic deformation of the molecular chains during which the bonds between carbon atoms distort and the chains begin to straighten. (This aspect of the deformation is elastic and the strain is recovered when the load is removed.) There is also a time-dependent element of strain, the retarded strain. This is due to two factors, one is a continued slow straightening of the molecular chains and the other is a relative sliding movement between molecules as the weak intermolecular van der Waal's bonds are broken. This relative sliding is a viscous flow and is irrecoverable.

8.3 Questions

Question 8.1

What mass of hydrogen peroxide, H_2O_2, would be needed as an initiator for the polymerisation of 10 kg of propylene, $CH_2 = CH.CH_3$, to produce an average degree of polymerisation of 750. Atomic mass numbers are: H = 1.008, C = 12.01, O = 16.00.

Question 8.2

Determine the average molecular weight of a sample of polyethylene if the polymerisation used hydrogen peroxide as initiator in the amount 5 g H_2O_2 per 10 kg ethylene. Assume atomic mass numbers are as for question 8.1.

Question 8.3

SBR is a synthetic rubber made by copolymerising equal molar quantities of styrene (CH_2=CH.C_6H_5) and butadiene (CH_2=CH—CH=CH_2).

(a) Calculate the average molecular weight for a degree of polymerisation of 600.

(b) What mass of sulphur per kg of SBR is needed to lightly vulcanise by cross-linking at one-fifth of the available sites, assuming that the cross-links are composed of S_2 chains?
   Atomic mass numbers are: H = 1.008, C = 12.01, S = 32.066.

Question 8.4

Nylon 6.6 is made by the condensation polymerisation of hexamethylene diamine, $NH_2.(CH_2)_6.NH_2$, and adipic acid, $COOH.(CH_2)_4.COOH$. Determine the degree of polymerisation in nylon 6.6 with an average molecular weight of 250 kg/mole. Atomic mass numbers are: H = 1.008, C = 12.01, O = 16.00, N = 14.008.

Question 8.5

What is the ratio of styrene, CH_2=CH.C_6H_5, to acrylonitrile, CH_2—CH.CN, in the copolymer SAN having a degree of polymerisation of 600 and an average molecular weight of 50000 g/mole. Atomic mass numbers: H = 1.008, C = 12.01, N = 14.008.

Question 8.6

A rubber band with an instantaneous modulus of elasticity of 4 MPa is stretched around a sheaf of papers and the instantaneous stress developed in the rubber is 2 MPa. The stress within the rubber is determined to be 1.9 MPa after six weeks. Assuming that the viscoelastic properties of the rubber can be represented by a Maxwell model, estimate the stress in the rubber after a period of one year.

Question 8.7

An amorphous thermoplastic material which can be represented by a Maxwell viscoelastic model has a tensile modulus of 1 GPa. When in a state of constant strain it is found that the stress reduces to 0.6 of its original value after 300 days. Estimate the viscosity of the material.

167

8.4 Answers to Questions

8.1 11.6 g H_2O_2 per kg polypropylene.

8.2 68027 g/mole.

8.3 **(a)** 47470 g/mole, **(b)** 81 g sulphur/kg SBR.

8.4 DP = 2209. (Remember that H_2O is lost in condensation polymerisation.)

8.5 Ratio PS/AN = 1.46/1.

8.6 1.28 MPa.

8.7 5.07×10^{16} Pa s.

9 Ceramics and Composites

9.1 Fact Sheet

(a) Ceramics

Ceramics are crystalline solids. Most modern industrial ceramics are the oxides, carbides or nitrides of metals. Brick, pottery and china are complex alumino-silicates. Ceramics are non-ductile and fracture in a brittle manner. They are comparatively weak in tension but their compressive strengths are of the order of 15 times greater than the tensile strength.

(b) Glasses

Glasses are amorphous solids (supercooled liquids) whose viscosities decrease as the temperature is raised. Commercial glasses are based on silica and window glass (soda glass) is a sodium-calcium silicate containing about 70 per cent silica.

(c) Creep

Glasses and ceramics are subject to creep under stress. This occurs at moderate temperatures for glass, because of the relatively low softening temperatures, but at high temperatures for ceramics. The steady state creep rate, $d\varepsilon/dt$, is given by: $d\varepsilon/dt = A\,\sigma^n \exp(-Q/R_0 T)$, where A and Q are constants, R_0 is the universal gas constant, T is temperature (K), σ is the stress and n is another constant, the time exponent. For glass and many ceramics $n = 10$.

(d) Composites

Composite materials may be classified as particulate or fibrous. An example of a particulate composite is a cermet cutting tool composed of hard carbide particles in a metallic matrix. Of the fibrous composites, the most widely used is fibre reinforced plastic (FRP). The main reinforcing fibres are glass or carbon and the main matrix materials are polyester or epoxy resins.

(e) Properties of fibre composites

Density, ρ_c, is given by the rule of mixtures as $\rho_c = \rho_f V_f + \rho_m (1 - V_f)$. For composites with the reinforcement in the form of long parallel fibres, the values of E_c and tensile strength, σ_c, in the fibre direction are given by:

$$E_c = E_f V_f + E_m (1 - V_f) \text{ and } \sigma_c = \sigma_f V_f + \sigma_m (1 - V_f)$$

where E_f and σ_f are properties of the fibre, E_m and σ_m are properties of the fibre and V_f is the fibre volume fraction.

Parallel fibre composites are highly anisotropic and the values of modulus and strength in a direction normal to the fibre direction are very much lower than those in the fibre direction, for example:

$$E_{c(transverse)} = \left(\frac{V_f}{E_f} + \frac{1 - V_f}{E_m} \right)^{-1}$$

9.2 Worked Examples

Example 9.1

(a) Distinguish between a glass and a ceramic material.

(b) (i) Define the modulus of rupture of a ceramic.
    (ii) How do ceramics fail?

(c) Why does glass have a low resistance to thermal shock and engineering ceramics have a high resistance?

(d) The window in a vacuum chamber is to be made of glass. Tests on a sample of the glass produce an equivalent tensile strength of 50 MPa after 6 minutes. Determine the maximum stress that can be applied to the window to meet a design life of 1000 hours given that the time exponent for glass, $n = 10$.

(Sheffield University)

Solution 9.1

(a) A ceramic possesses a crystalline structure while a glass has an amorphous structure. Consider silica, SiO_2. The structure of silica consists of covalently bonded SiO_4 tetrahedra. In crystalline silica, the tetrahedra are linked together in such a way that there is full crystallinity, but in silica glass, while there is a short range order, in that there are SiO_4 units, there is no long range order or crystallinity and the tetrahedra form an amorphous structure. This difference is shown

170

schematically in the diagram below. *Note that for clarity in a two-dimensional sketch each silicon atom is shown bonded to three rather than four oxygen atoms.*

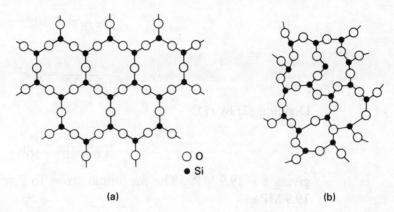

○ O
● Si

(a)   (b)

Figure 9.1 *Schematic representation of (a) crystalline silica, (b) silica glass*

(b)   (i)   The modulus of rupture is the maximum tensile stress developed in the surface of a beam-type specimen when tested to failure in bending with a symmetrical three-point loading arrangement. For a specimen of width, b, and thickness, d, the modulus of rupture is given by $3FL/2bd^2$ (see the diagram below).

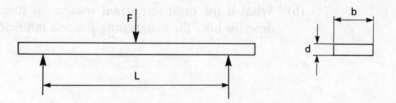

Figure 9.2 *Modulus of rupture test arrangement*

(ii)   Ceramics are non-ductile materials and fail through brittle fracture. As there is no ductility, a crack can propagate through the material with little absorption of energy. Ceramic materials contain internal cracks or flaws most of which are generated during the processing and forming of the material. The size of the internal cracks is the controlling factor over the tensile strength of ceramics.

(c)   The resistance of a material to thermal shock is related to its coefficient of linear expansion. If a body is cooled through a temperature interval of θ, there will be a contraction strain of $\alpha\theta$, where α is the expansion coefficient. In a ceramic or glass, where the thermal conductivity is low, the surface layers cannot contract when the material is cooled suddenly as the interior of the body is still hot. This has the effect of creating a tensile strain of $\alpha\theta$ in the surface layers equivalent to a surface tensile stress of $E\alpha\theta$. The material will crack and fail if this stress is greater than the tensile strength of the material. The tensile strengths of glasses is less than those for many industrial ceramics, while the expansion coefficients for glasses are higher than for many ceramics. The thermal shock resistance of glass is, therefore, lower than that for ceramics.

(d)   The steady state creep rate of a glass at a stress σ can be expressed by: $d\varepsilon/dt = B\,\sigma^n$ where B is a constant and n is the time exponent.

171

Limiting creep strain is reached in 6 min (360 s) at a stress of 50 MPa.
Limiting creep strain is reached in 1000 hours (3.6×10^6 s) at a stress of σ

$$\frac{1}{360} = B \, 50^{10} \tag{1}$$

$$\frac{1}{3.6 \times 10^6} = B \, \sigma^{10} \tag{2}$$

Dividing (2) by (1),

$$\frac{360}{3.6 \times 10^6} = \frac{\sigma^{10}}{50^{10}}$$

giving $\sigma = 19.9$ MPa. The maximum stress to give a design life of 1000 hours is 19.9 MPa.

Example 9.2

(a) Explain why window glass shows viscous behaviour at high temperatures, for example 850 K, and brittle behaviour at room temperature.

(b) What is the most important reason for toughening such window glass and describe how the toughening process influences the mechanical properties?

(City University)

Solution 9.2

(a) Glasses are based on silica and have amorphous structures (see solution 9.1(a)). When cooled from a high temperature, at which the glass is a low viscosity liquid, no structural changes occur and the cooling curve shows no discontinuities.

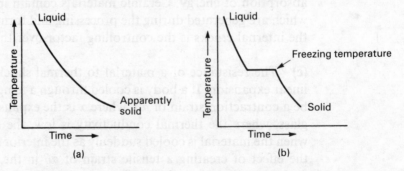

Figure 9.3 *Cooling curves: (a) glass, (b) crystalline material*

As the temperature of a glass falls, the viscosity increases steadily, but the material still has the amorphous fluid structure and is, in effect, a supercooled liquid. At 850 K, window glass has a viscosity of about 10^{10} poise and can creep or flow in a viscous manner. The value of viscosity at which viscous flow is, in effect, non-existent is about 10^{17} poise. At room temperature, the viscosity of glass is higher than this and the material behaves as a brittle solid.

(b) Glass is weak in tension and the tensile strength is reduced considerably by the presence of micro-sized surface defects such as scratches. The surface of window glass can be scratched by wind-borne particles, thus reducing its susceptibility to failure. The toughening process for glass, by inducing high compressive stresses in the surface layers, greatly increases the level of applied tensile stress needed to cause failure, as the first effect of the applied stress will be to reduce the residual compressive stress in the surface. (Further information on the toughening process for glass is given in solution 9.4.)

Example 9.3

(a) The processing of a ceramic body takes place in three stages, forming, drying and firing. Describe plastic forming, the drying process and firing.

(b) A laboratory sample of dried, but unfired, whiteware body has the following weight:

dry 873 g
saturated (with kerosene) 898 g
suspended in kerosene 587 g
mass of 170 cm^3 of kerosene = 141 g.

Calculate: (i)   the apparent porosity,
            (ii) the apparent density,
            (iii) the bulk density,
            (iv) the apparent volume,
            (v)   the bulk volume.

(Kingston Polytechnic)

Solution 9.3

(a) The question refers to plastic forming, which is applicable to clays and not to the newer industrial ceramics. The clay minerals are hydrated alumino-silicates which have plate-type crystals. These plate crystals are polarised with one surface of each plate being positively charged, the other bearing a negative charge. This polarisation allows the clay to absorb water molecules, also polar, between the layers. This provides lubrication permitting easy interlayer sliding. With the correct water content, a clay is plastic and can be formed with relative ease. Clay shapes can be formed by moulding, extrusion or turning on a potter's wheel. After forming to shape, the clay product is dried. This is the loss of excess water by evaporation and it leaves the product sufficiently strong to be handled. After drying, the clay articles are placed in a kiln and fired at temperatures in the range 800–1500°C, depending on the exact composition of the clay. During the firing process, all remaining water is lost, then water of crystallisation is expelled causing a recrystallisation to occur and a hard, rigid, though brittle, structure to be formed. The firing temperature is sufficiently high for a molten silicate glass to form and be drawn by capillary action into many of the spaces between the solid crystals. The changes during firing are accompanied by a major shrinkage but the fired product is still porous. The porosity with some clay products may be as high as 15 or 20 per cent. Finally, in many cases the articles are glazed. A slurry of a glass is applied to the surface and the material refired. This produces a non-porous layer over the surface of the clay article.

An alternative forming process for clay materials is slip casting. The slip is a fluid slurry of clay in water and this is poured into a porous plaster mould. Water is absorbed rapidly into the mould from the slip, and the surface layers of the slip become solid. When the desired wall thickness has solidified excess slurry is poured from the mould. After a suitable time has elapsed, the clay shell is dry enough for the mould to be opened and the shell removed. This is a process suitable for the production of complex and hollow shapes.

(b)   Density of kerosene = $141 \div 170 = 0.829 \, g/cm^3 = 829 \, kg/m^3$.

The dry sample can absorb $898 - 873 = 25 \, g$ kerosene into its open pores. (There may be some closed pores into which the kerosene cannot penetrate.) So, volume of open porosity is $25 \div 0.829 = 30.16 \, cm^3$.

Difference between saturated wt. and wt. in kerosene = $898 - 587 = 311 \, g$.

Volume of kerosene displaced = $311 \div 0.829 = 375.15 \, cm^3$ = bulk volume of the sample (including open and closed porosity).

Difference between dry weight and weight in kerosene = $873 - 587 = 286 \, g$.

Volume of kerosene displaced = $286 \div 0.829 = 345.00 \, cm^3$ = apparent volume of sample (excluding open porosity but including any possible closed porosity).

(i)   The apparent porosity = (vol. of open porosity $\div$ bulk vol.) $\times 100$
$= (30.16 \div 375.15) \times 100 = 8.04$ per cent.

(ii)   The apparent density = dry weight $\div$ apparent vol. $= 873 \div 345.00$
$= 2.53 \, g/cm^3 = 2530 \, kg/m^3$.

(iii)   The bulk density = dry weight $\div$ bulk vol. $= 873 \div 375.15$
$= 2.327 \, g/cm^3 = 2327 \, kg/m^3$.

(iv)   The apparent volume = $345.00 \, cm^3$.

(v)   The bulk volume = $375.15 \, cm^3$.

Example 9.4

(a)   Briefly describe the structure changes which take place when:

(i)   wet clay is processed to make a solid ceramic article,

(ii)   an oxide powder is pressed and sintered to form a solid ceramic component,

(iii)   a molten silicate cools to form a glass, and

(iv)   a glass is thermally toughened.

(b)   A modern ceramic based on silica is a mixture of crystalline and amorphous phases. Describe the main structure difference between the two phases.

(City University)

Solution 9.4

(a) (i) Refer to part **(a)** of solution 9.3.

(ii) An oxide powder, for example alumina, for the manufacture of ceramic components is produced to a very fine particle size, usually 1 μm or less. The powder is then pressed to shape in a die. Ceramic powders do not show plasticity and a small amount of a binding agent is often used to aid compaction and produce a compact with sufficient 'green' strength to be handled for transfer to a sintering furnace. The temperature required for sintering is of the order of two-thirds of the melting temperature (K) and at this temperature the individual powder particles bond together. The mechanism is that bonding reduces the total particle surface area, hence the total surface energy of the material is reduced. There is also a movement of atoms by diffusion processes to close up some of the pore spaces between particles and this reduces surface area still further. This process of densification is accompanied by some shrinkage of the compact. In a similar manner to the phenomenon in metals, grain growth can occur at the sintering temperatures and the grain size of the sintered product may be larger than the powder particle size. Other processes which may be used for the production of ceramic components are hot pressing and hot isostatic pressing (HIP) in which the compaction and sintering are combined in one operation. The combination of pressure and temperature accelerates the sintering process and gives a product of higher density.

(iii) The cooling curve (temperature–time) obtained when a glass is cooled from the fully molten state is a smooth curve with no discontinuities. The material does not solidify at a specific temperature. Instead, as the temperature falls so the viscosity of the fluid increases. The structure remains amorphous at all stages and, at ordinary temperatures, the material is, in effect, a supercooled fluid. The material is deemed to be solid when the viscosity is very high, namely about 10^{17} poise.

(iv) Thermal toughening of glass produces a situation where the surface layers of the glass contain residual compressive stresses but the interior of the section contains residual tensile stresses. Failure of glass is due to tensile forces and normally starts from scratches or other defects on the surface. In the case of toughened glass, a high level of applied force is needed to overcome the compressive stresses in the surface and give a net tensile stress. If, however, a scratch is made of sufficient depth to penetrate beyond the compressive surface zone the glass will then shatter instantaneously. Toughened glass is produced by heating it to a temperature sufficiently high for stress relief to occur (this is about 450–500°C for window glass, and is termed the annealing point). The glass is then cooled rapidly by an air or oil quench. The surface layers become rigid while the centre is still hot. As the centre cools and contracts, it induces tensile stresses in the centre and compressive stresses in the surface zone.

(b) The structure of a ceramic is crystalline while that of a glass is amorphous. (Refer to solution 9.1**(a)** for greater detail.) During the firing of clays some of the constituents form a glass phase at the firing temperature and this glass flows into the spaces between crystalline particles and binds them together.

Example 9.5

(a) A sample of alumina powder has an average particle diameter of 10^{-6} m. Calculate the surface area per kilogramme of powder if the density of alumina is $3.9\,Mg\,m^{-3}$.

(b) If the surface energy of alumina is $1\,J\,m^{-2}$ and the grain boundary energy is $0.5\,J\,m^{-2}$, calculate the available energy per kilogramme of powder to drive the sintering process if the surface and grain boundary areas are the same.

Solution 9.5

(a) Assume all particles are spherical and of 1 μm diameter.

$$
\begin{aligned}
\text{Volume of one particle} &= 4/3\,\pi r^3 = 5.24 \times 10^{-19}\,m^3. \\
\text{Number of particles per } m^3 &= 1.91 \times 10^{18}. \\
\text{Number of particles per kg} &= 1.91 \times 10^{18} \div 3900 = 4.90 \times 10^{14}. \\
\text{Surface area of a particle} &= 4\pi r^2 \\
\text{Surface area per kg} &= 4\pi \times (0.5 \times 10^{-6})^2 \times 4.90 \times 10^{14} \\
&= 1538\,m^2.
\end{aligned}
$$

(b) Before sintering, the surface energy is $1\,J/m^2$. After sintering, the particles are fused together and the grain boundaries have an energy of $0.5\,J/m^2$, so that the energy available to drive the sintering process is $0.5\,J/m^2 = 0.5 \times 1538 = 769\,J/kg$ powder.

Example 9.6

(a) Two ceramics of engineering importance are cubic zirconia, ZrO_2, and alumina, Al_2O_3. The structure of zirconia is a FCC lattice of Zr^{4+} ions with the O^{2-} ions located at the tetrahedral sites. The structure of alumina is a HCP lattice of O^{2-} ions with two-thirds of the octahedral sites occupied by Al^{3+} ions.

Sketch the unit cells of zirconia and alumina and briefly explain why only two thirds of the octahedral sites in alumina are filled with Al^{3+} ions.

(b) A ferrospinel is fabricated by sintering. If the porosity at the green stage is 23 per cent, what linear shrinkage should be allowed for if the total porosity after sintering is 2 per cent?

(Kingston Polytechnic)

Solution 9.6

(a) A tetrahedral site in FCC occurs at $\frac{1}{4},\frac{1}{4},\frac{1}{4}$ and there are 8 such sites in a unit cell. An octahedral site in HCP occurs at $\frac{1}{2},\frac{1}{2},0,\frac{1}{3}$ in a Miller–Bravais cell and there are six possible sites of this type. The unit cells for zirconia, ZrO_2, and alumina, Al_2O_3, are illustrated below.

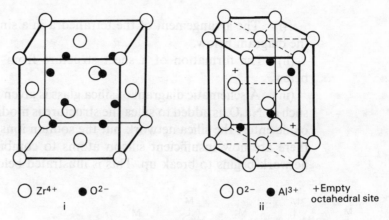

Figure 9.4 *(i) ZrO₂ unit cell; (ii) Al₂O₃ unit cell*

Note that in the zirconia cell, the zirconium ions form an FCC lattice, therefore the cell contains four Zr ions (see chapter 2 for proof of this) while the eight oxygen ions are wholly contained within the unit cell, giving a ratio of Zr to O ions of 1:2. Similarly, the hexagonal unit cell wholly contains four aluminium ions and the equivalent of six oxygen ions. This gives the ratio Al/O of 2:3. There are six possible octahedral sites within the cell but only four of these are filled with Al ions. If all six sites were occupied, the bonding requirements, in terms of chemical valencies, could not be satisfied.

(b) In the green state 77 per cent of the volume is material, the remainder porosity. With 2 per cent porosity in the sintered state the volume, as a percentage of the green volume is 77 ÷ 0.98 = 78.6 per cent so the volume shrinkage during sintering is 21.4 per cent. Assuming that shrinkage is uniform in all directions, the linear shrinkage is the cube root of 21.4 = 2.78 per cent = 27.8 mm/m.

Example 9.7

(a) Sketch the fundamental structural unit for silica and show how a number of such units may be combined to produce:

 (i)   a single chain structure such as $Ca^{2+}[SiO_3]^{2-}$ (Portland cement),
 (ii) a sheet material such as $(Mg_3[OH]_2)^{4+}([Si_2O_5]^{2-})_2$ (talc),
 (iii) an amorphous glass containing sodium.

(Southampton University)

Solution 9.7

(a) The fundamental structural unit for silica is the SiO_4 tetrahedron, in which a silicon atom is bonded covalently to four oxygen atoms, each situated at the corner of a tetrahedron. These tetrahedra can be built into a variety of structures, giving single chains, double chains, sheet lattices and full three-dimensional crystal structures. Substitution of ions of other metallic elements in place of silicon can produce a wide range of silicates.

(i)   The arrangement of the tetrahedra in a single chain structure is shown in the diagram below.

(ii)   The formation of a sheet structure from tetrahedral units is illustrated below.

(iii)   A schematic diagram of silica glass is given in solution 9.1. When an oxide, such as Na_2O, is added to silica the structure is modified. The oxygen of the sodium oxide enters the silica network but the sodium ions enter holes in the network. As there are now insufficient silicon atoms to combine with the extra oxygen, the network begins to break up. This is illustrated below.

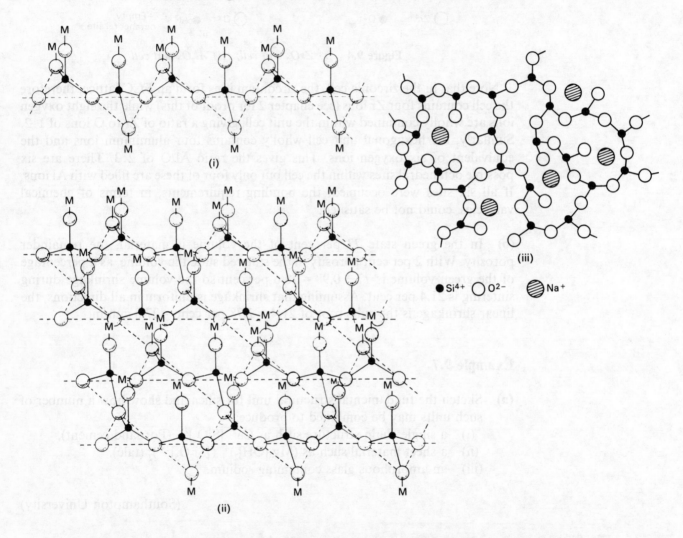

● Si^{4+} ○ O^{2-} ◐ Na^+

Figure 9.5   *Silicate structures (i) single chain, (ii) sheet, (iii) soda glass. (In (i) and (ii) metal atoms may be attached at points marked M.)*

Example 9.8

(a)   For a continuously aligned fibre composite, calculate the maximum theoretical fibre volume fraction.

(b)   The fibre volume fraction for a continuously aligned glass fibre/polyester matrix composite was found to be 55 per cent. How could this be determined experimentally?

(c) For a continuously aligned fibre composite derive an expression for E_c, the composite modulus, in terms of E_f and E_m, the moduli of the fibres and matrix respectively, and V_f, the volume fraction of the fibres.

(d) Plot the modulus of a continuously aligned boron fibre/epoxy composite in which $E_f = 350\,GPa$ and $E_m = 2.5\,GPa$, as a function of the fibre volume fraction.

(Kingston Polytechnic)

Solution 9.8

(a) In calculating the maximum theoretical fibre volume fraction the following assumptions are made: (1) all fibres are of circular cross-section and of the same size, (2) the fibres are packed in a hexagonal packing (see diagram), and (3) the film of resin between fibres is infinitely thin.

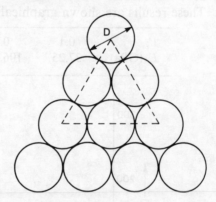

Figure 9.6

The diagram illustrates the appearance of a cross-section with fibres packed in a hexagonal arrangement. Consider a triangular element. This element contains $\{(3 \times 1/6) + (3 \times \frac{1}{2})\} = 2$ circles of diameter D.

The area of this element $= D^2\sqrt{3}$.

The density of packing is

$$\frac{\text{area of 2 circles}}{\text{area of triangle}} = \frac{2 \times \pi D^2}{\sqrt{3}D^2 \times 4} = 0.907$$

The maximum theoretical fibre volume fraction is 0.907.

(b) The fibre volume fraction of a glass fibre/epoxy composite can be calculated after determining the density of the composite. The density, ρ, of glass fibre is about $2500\,kg/m^3$ and ρ for epoxy resin is about $1300\,kg/m^3$. The contribution to the final density made by the fibre is $\rho_f x$, where x is the fibre volume fraction. That made by the matrix is $\rho_m (1 - x)$. So $\rho_c = \rho_f x + \rho_m(1 - x)$ from which $x = (\rho_c - \rho_m)/(\rho_f - \rho_m)$.

(c) When a force, F, parallel to the fibre direction, acts on a fully aligned continuous fibre composite with good bonding between fibres and matrix, the same strain, ε, will be generated in both fibres and matrix and the force will be divided between fibre and matrix such that:

$$F = F_f + F_m$$

where F_f and F_m are the forces carried by fibres and matrix respectively.

Force is equal to stress × cross-sectional area and the area is directly related to the volume of each component, so:

$$\sigma_c = \sigma_f V_f + \sigma_m(1 - V_f)$$

where V_f is the fibre volume fraction. But

$$\sigma = E\varepsilon, \text{ so } E_c\varepsilon = E_f\varepsilon V_f + E_m\varepsilon(1 - V_f)$$

Therefore

$$E_c = E_f V_f + E_m(1 - V_f)$$

(d) Using the expression developed in (c) above values for E_c can be calculated for several volume fractions. These results are:

These results are shown graphically below.

V_f	0.1	0.3	0.5	0.7	0.9
E_c (GPa)	37.25	106.75	176.25	245.75	315.25

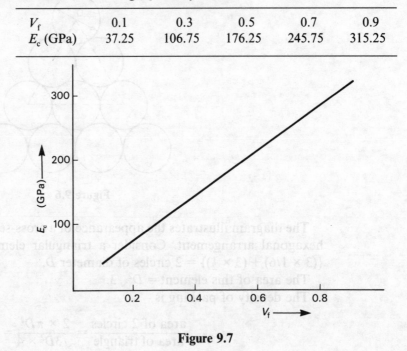

Figure 9.7

Example 9.9

(a) Discuss the advantages of a composite material over a single phase material, with particular reference to (i) high impact polystyrene and (ii) glass-filled nylon. Give two main factors that need to be controlled to achieve a successful composite. What common metallurgical alloy could be classified as a composite and why?

(b) Give the formulae used to calculate the values of Young's modulus and tensile strength of a glass-filled polyester resin.

Indicate graphically the effect of increasing the volume fraction of glass on (i) the brittleness and (ii) the tensile strength of the composite and state any assumptions made.

(c) Calculate the strength of composites containing glass volume fractions of (i) 40 per cent and (ii) 60 per cent, given that the tensile strengths of glass fibre and resin are 3000 MPa and 30 MPa respectively.

(Trent Polytechnic)

Solution 9.9

(a) A composite can have advantages over a single phase material. In the case of a composite made from a soft ductile material and a strong, but brittle, material the resulting composite may possess a strength based on the relative proportions of the materials used yet have a toughness exceeding that of either component (see part **(b)** (i) of this solution). There are many types of composites in use. For example, high impact polystyrene (HIPS) is a composite of polystyrene, a brittle glassy material at room temperatures, and styrene/butadiene rubber (SBR). In this case, small particles of SBR are dispersed throughout the polystyrene and then treated so that a graft copolymer is formed at the interface between the two phases. This produces a material with between five and ten times the impact strength of pure polystyrene, although the tensile strength is reduced to about one-third of that of polystyrene. In glass-filled nylon, on the other hand, the nylon matrix is greatly strengthened by the presence of glass. In this case, the glass is in the form of small chopped fibres and parts can be made by conventional thermoplastic moulding processes. In this case, the tensile strength of the nylon may be doubled and the impact strength maintained relatively constant even though the presence of the glass reduces the percentage elongation value of the material very considerably.

In order to achieve a successful composite, there must be good interfacial bonding between the separate phases and the size, shape and distribution of the composite constituents need to be closely controlled.

A common group of metallurgical materials, effectively, composite materials is steel. One of the constituents of steels, in the annealed or normalised condition, is the eutectoid pearlite. This is a duplex constituent consisting of ferrite, a soft ductile phase, and cementite, Fe_3C, an extremely hard and brittle phase. The structure of pearlite is of thin alternating lamellae of the two phases and this composite constituent is hard, strong and yet tough.

(b) Young's modulus for a fibre-filled composite, E_c, is given by the expression $E_c = E_f V_f + E_m(1 - V_f)$ where E_f and E_m are the moduli for fibre and matrix respectively and V_f is the fibre volume fraction (see example 9.8 for derivation).

Similarly, for tensile strength, σ, $\sigma_c = \sigma_f V_f + \sigma_m(1 - V_f)$. Here σ_f is the fracture strength of the brittle fibre material and σ_m is the yield strength of the matrix.

(i) The toughness of a fibre-reinforced composite increases as the fibre volume fraction increases. This may seem surprising, considering that the fibres tend to be brittle and the matrix is tough, but a fracture in a fibre composite can only propagate by either the fibres pulling out of the matrix as the crack develops or by the fibres breaking. A considerable amount of energy is absorbed in the pull-out of fibres.

(ii) The tensile strength of a fibre composite will increase linearly as the fibre volume fraction is increased.

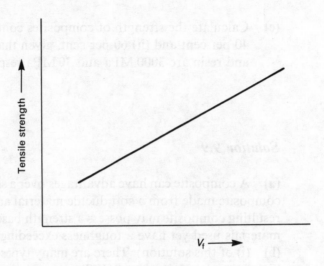

Figure 9.8

(c)   From $\sigma_c = \sigma_f V_f + \sigma_m (1 - V_f)$
   (i) $V_f = 0.4$ $\sigma_c = (3000 \times 0.4) + (30 \times 0.6) = 1218$ MPa.
   (ii) $V_f = 0.6$ $\sigma_c = (3000 \times 0.6) + (30 \times 0.4) = 1812$ MPa.

Example 9.10

(a)   Briefly describe the advantages of a composite material. In relation to a fibre-filled polymer, give two important factors which will control the properties of the composite.

(b)   A composite is made by taking an epoxy resin and adding 10 per cent by volume glass fibre and 5 per cent by volume carbon fibre. Given that the values of E for glass, carbon and resin are 85 GPa, 300 GPa and 5 GPa respectively, calculate the value of E for the composite, stating any assumptions made.

(Trent Polytechnic)

Solution 9.10

(a)   Refer to part (a) of example 9.9.

(b) $E_c = E_f V_f + E_m (1 - V_f)$
   For the glass/carbon/epoxy material
$$E_c = (85 \times 0.1) + (300 \times 0.05) + (5 \times 0.85) = 27.75 \text{ GPa}.$$

182

The assumptions made for the above calculation were: (1) fibres are long and continuous, (2) all fibres are aligned parallel, and (3) there is full bonding between fibres and matrix resin.

Example 9.11

(a) Discuss the role of composite materials in engineering, illustrating your answer by referring to *either* reinforced concrete *or* high-stiffness reinforced polymers.

(b) Glass fibres provide longitudinal reinforcement for a nylon material subject to a tensile load. The fibre diameter is 20 μm and the volume fraction is 0.45.
  (i)   What fraction of the load is carried by the glass?
  (ii) What is the stress in the glass when the average stress in the composite is 14 MPa?
(Take Young's modulus of glass fibres as 70 000 MPa and that of nylon as 2800 MPa.)

(Southampton University)

Solution 9.11

(a) Composite materials have an important role in engineering. There are many instances where the combination of properties required by the engineer can only be available through manufacturing a composite. Concrete, itself a composite material composed of sand, aggregate and cement, is relatively strong in compression, with strengths of 50–80 MPa, but with tensile strengths about one-tenth of this. Plain reinforced concrete is concrete reinforced with steel, a material with both a high tensile strength and a high elastic modulus. Reinforced concrete can accept much higher tensile loadings without failure than can plain concrete. In the manufacture of a concrete beam, the steel is positioned in that part of the beam which, under the influence of bending forces, will contain tensile stresses.

Polymer materials, such as polyester and epoxy resins, are of low density and tough but have relatively low strength and a low stiffness. The value of E for these materials is about 3 GPa. Glass and carbon fibres possess high strengths and have high moduli (E for glass is 70–80 GPa and for Type I carbon fibre is 400 GPa) but these materials are non-ductile. Fibre/resin composites can be manufactured which are of high strength and stiffness coupled with low density. A Type I carbon fibre reinforced epoxy with long parallel fibres and a fibre volume fraction of 0.5 can have a maximum E value of 200 GPa and a density of about 1700 kg/m^3. However, for a composite made with long fibres lying in several directions within a plane the average value of E would be nearer 70 GPa. The specific modulus, E/ρ, for such a material would be about 40 GPa kg^{-1} m^3, which compares with values of the order of 25 GPa kg^{-1} m^3 for aluminium and steel. If considering a plate in bending it is more relevant to take the ratio $E^{\frac{1}{3}}/\rho$ when comparing the relative merits of different materials. This gives a value of 2.4 for the carbon fibre/epoxy composite compared with 1.5 for aluminium and 0.75 for steels. This factor is the reason for the development and use of such fibre composites for high stiffness applications in aerospace such as structural panels and cabin flooring.

(b) (i) The total force is distributed such that $F_T = F_f + F_m$.

In a longitudinally reinforced composite with long continuous fibres the strain in the fibres is the same as the strain in the matrix. Strain, $\varepsilon = \sigma/E$ so $\varepsilon = \sigma_f/E_f = \sigma_m/E_m$ or $\sigma_m = (E_m/E_f)\,\sigma_f = (2800/70\,000)\,\sigma_f = 0.04\,\sigma_f$.

But $F = \sigma \times \text{csa} \equiv \sigma \times \text{volume fraction}$, so $F_T = (\sigma_f \times 0.45) + (\sigma_m \times 0.55) = 0.45\,\sigma_f + (0.55 \times 0.04)\,\sigma_f = 0.472\,\sigma_f$.

The proportion of the load carried by the fibres is $0.45/0.472 = 0.953$ or 95.3 per cent.

(ii) $E_c = E_f V_f + E_m(1 - V_f) = (70\,000 \times 0.45) + (2800 \times 0.55) = 33\,040$ MPa.
Strain $\varepsilon = \sigma/E = 14/33\,040 = 4.237 \times 10^{-4} = \varepsilon_f = \varepsilon_m$
Stress $\sigma = \varepsilon E$ so stress in glass, $\sigma_f = 4.237 \times 10^{-4} \times 70\,000 = 29.66$ MPa.

Example 9.12

(a) The use of fibre-reinforced plastics (FRP) for engineering applications is increasing at a rate of 15–20 per cent per annum. Suggest reasons for this and discuss, briefly, the main advantages and limitations of FRP materials.

(b) From the data below determine the densities and maximum values of Young's modulus and tensile strength for uniaxially aligned fibre/epoxy composites based on each of the three fibre types. (Assume a fibre volume fraction of 0.45 in each case.)

(c) Discuss the relative merits of the three composites for use as lightweight floor panels in aircraft.

(City University)

Material	Density (kg/m^3)	Tensile strength (MPa)	E (GPa)
Epoxy resin	1300	65	4
E-glass fibre	2500	2000	70
Type I carbon fibre	2000	2200	400
Type II carbon fibre	1700	3300	200

Solution 9.12

(a) *Advantages.* FRP materials offer potential for low density, high strength and high modulus materials. They are relatively easy to fabricate into simple and complex shapes. GFRP materials are relatively low cost but considerably higher costs are incurred with CFRP.

Limitations. The highest strength arrangement, namely continuous parallel fibre orientation, gives a highly anisotropic material. Anisotropy can be reduced by using random orientation of fibres or by making cross-ply laminates but this causes a major reduction from maximum potential strength. The FRP materials are not suitable for use at elevated temperatures.

(b) The expressions: $\rho_c = \rho_f V_f + \rho_m(1 - V_f)$
$E_c = E_f V_f + E_m(1 - V_f)$ and
$\sigma_c = \sigma_f V_f + \sigma_m(1 - V_f)$ are used.

For epoxy/e-glass $\rho_c = (2500 \times 0.45) + (1300 \times 0.55)$ $= 1840 \, \text{kg/m}^3$
$E_c = (70 \times 0.45) + (4 \times 0.55)$ $= 33.7 \, \text{GPa}$
$\sigma_c = (2000 \times 0.45) + (65 \times 0.55)$ $= 935.75 \, \text{MPa}$

For epoxy/Type I C $\rho_c = (2000 \times 0.45) + (1300 \times 0.55)$ $= 1615 \, \text{kg/m}^3$
$E_c = (400 \times 0.45) + (4 \times 0.55)$ $= 182.2 \, \text{GPa}$
$\sigma_c = (2200 \times 0.45) + (65 \times 0.55)$ $= 1025.75 \, \text{MPa}$

For epoxy/Type II C $\rho_c = (1700 \times 0.45) + (1300 \times 0.55)$ $= 1480 \, \text{kg/m}^3$
$E_c = (200 \times 0.45) + (4 \times 0.55)$ $= 92.2 \, \text{GPa}$
$\sigma_c = (3300 \times 0.45) + (65 \times 0.55)$ $= 1520.75 \, \text{MPa}$

(c) The requirements for aircraft floor panels are low density and high stiffness, as weight saving is very important in aircraft construction. The epoxy/glass has the highest density and the lowest modulus. If used a larger sectional thickness would be required to give the necessary stiffness than if the other materials were used. This would impose a weight penalty.

Considering the epoxy/carbon materials, the Type I fibre gives a higher modulus, but lower strength, than the Type II fibre. A floor panel is a plate in bending for which the ratios $E^{\frac{1}{3}}/\rho$ and $\sigma^{\frac{1}{2}}/\rho$ are important parameters. These ratios for the two types of carbon composites are:

	Type I carbon	Type II carbon
$E^{\frac{1}{3}}/\rho$	3.51	3.05
$\sigma^{\frac{1}{2}}/\rho$	19.8	26.3

From the above table, it can be seen that use of the Type II carbon would give the lowest weight panel. It has a lower modulus but the stiffness of panels could be improved by incorporating stiffening ribs in the design. As weight saving is important, coupled with the fact that Type I carbon fibre is much more expensive than the Type II fibre it is likely that an epoxy/Type I carbon fibre composite would be preferred for this application.

9.3 Questions

Question 9.1

The density of silicon carbide, SiC, powder is $3200 \, \text{kg/m}^3$, SiC powder is compacted and sintered to form a ceramic component. The component has a dry weight of 360 g and a weight, when saturated in water of 385 g. The weight of the component when suspended in water is 224 g.

Calculate the apparent porosity and the true total porosity of the sintered compact.

Question 9.2

The viscosities of window glass at 1450°C and 780°C are 100 and 10^6 poise respectively. Below what temperature would glass not creep? Assume no creep at viscosities of 10^{17} poise or greater.

Question 9.3

The tensile strength of glass, as measured in a short-term test (1 min) is recorded as 55 MPa. What would be the maximum continuous tensile stress the glass should be subjected to for a component life of: **(a)** 1000 hours, and **(b)** 10 000 hours? Assume the time exponent for glass = 10.

Question 9.4

A cermet cutting tool material has the following weight analysis: tungsten carbide—75 per cent; titanium carbide—10 per cent; cobalt—15 per cent.

Determine the density of the composite, assuming full densification during sintering and given that ρ for WC, TiC and Co are 15 770, 4940 and 8900 kg/m^3 respectively.

Question 9.5

A sample of glass-filled PA 66 is found to have a density of 1515 kg/m^3. What is the volume fraction of glass fibre in the nylon? ρ for PA 66 = 1135 kg/m^3, ρ for glass = 2500 kg/m^3.

Question 9.6

A fibre-reinforced composite material is made from a polyester resin and long uniaxially-aligned glass fibres with a fibre volume fraction of 45 per cent.

Estimate the maximum strength of the composite and the value of E for the composite both parallel to and normal to the fibre direction.

	Polyester resin	Glass Fibre
E (GPa)	2.8	70
Tensile strength (MPa)	65	1800

Question 9.7

A component is to be manufactured from a uniaxially-aligned continuous fibre composite material. Two composites are available, one containing 40 per cent by volume of glass fibre and the other containing 40 per cent by volume of carbon fibre. A minimum tensile strength of 700 MPa and a minimum Young's modulus of 50 GPa is required. Determine which of the two materials is to be recommended for the application by making use of the table of mechanical properties given below.

Material	Tensile strength (MPa)	E (GPa)
Matrix for glass composite	60	3
Matrix for carbon composite	15	3
Glass fibre	3500	62
Carbon fibre	2000	415

9.4 Answers to Questions

9.1 Apparent porosity 15.5 per cent, total porosity 30.1 per cent.
9.2 213°C (486 K).
9.3 (a) 18.3 MPa, (b) 14.54 MPa.
9.4 13 660 kg/m^3.
9.5 0.28.
9.6 $\sigma = 846$ MPa, $E = 33$ GPa (parallel), $E = 1.47$ GPa (normal).
9.7 The carbon fibre composite. Both composites meet the minimum strength requirement but the glass fibre composite with $E = 26.6$ GPa does not meet the requirements.

10 Fracture, Fatigue and Creep

10.1 Fact Sheet

(a) Fracture

Fractures which are the result of a static overload are described as either ductile or brittle. A characteristic feature of a ductile fracture is plastic deformation prior to failure. In the case of a brittle fracture, there is little, if any, plastic deformation prior to fracture.

A. A. Griffith postulated that brittle materials fracture at stresses well below the theoretical failure stress because of the presence of microcracks within the material. These cracks have a stress intensification effect and the material fails when the strain energy is sufficient to provide the surface energy for the new surfaces created by fracture. The Griffith fracture stress, σ_f, is given by the relationship $\sigma_f = (2\gamma E/\pi a)^{1/2}$ where γ is the surface energy, E is the modulus of elasticity and a is one-half of the crack length.

(b) Fast fracture

Fast fracture, a catastrophic failure, can occur in metals containing small cracks or flaws, which in other circumstances would be expected to plastically deform prior to failure. The fracture toughness of a metal, K_c (units $Pa\, m^{1/2}$), is an important property of the material. The stress for fast fracture, σ_f, is given by the expression: $\sigma_f = K_c/\sqrt{(\pi a)}$ where a is one half of the crack length. When a is small σ_f will be greater than σ_y, the yield strength of the metal, but when the crack reaches a critical size the value of σ_f will be equal to σ_y and fast fracture will occur with no plastic deformation.

(c) Fatigue

Fatigue is the response of a material to dynamic loading conditions. A material subjected to repeated cyclical stressing may fail after a number of cycles even though the maximum stress in any one cycle is considerably less than the fracture stress of the material, as determined in short term static tests. Fatigue testing generally involves subjecting a test-piece to alternating stress cycles with a mean stress of zero, the results being plotted in the form of an *S–N* curve. *S–N* curves for two materials are shown in the figure below. Most steels give a curve of type (i) with a definite fatigue limit which is usually about one-half of the tensile strength. Many non-ferrous metals show curves of type (ii) with no definite fatigue limit.

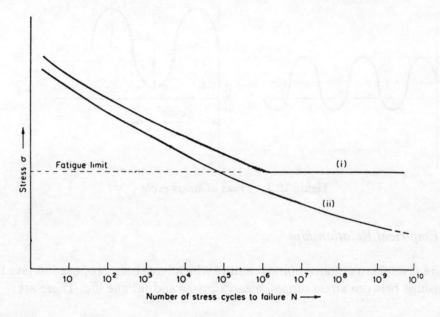

Figure 10.1 S–N *curves: (i) metal with fatigue limit; (ii) metal with no fatigue limit*

(i) Types of Stress Cycle

Stress cycles are described as *alternating*, when the mean stress, σ_m, is zero, *repeating*, when the minimum stress, σ_{min}, is zero, and *fluctuating*, when the mean stress, σ_m, has some value other than zero. These cycle types are shown in the figure below. The stress range of a cycle, $\Delta\sigma$, is $(\sigma_{max} - \sigma_{min})$, the cyclic stress amplitude, $\sigma_a = \frac{1}{2}(\sigma_{max} - \sigma_{min})$, and the mean cycle stress, $\sigma_m = \frac{1}{2}(\sigma_{max} + \sigma_{min})$.

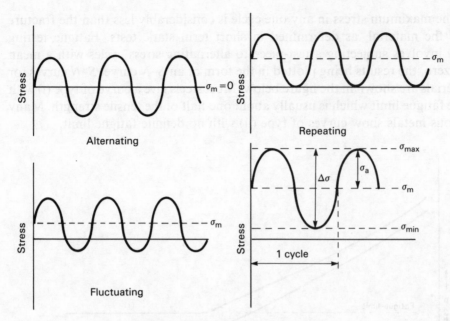

Figure 10.2 *Types of stress cycle*

(ii) Empirical Relationships

There are several laws of an empirical nature which have been proposed to give the relationships between stress ranges, mean stresses and fatigue life. These are:

1. The modified Goodman equation:

$$\frac{\sigma_a}{\sigma_{FL}} + \frac{\sigma_m}{\sigma_{TS}} = 1$$

2. The Gerber parabolic equation:

$$\frac{\sigma_a}{\sigma_{FL}} + \left(\frac{\sigma_m}{\sigma_{TS}}\right)^2 = 1$$

3. The Soderberg equation:

$$\frac{\sigma_a}{\sigma_{FL}} + \frac{\sigma_m}{\sigma_{Y}} = 1$$

In the above equations, σ_{FL} is the fatigue strength as determined in tests with a mean stress of zero, σ_{TS} is the tensile strength, and σ_{Y} is the yield strength of the material.

4. Miner's law of cumulative fatigue. Miner's cumulative fatigue law is an empirical rule used to estimate the fatigue life of a component when subjected to a series of different loading cycles. For example, if stressed for n_1 cycles in a regime which would cause failure in a total of N_1 cycles and for n_2 cycles in a regime where failure would occur after N_2 cycles, then n_1/N_1 of the fatigue life of the component would be used up in the first case and the fraction n_2/N_2 of the fatigue life used in the second instance. Miner's rule can be expressed by stating that failure will occur when $\Sigma(n/N) = 1$.

(iii) Surface Defects

Surface defects will act as points of stress concentration and points for the initiation of fatigue cracks. The two factors are interdependent and both contribute to the stress intensity factor, ΔK, the relationship being: $\Delta K = C\Delta\sigma\sqrt{(\pi d)}$, where $\Delta\sigma$ is the cyclic stress range, d is the depth of a surface flaw (or depth of a trough in a machined surface profile) and C is a material constant. Catastrophic failure will occur when ΔK reaches a critical value, this value being a function of the material.

(d) Creep

Creep is the continued slow straining of a material under constant load. This is of consequence with many thermoplastics at ordinary temperatures but does not become significant for ceramics, glasses and the majority of metallic materials until the temperature is raised. A typical creep curve showing the development of strain with time at a constant stress and temperature is shown in the figure. The rate of steady state creep is affected by variations of stress and temperature.

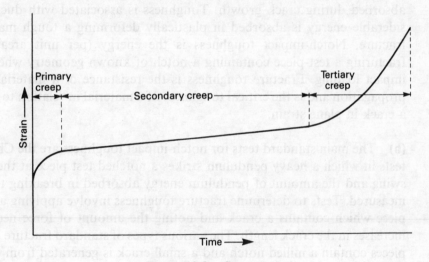

Figure 10.3 *Creep curve*

(i) Stress

An increase in stress, σ, will increase the rate of creep strain, $d\varepsilon/dt$, following the relationship: $d\varepsilon/dt = C\sigma^n$, C and n being constants for the material.

(ii) Temperature

The creep strain rate increases exponentially with temperature according to an Arrhenius-type relationship: $d\varepsilon/dt = A\exp(-B/T)$, where A and B are material constants and T is temperature (K).

10.2 Worked Examples

Example 10.1

(a) What is meant by the term toughness used in connection with materials? Distinguish clearly between notch-impact toughness and fracture toughness.

(b) Explain how both notch-impact toughness and fracture toughness may be determined.

(c) A notch-impact test sample of 10 mm square cross section with a standard milled V-notch 2 mm deep absorbs 115 J of energy in fracture. How should this result be expressed?

Solution 10.1

(a) The term toughness relates to the amount of energy required to initiate and propagate fracture. A material is said to be tough when a large amount of energy is absorbed during crack growth. Toughness is associated with ductility and considerable energy is absorbed in plastically deforming a tough material prior to fracture. Notch-impact toughness is the energy (per unit area) absorbed in fracturing a test-piece containing a notch of known geometry when subjected to impact loading. Fracture toughness is the resistance of a material to fast crack propagation and is the critical toughness of a material in relation to the opening of a crack in plane strain.

(b) The main standard tests for notch-impact toughness are the Charpy and Izod tests in which a heavy pendulum strikes a notched test piece at the bottom of its swing and the amount of pendulum energy absorbed in breaking the test-piece is measured. Tests to determine fracture toughness involve applying a load to a test-piece which contains a crack and noting the amount of force necessary to give increases in the crack length. The various types of standard fracture toughness test-pieces contain a milled notch and a small crack is generated from the root of the notch by a fatigue process prior to conducting the fracture toughness test.

(c) Notch-impact test results should be expressed as energy for fracture per unit area of cross-section (J/m^2).

The effective cross-sectional area of the test-piece (area below the notch is $10 \times 8 = 80 \text{ mm}^2$ so the notch impact value is $115 \div 80 \times 10^{-6} = 1438 \text{ kJ/m}^2$.

Example 10.2

(a) Distinguish between the failure of ductile and brittle materials in:
   (i) a tensile test, and (ii) a notch-impact test.

(b) Plot the Charpy impact test data given in the table below and obtain the ductile-brittle transition temperature.

(Kingston Polytechnic)

Test temperature (°C)	Energy absorbed (J)	Test temperature (°C)	Energy absorbed (J)
95	164	5	50
80	164	− 10	34
70	157	− 20	25
60	149	− 30	18
50	149	− 40	12
40	123	− 50	12
20	84		

Solution 10.2

(a) Failure of a ductile material is preceded by plastic deformation whereas failure of a brittle material is preceded by little, if any, plastic deformation. As metals can show a wide range of properties from high ductility to a brittle nature, the behaviour in tensile and notch-impact tests will be discussed in relation to metals.

(i) *Tensile tests.* The characteristic fracture of a ductile metal in a tensile test to failure is the cup and cone fracture. When the yield point is exceeded and plastic deformation occurs, the test-piece begins to neck. The stress in the necked portion builds up to a high level and small cavities begin to form within the test-piece. Finally, failure by shear occurs at an angle of about 45° to the axis of stress giving the cup and cone fracture (see the diagram below). The centre part of the fracture zone has a fibrous appearance. A very hard and strong metal which cannot deform plastically to any significant extent will fail in a brittle manner giving either a shear type or cleavage type fracture (see the diagram below). A brittle fracture surface is often granular in appearance and may show a bright appearance due to reflection of light from individual cleaved crystal surfaces.

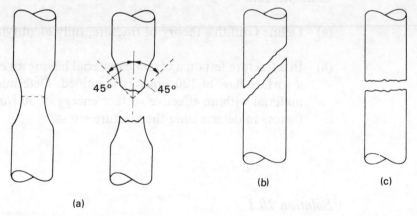

Figure 10.4 *Tensile fractures: (a) ductile; (b) brittle shear; (c) brittle cleavage*

(ii) *Notch-impact tests.* A ductile metal sample will absorb a large amount of energy in a notch-impact test of the Charpy or Izod type. The fracture surface will have a torn fibrous appearance and evidence of considerable plastic deformation will be observed in the material opposite the notch. A brittle metal, on the other hand, will absorb little energy in fracture. The metal cleaves in a straight line from the notch and the surface has a bright crystalline appearance.

(b) A plot of the Charpy impact test data is shown in the figure below.

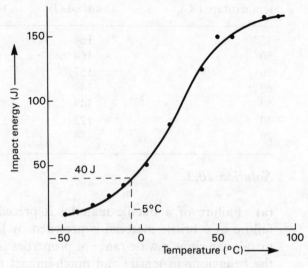

Figure 10.5

The value of the transition temperature may be obtained by using more than one criterion. One standard is based on examination of the fracture surfaces and quotes the temperature at which approximately one-half of the surface is of the cleavage type and one-half is a fibrous fracture. The other criterion is to quote the temperature at which the absorbed energy for a standard sized Charpy test-piece is 40 J. Obviously, only the latter method can be used in this example and the transition temperature read from the graph is − 5°C.

Example 10.3

(a) Define Griffith's theory of fracture, fully identifying each of the parameters.

(b) In a fracture test on a ceramic material having an elastic modulus of 400 GPa, a surface flaw of 120 μm was identified. Determine the fracture stress for a material with an effective surface energy of 30 J/m². What are the dominant factors in determining the fracture stress?

(Sheffield University)

Solution 10.3

(a) A material will fail through brittle fracture at a stress which is generally much lower than the theoretical value based on interatomic bond strengths. A. A. Griffith postulated that materials contained small cracks and these served as major stress concentrators. When a crack propagates, new surfaces are created giving an increase in surface energy and Griffith stated that brittle failure will occur when the strain energy released during the process is equal to the energy required in the creation of new surfaces. The Griffith equation is:

$$\sigma_f = \left(\frac{2\gamma E}{\pi a}\right)^{1/2}$$

where σ_f is stress to cause brittle fracture (Pa), E is the modulus of elasticity (Pa), γ is the surface energy ($J\,m^{-2}$) and a is one-half of the crack length (m).

(b) Substituting the given data in the Griffith equation, remembering that a is equal to $120 \times 10^{-6} \div 2\,m$, we have:

$$\sigma_f = \left(\frac{2 \times 30 \times 400 \times 10^9}{\pi \times 60 \times 10^{-6}}\right)^{1/2} = 357\,MPa$$

In the above solution, it is assumed that the crack is lying normal to the direction of stress. The fracture strength will be higher if the crack is lying at some other angle. Materials with high moduli and surface energies will tend to have higher fracture stresses. The size of flaw or crack is also very important, an increase in size reducing the fracture strength.

Example 10.4

A steel has a yield strength of 550 MPa and a fracture toughness of $40\,MPa\,m^{1/2}$. What will be the limiting design stress if the maximum tolerable crack is 3.0 mm in length and no plastic deformation is permitted?

(Southampton University)

Solution 10.4

The stress required to cause fast fracture, σ_f, is given by:

$$\sigma_f = \frac{K_c}{\sqrt{\pi a}}$$

where K_c is the fracture toughness and a is one-half of the crack length.
Using the given data

$$\sigma_f = \frac{40 \times 10^6}{\sqrt{(\pi \times 1.5 \times 10^{-3})}} = 583\,MPa$$

This means that $\sigma_f > \sigma_Y$. As no plastic deformation is permitted, the limiting stress for design purposes will be the yield stress of 550 MPa so that if a design code stipulated a Factor of Safety of 2 then the maximum design stress would be $550 \div 2 = 275\,MPa$.

Example 10.5

(a) (i) Sketch and define the various points on the Charpy impact temperature transition curve for a plain carbon steel.
     (ii) What alloying elements may be added to the steel in order to improve its toughness?

(iii)   What is the influence of alloying elements on the curve?

(b)   An aluminium alloy ($\sigma_Y = 400\,\text{MN/m}^2$, $K_c = 32\,\text{MN/m}^{3/2}$) and a steel ($\sigma_Y = 1050\,\text{MN/m}^2$, $K_c = 150\,\text{MN/m}^{3/2}$) are being considered as possible materials for a pressure vessel. Comment on the safety aspects of using these materials under (i) static loading and (ii) fatigue loading conditions.

Solution 10.5

(a)   (i)   The general form of the Charpy impact temperature curve for a plain carbon steel is shown in the diagram below.

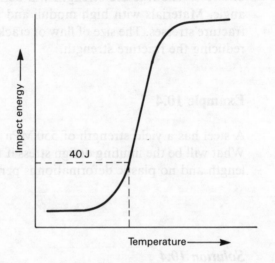

Figure 10.6

It will be noted that there is a transition from brittle failure to tough or ductile failure over a relatively small range of temperature. This transition range is about 25°C. Within this range of temperature, the fracture appearance is part brittle and part tough. The transition temperature may be determined by quoting the temperature at which either the fracture appearance shows brittle and tough characteristics in approximately equal proportions or the impact energy for a standard sized test-piece is 40 J. The transition temperature for a plain carbon steel is close to 0°C.

(ii)   Nickel and, to a lesser extent, manganese are two alloying elements which will improve the toughness of a steel.

(iii)   Both of the above mentioned alloying elements will have two effects on the Charpy impact curve. They will raise the Charpy values to some extent at all temperatures but, perhaps, the most important effect is that they reduce the value of the transition temperature, that is, move the curve towards the left. Nickel alloy steels are to be recommended for applications where steels are to be used in sub-zero temperatures.

(b)   The fast fracture stress, σ_f, is given by $\sigma_f = K_c/\sqrt{(\pi a)}$. The largest size defect which can be tolerated if fast fracture is not to occur before yielding can be determined by making $\sigma_f = \sigma_Y$. Then

$$2a = \frac{2}{\pi}\left(\frac{K_c}{\sigma_Y}\right)^2$$

For aluminium,

$$2a = \frac{2}{\pi}\left(\frac{32}{400}\right)^2 = 4.07 \times 10^{-3}\,\text{m} = 4.07\,\text{mm}$$

and for steel

$$2a = \frac{2}{\pi}\left(\frac{150}{1050}\right)^2 = 0.013\,\text{m} = 13\,\text{mm}$$

The above calculation indicates that the steel will offer a considerably greater safety margin than the aluminium under static loading conditions as the size of defect needed to give fast fracture before the onset of yielding is about three times larger and, in consequence, it will prove easier to detect defects before they reach critical size.

In a fatigue situation, a crack may start at the surface of the component and grow as the number of stress cycles increases. Although the cyclic load range may remain constant, the stress intensity will increase as the crack increases in size. The cyclic stress intensity, ΔK, is given by $\Delta K = \Delta\sigma\sqrt{(\pi a)}$, where $\Delta\sigma$ is the cyclic stress range and a is the depth of a surface crack. The rate of crack growth, $\mathrm{d}a/\mathrm{d}N$ is given by the expression $\mathrm{d}a/\mathrm{d}N = A\,\Delta K^m$, where A and m are material constants. No information is given to compare the crack growth rates of the aluminium alloy and the steel.

Example 10.6

(a) Briefly explain why both applied stress and machined surface profile are mutually important safe-life design parameters.

(b) The threshold intensity factor range ΔK for a steel may be assumed to be $5\,\text{MN/m}^{3/2}$. Given that $\Delta K = 1.12\,\Delta\sigma\sqrt{(\pi d)}$ where $\Delta\sigma$ is the cyclic stress range applied to a steel component and d is the depth of a surface defect, determine the safe cyclic stress range which can be applied to the following situations and sketch a graph of $\Delta\sigma$ versus d.

Component	d
A ground and polished crankpin	1 μm
A machine-turned rotating shaft	10 μm
A rough-turned pulley wheel	100 μm
A gouged-out defect on a flywheel shaft	1 mm
A weld-induced crack in a rock-crushing plant	10 m
An underwater crack in an oil platform rig	100 mm

(Sheffield University)

Solution 10.6

(a) In a regime likely to cause failure by fatigue, the higher the level of stress the shorter will be the fatigue life of the component. Similarly, the surface profile is important. Irregularities in the surface act as points of stress concentration and points for the initiation of fatigue cracks. The two factors are interdependent and both contribute to the stress intensity factor, ΔK, the relationship being $\Delta K = C\Delta\sigma\sqrt{(\pi d)}$ where $\Delta\sigma$ is the cyclic stress range, d is the depth of a surface flaw (or depth of a trough in a machined surface profile) and C is a material constant. Catastrophic failure will occur when ΔK reaches a critical value, this value being a function of the material. It will be seen that an increase in either or both $\Delta\sigma$ and d will generate an increase in ΔK.

(b) The equation $\Delta K = 1.12\,\Delta\sigma\sqrt{(\pi d)}$ can be rewritten as $\Delta\sigma = \Delta K \div 1.12\sqrt{(\pi d)}$. Substituting the various values for d given in the table this gives:

when $d = 1\ \mu m$	$\Delta\sigma =$	2519 MPa
$d = 10\ \mu m$	$\Delta\sigma =$	796 MPa
$d = 100\ \mu m$	$\Delta\sigma =$	252 MPa
$d = 1\ mm$	$\Delta\sigma =$	80 MPa
$d = 10\ mm$	$\Delta\sigma =$	25 MPa
$d = 100\ mm$	$\Delta\sigma =$	8 MPa

A graphical representation of the relationship between $\Delta\sigma$ and d is shown below.

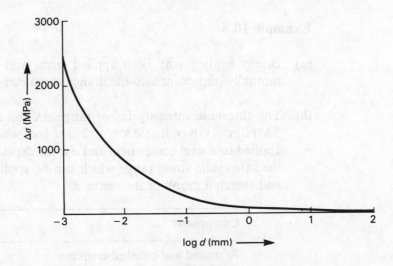

Figure 10.7

Example 10.7

(a) Define the term fatigue.

(b) With the aid of sketches, define the following terms as applied to fatigue testing: (1) stress range, (ii) mean stress, (iii) alternating stress, (iv) cycle.

(c) Using the modified Goodman law, calculate the maximum mean stress a steel

198

shaft is able to withstand when it is subjected to a stress range of 200 MN/m². The tensile strength of the steel shaft is 500 MN/m² and the fully reversed fatigue strength is 250 MN/m². Assume a factor of safety of 1.5 in order to avoid failure.

(d) Indicate three different ways of improving the fatigue strength of a steel component.

(Southampton University)

Solution 10.7

(a) Fatigue is the failure of a material after repeated cyclical stressing even though the maximum stress in any one stress cycle may be considerably lower than the fracture stress of the material, as determined in a static test.

(b)   (i) The stress range is $\sigma_{max} - \sigma_{min}$.
    (ii) The mean stress is $(\sigma_{max} + \sigma_{min}) \div 2$.
    (iii) The term alternating stress refers to stress cycling where the mean stress is zero, that is σ_{max} and σ_{min} have equal values but one is a tensile stress and the other is compressive.
    (iv) A cycle is the period between two successive applications of σ_{max}.

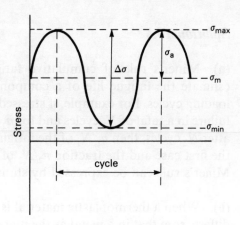

Figure 10.8

(c) The modified Goodman equation is:

$$\frac{\sigma_a}{\sigma_{FL}} + \frac{\sigma_m}{\sigma_{TS}} = 1$$

Substituting the given data and assuming a factor of safety of 1.5:

$$\frac{100}{250} + \frac{1.5\sigma_m}{500} = 1$$

from which the maximum mean stress, σ_m is 200 MN/m².

199

(d) (i) Prepare the component with a highly polished surface free from incidental scratches and other surface defects.

(ii) Peen the surface of the steel component. This will induce residual compressive stresses within the surface layers and improve resistance to fatigue. (Nitriding the steel will also induce surface compressive stresses and thus improve fatigue resistance.)

(iii) Manufacture the component from a low alloy steel containing nickel. Nickel steels have an improved resistance to fatigue.

Example 10.8

(a) Define Miner's rule of cumulative fatigue damage clearly identifying each of the parameters.

(b) Briefly describe the effects of fatigue cycling on a plastic at a constant stress range.

(c) (i) What parameters influence the creep behaviour of a material?
(ii) When is it necessary to consider the effects of creep on a material?
(iii) How can the creep range of a steel be extended?

(Sheffield University)

Solution 10.8

(a) Miner's rule of cumulative fatigue damage is an empirical rule used to estimate the fatigue life of a component when subjected to a series of different loading cycles. For example, if stressed for n_1 cycles in a regime which would cause failure in a total of N_1 cycles and for n_2 cycles in a regime where failure would occur after N_2 cycles, then n_1/N_1 of the fatigue life of the component would be used up in the first case and the fraction n_2/N_2 of the fatigue life used in the second instance. Miner's rule can be expressed by stating that failure will occur when $\Sigma(n/N) = 1$.

(b) When a thermoplastic material is subject to stress cycling, the strain response differs from that in a metal as the material is viscoelastic. At very slow cyclic rates, relaxation can occur and the material behaves more as a viscous fluid while, at high cyclic loading rates, viscous response is almost absent and the material behaves in a nearly elastic manner. The high internal friction of thermoplastic materials means that, if the amount of cyclic strain is great, there can be a significant rise in temperature of the material. An example of this is the large increase in temperature which can occur in vehicle tyres during a high-speed drive, particularly if the tyres are underinflated and the strain per cycle is considerable.

(c) (i) The rate of creep of a material is influenced by both stress and temperature. An increase in stress causes an increase in creep rate. At a constant temperature, the steady state creep strain rate, $d\varepsilon/dt$, is related to the stress, σ, by the expression: $d\varepsilon/dt = C\,\sigma^n$, where C and n are material constants. An increase in temperature has a major effect on creep strain rates and the relationship is of the

Arrhenius type: $d\varepsilon/dt = A \exp(-B/T)$, where T is the temperature (K) and A and B are material constants.

(ii)   For ceramics, glasses and metals, other than those of low melting temperature such as lead, creep is an elevated temperature phenomenon but many thermoplastic materials are subject to creep under the influence of comparatively low stresses at ordinary temperatures. Consideration of creep must be taken into account wherever a material will be subject to static load over a long period of time at a temperature at which slow continuous straining can occur.

(iii)   Similar factors to those which affect static strength may influence the creep strength of metals, namely those structural features which impede dislocation motion. The creep strength of a steel could be improved by alloying to give a dispersion strengthened material. At very high temperatures, however, the main mechanism of creep is viscous grain boundary flow and at these temperatures the creep strength of an alloy can be improved by either directional solidification to give a structure with few grain boundaries lying normal to the stress axis, or by the manufacture of single crystal components, where there are no grain boundaries. This latter technique is now being used for the manufacture of turbine blades for aircraft gas turbines.

Example 10.9

(a)   Define the term *creep*.

(b)   Indicate with the aid of sketches the progressive nature of creep.

(c)   Sketch isochronous and isometric creep curves clearly indicating their derivation.

(d)   Creep tests on a stainless steel at 550°C produced a strain of 0.12 after 300 hours when subjected to a stress of 350 MN/m² and a strain of 0.08 after 1200 hours when stressed to 245 MN/m². Assuming steady-state creep, calculate the time to produce 0.1 per cent strain in a link bar of the same material when stressed to 75 MN/m² at 550°C.

(Sheffield University)

Solution 10.9

(a)   Creep is the slow continued straining of a material under the influence of a constant load. Creep of some thermoplastic materials and soft metals, such as lead, can be significant at ordinary temperatures but for most metals, ceramics and glasses creep is a phenomenon that only occurs at elevated temperatures. Steady-state creep rates vary exponentially with temperature according to an Arrhenius-type expression: creep rate $d\varepsilon/dt = A \exp(-B/t)$.

(b)   A typical creep curve for a material subject to a constant load at constant temperature is shown in the figure below. There are three stages of creep, primary or transient, secondary or steady state, and tertiary. The last phase leads to rapid failure.

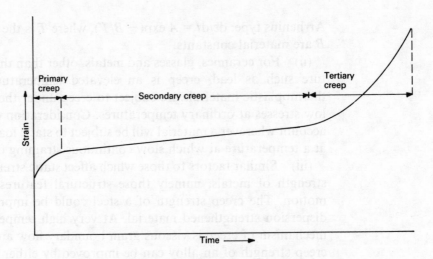

Figure 10.9 *Typical creep curve*

(c) The type of creep curve shown in part (b) is the result of one single test on a material at one temperature and load. Very many test results are required at various loads and temperatures to give a full picture of the creep behaviour of a material. The data obtained from a large number of tests for a material may be presented in a variety of ways, including the time required to produce some specified value of strain, the creep strain which occurs in some specified time and the time necessary for failure by fracture. Such curves may be plotted as isochronous stress–strain curves or isometric stress–time curves. The diagrams below show: (a) a family of strain-time creep curves for a material showing the effect of an increasing stress at a constant temperature; (b) isochronous stress–strain curves derived from the family of curves in (a); (c) isometric stress-time curves derived from the family of curves in (a).

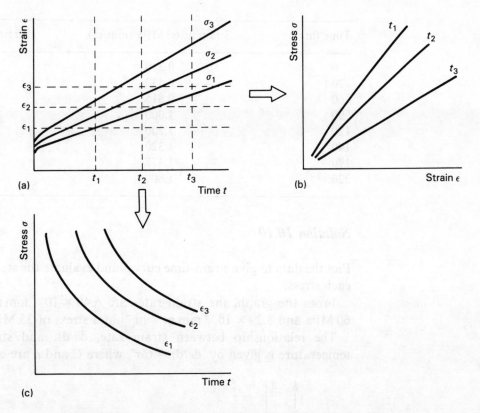

(a) (b) (c)

Figure 10.10 *Derivation of isochronous and isometric creep curves*

(d)   At 550°C and a stress of 350 MPa, the creep rate is $0.12 \div 300 = 4 \times 10^{-4}$/hr, while at 550°C and a stress of 245 MPa the creep rate is $0.08 \div 1200 = 6.67 \times 10^{-5}$/hr.

The relationship between strain rate, $d\varepsilon/dt$, and stress, σ, at a constant temperature is given by: $d\varepsilon/dt = C\sigma^n$, where C and n are constants.

Substituting in this expression we have:

$$4.00 \times 10^{-4} = C \times 350^n \text{ or } \log(4.00 \times 10^{-4}) = \log C + n \log 350 \qquad (1)$$

$$6.67 \times 10^{-5} = C \times 245^n \text{ or } \log(6.67 \times 10^{-5} = \log C + n \log 245 \qquad (2)$$

Subtracting (1) from (2), we have $0.776 = 0.154n$ from which $n = 5.04$ and $\log C = -16.22$.

For a stress of 75 MPa let the strain rate be x/hr. We have: $\log x = -16.22 + (\log 75 \times 5.04)$, from which $x = 1.67 \times 10^{-7}$/hr.

Straining by creep at this rate would produce a strain of 0.001 (0.1 per cent) in a time of $0.001 \div 1.67 \times 10^{-7} = 5988$ hours.

Example 10.10

The following data were obtained for the creep of an aluminium alloy when tested at 200°C. Plot the results and then calculate the value of stress that would give rise to a minimum creep rate of $4.8 \times 10^{-3} \text{ mm m}^{-1} \text{ hr}^{-1}$.

203

Time (hr)	Strain at 60 MPa (mm/m)	Strain at 35 MPa (mm/m)
0	0.320	0.108
20	0.532	0.215
60	0.815	0.332
90	1.000	0.400
120	1.200	0.477
140	1.320	0.532
170	1.477	0.610
220	1.800	0.723

Solution 10.10

Plot the data to give strain-time curves and evaluate the steady-state creep rates for each stress.

From the graph, the strain rates are 6.40×10^{-3} mm m^{-1} hr^{-1} at a stress of 60 MPa and 3.29×10^{-3} mm m^{-1} hr^{-1} at a stress of 35 MPa.

The relationship between strain rate, $d\varepsilon/dt$, and stress, σ, at a constant temperature is given by: $d\varepsilon/dt = C\sigma^n$, where C and n are constants.

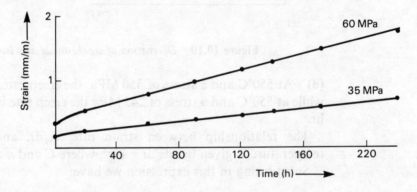

Figure 10.11

Substituting in this expression we have:

$$6.40 \times 10^{-3} = C \times 60^n \text{ or } \log(6.40 \times 10^{-3}) = \log C + n \log 60 \qquad (1)$$

$$3.29 \times 10^{-3} = C \times 35^n \text{ or } \log(3.29 \times 10^{-3}) = \log C + n \log 35 \qquad (2)$$

Subtracting (1) from (2), we have $0.289 = 0.235n$, from which $n = 1.235$ and $\log C = -11.80$.

For a strain rate of 4.8×10^{-3} m m^{-1} hr^{-1}, let the stress be x MPa. We have: $\log(4.8 \times 10^{-3}) = -2.319 = -11.80 + (1.235 \times \log x)$, from which $x = 47.5$ MPa.

Example 10.11

When tested at a stress of 100 MPa, the steady-state creep rate of a material is 1.0×10^{-4}/s at 900 K and is 7.5×10^{-9}/s at 750 K. Calculate the maximum working temperature if the limiting creep rate is 1.0×10^{-7}/s.

Solution 10.11

The Arrhenius expression $d\varepsilon/dt = A \exp(-B/T)$ applies.

$$1.0 \times 10^{-4} = A \exp(-B/900) \tag{1}$$

$$7.5 \times 10^{-9} = A \exp(-B/750) \tag{2}$$

Dividing (1) by (2), $1.0 \times 10^{-4} \div 7.5 \times 10^{-9} = 13.33 \times 10^3 = \exp\{B(1/750 - 1/900)\}$, from which $B = 42.75 \times 10^3$.

Substituting this value in (1) gives $A = 4.23 \times 10^{16}$.

Let the temperature at which creep strain rate is $1.0 \times 10^{-7}/s$ be T. Then $1.0 \times 10^{-7} = 4.23 \times 10^{16} \exp(-42.75 \times 10^3/T)$, from which $T = 786$ K.

The maximum working temperature at a stress of 100 MPa if the creep strain rate is not to exceed $1.0 \times 10^{-7}/s$ is 786 K.

10.3   Questions

Question 10.1

(a) Determine the fracture stress of a glass if it contains a series of microcracks with a maximum dimension of $10\,\mu m$.

(b) A fine surface scratch of depth 0.3 mm is made in the surface of the glass. What will be the likely fracture stress in this case?

Assume E for glass = 70 GPa and the surface energy of glass = $0.6\,J/m^2$.

Question 10.2

An aluminium alloy with a yield strength of 475 MPa and a fracture toughness, K_c, of 21 MPa m$^{1/2}$ is suggested for the manufacture of a structural component with a maximum design stress of $\sigma_Y/2$. The inspection facilities available are capable of detecting defects of 3 mm length or greater. Determine whether the inspection capability is sufficiently sensitive to detect flaws before they reach the critical dimensions for fast fracture.

Question 10.3

If a steel component was found to contain a small surface crack, calculate the critical crack length for brittle fracture, assuming: (i) the fracture toughness, $K_c = 150$ MPa m$^{1/2}$, and (ii) the maximum applied stress is limited by the yield stress of the steel $\sigma_Y = 1200$ MPa.

Question 10.4

Estimate the maximum safe cyclic stress range which can be applied to a steel shaft of 20 mm diameter if complete failure is not to occur before a fatigue crack has developed to at least one-quarter of the diameter. Assume that the relationship $\Delta K = 1.1\, \Delta\sigma\sqrt{(\pi d)}$ holds and that ΔK for the steel is $5\,\text{MPa m}^{1/2}$.

Question 10.5

A steel component is subject to a static tensile stress of 225 MPa with a superimposed cyclic stress. Estimate the maximum range of the cyclic stress using: **(a)** the modified Goodman law and **(b)** the Soderberg law. The steel has a static tensile strength of 640 MPa, a tensile yield strength of 510 MPa and a fatigue limit of 320 MPa.

Question 10.6

A steel with a tensile strength of 900 MPa and a fatigue strength (for 10^6 cycles) of 450 MPa is subjected to a series of alternating stress cycles as follows: 10 000 cycles at $\sigma_{max} = 575\,\text{MPa}$ and 10 000 cycles at $\sigma_{max} = 550\,\text{MPa}$. Estimate the number of additional stress cycles the steel can endure at a value of $\sigma_{max} = 500\,\text{MPa}$.

Question 10.7

The steady state creep rates for a steel obtained at a temperature of 510°C over a range of stresses are as follows: $1.69 \times 10^{-5}/\text{h}$ at 180 MPa; $3.22 \times 10^{-5}/\text{h}$ at 200 MPa; $7.55 \times 10^{-5}/\text{h}$ at 240 MPa; $1.41 \times 10^{-4}/\text{h}$ at 265 MPa.
(a) Does steady state creep at 510°C obey a simple power law and, if so, evaluate the exponent?
(b) Estimate the maximum stress to which the steel can be subjected if the limiting strain rate is $1.65 \times 10^{-4}/\text{h}$.

Question 10.8

The steady state creep strain rates for an alloy at several temperatures and under a constant stress of 105 MPa were determined and are given below:

Temperature (°C)	180	220	260
Strain rate (s⁻¹)	4.72×10^{-8}	2.08×10^{-7}	7.34×10^{-7}

Estimate the life of the material when stressed at 105 MPa at a temperature of 160°C if the total creep strain is not to exceed 0.01.

10.4 Answers to Questions

10.1 **(a)** 73.1 MPa; **(b)** 9.4 MPa. (Note: The term a in the Griffith equation is one-half of the crack length in **(a)** and the crack depth in **(b)**.)
10.2 Critical flaw size is 4.98 mm. Inspection facility is adequate.

10.3 9.95 mm.

10.4 36 MPa.

10.5 **(a)** 416 MPa, **(b)** 358 MPa.

10.6 74.5×10^3 cycles. (Note: Use Miner's law of cumulative fatigue.)

10.7 **(a)** Plot log strain rate against log stress. A linear plot confirms a simple power law, the slope being equal to the exponent $n = 5.5$. **(b)** 275 MPa.

10.8 4.93×10^5 s (137 hr).

11 Hardness and Tensile Testing

11.1 Fact Sheet

(a) Hardness

The hardness of metals can be defined as resistance to plastic deformation and test methods are based on forcing an indenter into the surface under a known load. Two such tests are the Brinell test and Vickers diamond test. In each case the hardness number is given by indenting force divided by the surface area of indentation.

(i) Brinell test

A hard steel ball indenter is used. Indenter diameters may be 1, 2, 5 or 10 mm.

$$\text{Hardness number, } H_B = \frac{2F}{\pi D[D - \sqrt{(D^2 - d^2)}]}$$

where F = indenting load (kgf), D = diameter of indenter (mm) and d = diameter of impression (mm).

(ii) Vickers diamond hardness test

A square pyramidal diamond indenter, with an included angle, $\theta = 136°$, between opposite faces is forced into the surface of a metal under a constant load for 15 s.

$$\text{Hardness number, } H_D = \frac{2F \sin(\theta/2)}{d^2} = \frac{1.854F}{d^2}$$

where F = indenting force (kgf) and d = mean length of impression diagonals (mm).

(iii) Meyer hardness analysis

The Meyer relationship for the Brinell test is $F = ad^n$ where F is the load (kgf), d is the diameter of the indentation and a and n are constants of the material and its condition. a is related to the resistance to indenter penetration and n is the work hardening index. The relationship can be written:

$$\log F = \log a + n \log d$$

Using a ball indenter of fixed diameter and a series of loads, the data recorded can be plotted as $\log F$ against $\log d$. A straight line should be obtained and the values of a and n determined.

(b) Tensile testing

The tensile test is used widely to determine the characteristics of metals and plastics materials. The following properties are usually determined: Young's modulus, E; yield stress or proof stress; tensile strength, percentage elongation on gauge length; percentage reduction in area.

(i) Determination of E

E can be evaluated from the slope of the linear elastic portion of the force–extension curve for the material:

$$E = \text{slope} \times (\text{gauge length/cross-sectional area, c.s.a.})$$

The force–extension curve for many soft thermoplastics does not possess a perfectly linear portion and it is customary to quote E as being the secant modulus at a strain of 0.2 per cent. See the figure below. For a gauge length of 50 mm a strain of 0.2 per cent is equivalent to an extension of 0.1 mm.

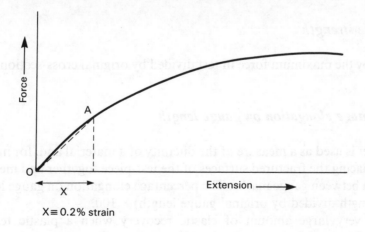

Figure 11.1

The secant modulus, E, is given by the slope of OA × (gauge length/c.s.a.).

(ii) Determination of yield and proof stress

Some materials, notably mild steel, show a sudden yield with a marked discontinuity on the force–extension curve. In these cases:

$$\text{yield stress} = \text{force at yield} \div \text{cross-sectional area}$$

For many materials, there is no sudden yield but a smooth transition from elastic to plastic behaviour. For these materials, it is customary to quote the nominal stress necessary to cause a specified amount of plastic strain. The specified strain may be 0.1, 0.2 or 0.5 per cent. The calculated value is expressed as either a percentage proof stress or a percentage yield stress, for example 0.1 per cent proof stress. It is obtained by constructing a line on the force–extension curve from an extension corresponding to a strain of 0.1 per cent and parallel to the elastic portion of the curve. The intersection of this line with the force–extension curve gives the proof force. See figure below.

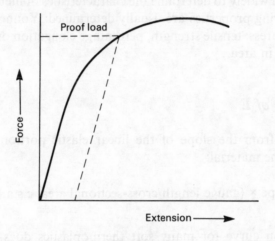

Figure 11.2

0.1 per cent proof stress = 0.1 per cent proof force ÷ original c.s.a.

(iii) Tensile strength

This is given by the maximum force in test divided by original cross-sectional area.

(iv) Percentage elongation on gauge length

This parameter is used as a measure of the ductility of a material and, for metals, is obtained by placing the fractured surfaces of the test-piece together and measuring the new length between gauge marks. The percentage elongation on gauge length is (increase in length divided by original gauge length) × 100.

There is a very large amount of elastic recovery when a plastic test-piece fractures and, for plastics, the value quoted is percentage elongation at break. This is based on the strained length at the moment of fracture. It is important that the original gauge length be quoted as the value of elongation for any material varies with gauge length. (See Barba's law below.)

(v) Percentage reduction in area

This is also a measure of the ductility of a metal and is used in connection with test-pieces of circular cross-section and is given by:

$$100 \times \{(\text{original c.s.a.} - \text{fracture c.s.a.}) \div \text{original c.s.a.}\}.$$

This quantity, unlike percentage elongation, is largely independent of test-piece dimensions.

(c) True stress–true strain

Force–extension data from a tensile test may be plotted in the form of stress and strain to give a nominal stress–strain curve in which nominal stress, $\sigma_n = F/A_o$, where F = force and A_o = original cross-sectional area, and nominal strain, $\varepsilon_n = (L - L_o)/L_o$, where L = extended length and L_o = original gauge length. The nominal stress–strain curve is not a true stress–strain curve because it is based on the original test-piece dimensions. The nominal stress–strain curve for a ductile metal shows a maximum before fracture. This is because, in a tensile test, the material becomes unstable and necks before fracture. A true stress–strain curve shows stress increasing steadily to fracture.

True stress, $\sigma_t = F/A_i$, where A_i is the instantaneous c.s.a.

True strain, $\varepsilon_t = dL/L = \ln(L/L_o)$ but $L/L_o = (1 + \varepsilon_n)$ so $\varepsilon_t = \ln(1 + \varepsilon_n)$ where L_o = initial gauge length and L = instantaneous gauge length.

True stress, $\sigma_t = F/A_i$. Assuming there is no volume change during plastic deformation $A_i L = A_o L_o$ or $A_i = A_o L_o/L$ so $\sigma_t = FL/A_o L_o$. But $L/L_o = (1 + \varepsilon_n)$, so

$$\sigma_t = \frac{F}{A_o}(1 + \varepsilon_n)$$

For most metals $\sigma_t = k\varepsilon_t^n$ where k and n are constants for the material. The constant n is the strain hardening exponent and the true stress–true strain equation is an empirical expression for work hardening. Instability and necking of a ductile metal occurs when $\varepsilon_t = n$ and at this point, the maximum on the nominal stress–strain curve, the maximum value of σ_n, the nominal tensile strength of the material, is given by:

$$\sigma_{max} = kn^n(1 - n)^{(1 - n)}$$

(d) Barba's law

The plastic extension of a tensile test-piece is not uniform and is greatest in the necked region. The percentage elongation value, if taken on a short gauge length, will be greater than if taken over a long gauge length. Barba's law is an empirical equation relating the percentage elongation to gauge length and the cross-sectional area of test-pieces. The equation is:

$$\text{Percentage elongation} = 100 \left(\frac{a\sqrt{A}}{L_o} + b \right)$$

where L_o = gauge length, A = c.s.a and a, b are material constants.

11.2 Worked Examples

Example 11.1

Indentation hardness tests are made on a sample of metal and the following results recorded:

(i) using Vickers diamond test with 30 kg load the mean lengths of diagonals were: 1st impression – 0.527 mm, 2nd impression – 0.481 mm, 3rd impression – 0.497 mm;

(ii) using Brinell test with 10 mm ball and 3000 kg load the diameter of impression was 4.01 mm.

Calculate the diamond and Brinell hardness numbers for the material and explain any variations in the results.

Solution 11.1

(i) $H_D = 1.854 \ F/d^2$. For the first impression, $H_D = (1.854 \times 30)/0.527^2 = 200$. Similarly, for the second impression $H_D = 240$ and for the third impression $H_D = 225$. The average of the three impressions gives $H_D = 221.7$.

(ii) $H_B = 2F/\{\pi D(D - \sqrt{(D^2 - d^2)})\}$
$H_B = (2 \times 3000) \div \{10\pi(10 - \sqrt{(100 - 4.01^2)})\} = 228$.

The small size of the indenter used in the Vickers test means that in an alloy an impression may be made on a non-representative hard or soft spot. A number of determinations may have to be made to obtain a true average value. Using a 10 mm diameter ball indenter the Brinell test gives a result more representative of the mean hardness of the material.

Example 11.2

The indenting loads normally used in connection with Vickers diamond tests are: 1 kg, 2.5 kg, 5 kg, 10 kg, 20 kg, 30 kg and 50 kg. If determinations are most accurate when impression diagonals are approximately 0.5 mm, what indenting loads should be selected for the testing of:

(i) aluminium samples with hardnesses of the order of $H_D = 20$,

(ii) brass samples with hardnesses of the order of $H_D = 60$, and

(iii) steel samples with hardnesses of the order of $H_D = 200$?

Solution 11.2

For the Vickers test, $H_D = 1.854 \ F \div d^2$, or $F = (H_D \times d^2) \div 1.854$.

Making $d = 0.5$ mm and substituting the various values of d, we have:

(i) for $H_D = 20$, $F = 2.69$ kg. The closest standard load is 2.5 kg.

(ii) for $H_D = 60$, $F = 8.1$ kg. The closest standard load is 10 kg.

(iii) for $H_D = 200$, $F = 26.9$ kg. The closest standard load is 30 kg.

From this, and using the expression $d = \sqrt{(1.854F \div H_D)}$, it can be calculated that d, the impression diagonal length in mm, will be:

(i) 0.48 mm when a 2.5 kg indenting load is used on material of $H_D = 20$,

(ii)   0.55 mm when a 10 kg indenting load is used on material of $H_D = 60$,

(iii)   0.53 mm when a 30 kg indenting load is used on material of $H_D = 200$.

The selected loads are (i) 2.5 kg for aluminium, (ii) 10 kg for brass, and (iii) 30 kg for steel.

Example 11.3

Samples of pure copper in both the annealed and cold-worked conditions were subjected to Brinell hardness tests, using a 1 mm diameter ball indenter, with various loads. The test data are given below.

(a)   Calculate the Brinell hardness of the copper samples.

(b)   Complete a Meyer analysis and determine the Meyer constants.

Material	Indenting load (kg)	Indentation diameter (mm)
Annealed copper	5	0.386
	10	0.540
	15	0.636
Cold worked copper	10	0.375
	20	0.527
	30	0.632

Solution 11.3

(a)   Using the expression $H_B = 2F/\{\pi D(D - \sqrt{(D^2 - d^2)})\}$,

For annealed copper, $H_B = 41.1$ (with 5 kg load)

$H_B = 40.2$ (with 10 kg load)

$H_B = 41.8$ (with 15 kg load)

Average value $H_B = 41.0$

For cold worked copper $H_B = 87.2$ (with 10 kg load)

$H_B = 84.8$ (with 20 kg load)

$H_B = 84.9$ (with 30 kg load)

Average value $H_B = 85.6$

(b)   Meyer's relationship is $F = ad^n$ or $\log F = \log a + n \log d$.

Plot graphs of $\log F$ against $\log d$ for both copper samples.

Annealed copper				Cold-worked copper			
F	$\log F$	d	$\log d$	F	$\log F$	d	$\log d$
5	0.699	0.386	-0.413	10	1.000	0.375	-0.426
10	1.000	0.540	-0.268	20	1.301	0.527	-0.278
15	1.176	0.636	-0.197	30	1.477	0.632	-0.199

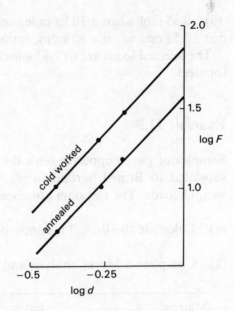

Figure 11.3

Slope of graph $= n$. Intercept with ordinate $= \log a$.
For annealed copper, $n = 2.2$; $\log a = 1.6$, $a = 39.8$.
For cold-worked copper, $n = 2.0$; $\log a = 1.86$, $a = 72.4$.

Example 11.4

(a) Discuss the significance of *gauge length* in the tensile testing of metals.

(b) A load of 1500 kg is applied to a rod of Monel metal of radius 0.8918×10^{-2} m. If the same load when applied to a rod of pure nickel is found to give the same amount of elastic strain, calculate the diameter of the nickel rod and the gauge length used. Young's modulus for Monel $= 179$ GN/m^2. Young's modulus for nickel $= 206$ GN/m^2.

(Salford)

Solution 11.4

(a) During a tensile test, necking occurs and plastic deformation is not uniform over the test-piece length and is greatest in the necked area. For test-pieces of the same cross-sectional area, percentage elongation values measured on a short gauge length will be greater than if measured over longer gauge lengths. For a declared result to have meaning the gauge length should be quoted. Barba stated that for a given material percentage gauge length values are comparable if the ratio of gauge length/cross-section area is maintained constant.

(b) $\sigma = F/A$ and for elastic deformation $\sigma/\varepsilon = E$.
Force $= 1500 \times 9.81 = 14.715$ kN c.s.a of Monel rod $= \pi(0.8918 \times 10^{-2})^2$.

Stress in Monel rod = $14715 \div \pi(0.8918 \times 10^{-2})^2$ = 58.89 MPa.

Strain, $\varepsilon = \sigma/E = 58.89 \times 10^6 \div 179 \times 10^9 = 3.29 \times 10^{-4}$.

Stress in nickel, $\sigma = \varepsilon \times E = 3.29 \times 10^{-4} \times 206 \times 10^9 = 67.78$ MPa

c.s.a. of nickel = $F/\sigma = 14715 \div 67.78 \times 10^6 = 2.171 \times 10^{-4}$ m² from which diameter of nickel rod = 16.63×10^{-3} m (16.63 mm).

There is no information from which to estimate the gauge length used.

Example 11.5

(a) List the main parameters which may be determined in a full tensile test.

(b) What are the main differences between the standard tensile test for metals and that for plastics.

(c) Evaluate the tensile properties of the material from the tensile test data given below. From the results identify the material tested.

(Polytechnic of Central London)

Test-piece dimensions: width = 12.61 mm, thickness = 3.47 mm, gauge length = 50 mm.

Force (N)	Extension (mm)	Force (N)	Extension (mm)	Force (N)	Extension (mm)
25	0.018	125	0.121	225	0.293
50	0.040	150	0.153	250	0.355
75	0.064	175	0.192	275	0.425
100	0.090	200	0.238	300	0.520

Maximum force in test = 1290 N

Length between gauge marks at break = 97 mm.

Solution 11.5

(a) The material parameters obtainable from a full tensile test are: the modulus of elasticity, E, the yield or proof stress, the tensile strength and the percentage elongation on gauge length and, for circular cross-section test-pieces, the percentage reduction in area.

(b) Thermoplastic materials are strain rate sensitive and testing standards specify the rates of strain to be used in standardised test procedures. Changes in strain rates have no significant effect on test results for metals. A further difference is that the percentage elongation for plastics is measured at the moment of fracture and includes both elastic and plastic strain, while for metals it is measured after elastic recovery has occurred.

215

(c) Plot the force–extension data. The graph is shown below.

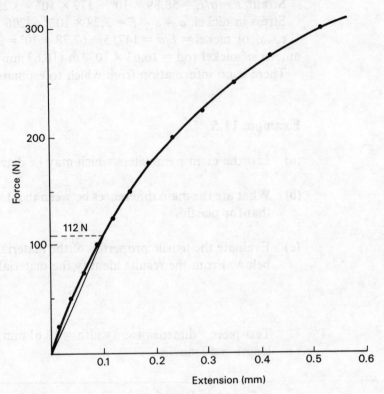

Figure 11.4

The general values and shape of the curve indicate a soft thermoplastic material.
(i) E. For a plastic, E is taken as the 0.2 per cent secant modulus.
0.2% of 50 mm = 0.1 mm. Force for an extension of 0.1 mm is 112 N.

$$E = \frac{F \times l}{e \times A} = \frac{112 \times 50}{0.1 \times 12.61 \times 3.47} = 1.28 \times 10^3 \text{ N/mm}^2 = 1.28 \text{ GPa}$$

(ii) Tensile strength = Max. load ÷ original c.s.a. = $1290 \div (12.61 \times 3.47) = 29.48 \text{ N/mm}^2 = 29.48 \text{ MPa}$.

(iii) Percentage elongation at break = $(L - L_o)/L_o \times 100 = (97 - 50)/50 \times 100 = 94\%$.

A proof stress value is not usually quoted for polymers.

The very low value of E, coupled with a low tensile strength and high percentage elongation values indicate that the material is a soft thermoplastic, probably high density polyethylene or polypropylene.

Example 11.6

A metal sample of width 12.2 mm, thickness 1.9 mm and gauge length 50 mm was tested to destruction in tension. The force–extension curve obtained is shown in the figure below. The maximum force recorded in the test was 1700 N and the final length between gauge marks was 72 mm.

From these results, determine values for:

(a) Young's modulus, E,

(b) 0.1 per cent proof stress,

(c) tensile strength, and

(d) percentage elongation on gauge length.

What type of material was tested?

(Polytechnic of Central London)

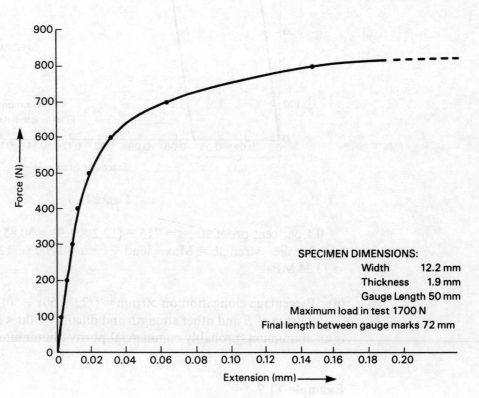

SPECIMEN DIMENSIONS:
Width   12.2 mm
Thickness   1.9 mm
Gauge Length 50 mm
Maximum load in test 1700 N
Final length between gauge marks 72 mm

Figure 11.5

Solution 11.6

(a) From graph, the slope of the linear elastic portion is:

$$400 \div 0.012 = 33333 \text{ N/mm}, \quad E = \text{slope} \times (\text{gauge length/c.s.a})$$

$$E = 33333 \times \frac{50}{12.2 \times 1.9} = 71.9 \times 10^3 \text{ N/mm}^2 = 71.9 \text{ MPa}$$

(b) 0.1 per cent of 50 mm = 0.05 mm. From 0.05 mm on the extension axis, draw a line parallel to slope of linear elastic portion of curve. This line intercepts curve at a point corresponding to a force of 715 N.

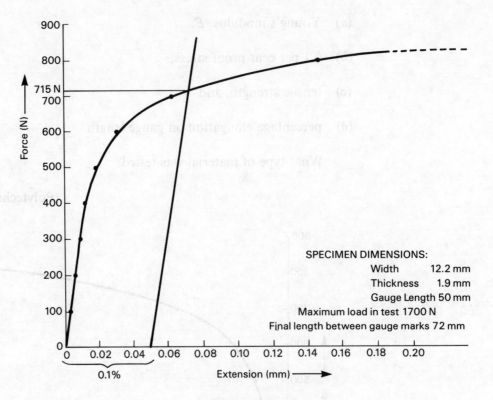

Figure 11.6

0.1 per cent proof stress = 715 ÷ (12.2 × 1.9) = 30.85 N/mm² = 30.85 MPa

(c) Tensile strength = Max load ÷ c.s.a = 1700 ÷ (12.2 × 1.9) = 73.34 N/mm² = 73.34 MPa.

(d) Percentage elongation on 50 mm = {(72 − 50) ÷ 50} × 100 = 44 per cent.
The value of E and other strength and ductility values indicate that the material is an aluminium, probably commercial purity aluminium in the annealed state.

Example 11.7

A tensile test on a polymer specimen 20 mm wide × 3 mm thick with a gauge length of 50 mm produced the load–extension curve shown in the figure below.

218

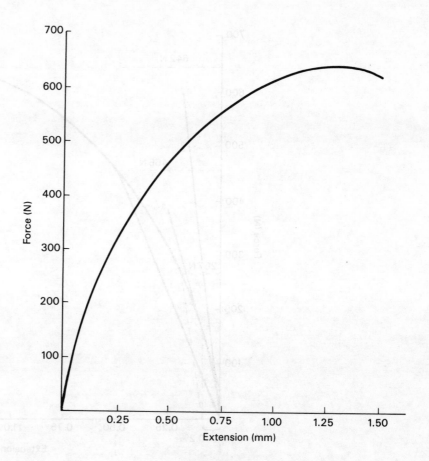

Figure 11.7

Determine: (i) tensile strength, (ii) initial modulus, (iii) tangent modulus at 0.2 per cent strain, (iv) secant modulus at 1.0 per cent strain, (v) 0.2 per cent proof stress, and (vi) percentage elongation.

(Sheffield University)

Solution 11.7

(i) From curve maximum load in test is 642 N.
Tensile strength = 642 ÷ (20 × 3) = 10.7 N/mm² = 10.7 MPa.

(ii) Initial modulus. Draw tangent to curve from origin.
Slope of tangent = 600/0.18 N/mm

$$\text{Initial modulus} = \frac{600 \times 50}{0.18 \times 20 \times 3} = 2.78 \times 10^3 \text{N/mm}^2 = 2.78 \text{ GPa}$$

(iii) 0.2 per cent of 50 mm = 0.1 mm. Draw tangent to curve at extension value of 0.1 mm. Slope of tangent = 340 ÷ 0.25 N/mm

$$\text{Tangent modulus at 0.2 per cent strain} = \frac{340 \times 50}{0.25 \times 20 \times 3} = 1.13 \text{ GPa}$$

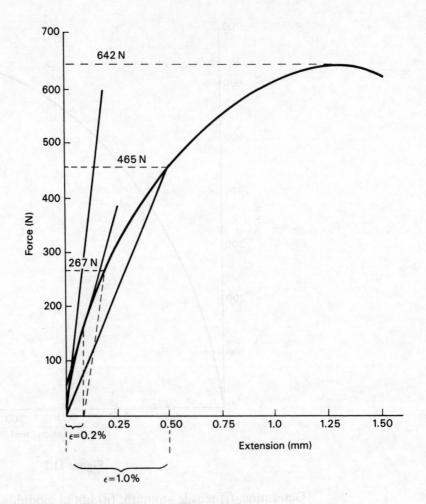

Figure 11.8

(iv) 1.0 per cent of 50 mm = 0.5 mm. An extension of 0.5 mm corresponds to a force of 465 N. Slope of secant = 465 ÷ 0.5 N/mm. 1 per cent secant modulus = 0.78 GPa.

(v) 0.2 per cent of 50 mm = 0.1 mm. Draw line parallel to initial slope from extension value of 0.1 mm. This cuts curve at a load of 267 N.

$$0.2 \text{ per cent stress} = 267 \div (20 \times 3) = 4.45 \text{ MPa}$$

(vi) From the results calculated above the material is a soft thermoplastic. Therefore the percentage elongation at break should be quoted. The extension at fracture point is 1.50 mm.

Percentage elongation at break = (1.5 × 1000) ÷ 50 = 3 per cent.

Example 11.8

The following data were obtained in a tensile test on a specimen of 15 mm diameter with a 50 mm gauge length.

Load (kN)	70	120	150	160	170	200	220	233	233	220
Extension (mm)	0.25	0.40	0.50	0.60	0.75	1.75	3.00	5.00	6.50	8.00

The specimen diameter after fracture was 12.45 mm.

Determine: (i) tensile strength, (ii) Young's modulus, (iii) 0.2 per cent proof stress, (iv) true stress at a nominal strain of 8.0 per cent, (v) percentage elongation, (vi) percentage reduction in area.

(Sheffield University)

Solution 11.8

Use the data to plot a force–extension diagram, as shown below.

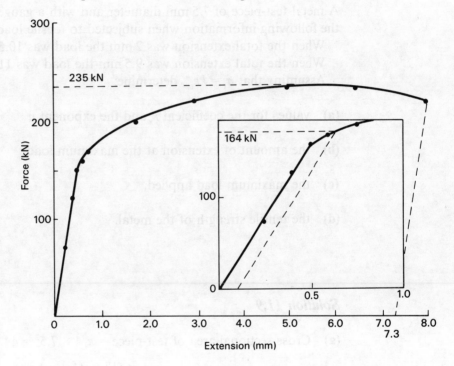

Figure 11.9

Cross-sectional area of test-piece = $\pi/4 \times 15^2$ = 176.7 mm^2

(i)   From curve maximum force = 235 kN

Tensile strength = $235 \times 10^3/176.7$ = 1330 MPa

(ii)   Slope of elastic portion of curve = $150 \times 10^3/0.5 = 300 \times 10^3$ N/mm

Young's modulus = $(300 \times 10^3 \times 50) \div 176.7$ = 84.9 GPa

(iii)   0.2 per cent of 50 mm = 0.1 mm. Draw line parallel to linear portion from extension of 0.1 mm. This cuts curve at a load of 164 kN.

0.2 per cent proof stress = 164000/176.7 = 928 MPa

221

(iv)   A nominal strain of 8 per cent ($\varepsilon_n = 0.08$) on a 50 mm gauge length equals an extension of 4 mm. From the force–extension curve, the force needed to give a 4 mm   extension = 230 kN. $\sigma_t = (F/A_o) \times (1 + \varepsilon_n) = (230000/176.7) \times 1.08 = 1406$ MPa.

(v)   On the force–extension curve, draw a line from the fracture point, parallel to linear elastic portion. This cuts the abscissa at an extension of 7.3 mm. Percentage elongation on 50 mm gauge length = $(7.3/50) \times 100 = 14.6$ per cent.

(vi)   Diameter after fracture = 12.45 mm. Area = $12.45^2 \times \pi/4 = 121.7$ mm^2. Percentage reduction in area = $\{(176.7 - 121.7) \div 176.7\} \times 100 = 31.1$ per cent.

Example 11.9

A metal test-piece of 7.5 mm diameter and with a gauge length of 50 mm yielded the following information when subjected to tensile loading.
  When the total extension was 2 mm the load was 10.5 kN.
  When the total extension was 9.5 mm the load was 11.1 kN.
  Assuming that $\sigma_t = k\varepsilon_t^n$, determine:

(a)   values for the coefficient k and the exponent n

(b)   the amount of extension at the maximum load,

(c)   the maximum load applied,

(d)   the tensile strength of the metal.

(Sheffield University)

Solution 11.9

(a)   Cross-sectional area of test-piece = $\pi/4 \times 7.5^2 = 44.18$ mm^2.

$$\sigma_t = (F/A_o)(1 + \varepsilon_n)$$

When $F = 10500$ N, $\varepsilon_n = 2/50 = 0.04$, so $\sigma_t = (10500/44.18) \times 1.04 = 247.2$ MPa and $\varepsilon_t = \ln(1 + \varepsilon_n) = 0.039$.
  When $F = 11100$ N, $\varepsilon_n = 9.5/50 = 0.19$, $\sigma_t = (11100/44.18) \times 1.19 = 299.0$ MPa and $\varepsilon_t = \ln(1.19) = 0.174$.
  Therefore $\log 247.2 = \log k + n \log 0.039$ and $\log 299 = \log k + n \log 0.174$. Solution of these two equations gives $k = 374.2$ MPa and $n = 0.128$.

(b)   At maximum load instability occurs and $\varepsilon_t = n$, so at maximum load, $\varepsilon_t = 0.128 = \ln(1 + \varepsilon_n)$, therefore $\varepsilon_n = 0.136$. A nominal strain of 0.136 = an extension of $(0.136 \times 50) = 6.8$ mm.

(c)   At maximum load, $\sigma_t = 374.2 \times 0.128^{0.128} = 287.6$ MPa. From $\sigma_t = (F/A_o)(1 + \varepsilon_n)$, maximum load $F = (287.6 \times 44.18) \div 1.136 = 11185$ N.

(d) Tensile strength $= F/A_o = 11185/44.18 = 253.2$ MPa.

Example 11.10

Two test-pieces of pure aluminium, each of 6 mm diameter are tested in tension. One, with a gauge length of 50 mm, showed an elongation value of 32 per cent while the other, with a gauge length of 100 mm, had an elongation value of 25 per cent. What would be the likely percentage elongation value obtained from a piece of aluminium of the same quality, but of rectangular section, 12.5 mm × 1.8 mm, and with a gauge length of 50 mm?

Solution 11.10

Using Barba's law, percentage elongation $= 100(a\sqrt{A}/L_o + b)$

c.s.a of test-pieces, $A = \pi/4 \times 6^2 = 28.27$ mm^2, so $\sqrt{A} = 5.317$

$32 = 100\{(5.317a/50) + b\}$ and $25 = 100\{(5.317a/100) + b\}$

from which $b = 0.18$ and $a = 1.32$.

For a rectangular section piece, $A = 12.5 \times 1.8 = 22.5$ mm^2, so $\sqrt{A} = 4.743$

percentage elongation $= 100\{(4.743 \times 1.32)/50 + 0.18\} = 30.5$ per cent

Example 11.11

(a) Explain how the tensile strength of a brittle material may be determined.

(b) A piece of glass of length 95 mm, width 15 mm and thickness 3 mm is simply supported over a span of 75 mm and a force applied at mid-span. The load needed to break the glass is measured as 35 N. Calculate the tensile strength (modulus of rupture) of the glass.

(c) A concrete cylinder of 100 mm diameter and 100 mm length is subjected to a diametral compressive force. The value of force at the failure point is 47.5 kN. Calculate the tensile strength of the concrete.

(Polytechnic of Central London)

Solution 11.11

(a) It is difficult to mount a brittle material so that it may be tested to destruction in uniaxial tension. Convenient test methods are to apply loads in such a way that a direct tensile stress is developed within some part of the test piece. Two such methods are: (i) to stress the test-piece as a simply supported beam with mid-span loading. Brittle materials tend to be stronger in compression than in tension and failure will occur when the tensile stress in one surface reaches the tensile strength of the material.

Another method is to subject a cylindrical shaped test-piece to diametral compression. Tensile stresses will be developed in the circumferential layers, being maximum at points on a plane normal to the compressive force. This method is used to determine the tensile strength of cement and concrete.

(b) The loading arrangement is as shown in the figure below. When a force F is applied at mid-span the maximum bending moment at the centre of the beam is $FL/4$. From the general bending equation, the direct stress, σ, developed in the material is given by $\sigma = My/I$ where y is the distance from the neutral surface. Maximum stress will be when $y = d/2$, d being the thickness of the beam. I for a rectangular section is $bd^3/12$. From this, it follows that the maximum direct stress developed by this loading configuration is given by $3FL \div 2bd^2$.

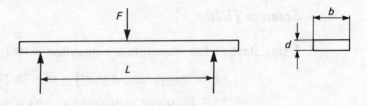

Figure 11.10

The tensile strength $= (3 \times 35 \times 0.075) \div (2 \times 0.015 \times 0.003^2) = 29.17$ MPa.

(c) In a split cylinder test the tensile stress developed at the cylinder surface is given by $2F/\pi LD$, so tensile strength $= (2 \times 47500) \div (\pi \times 0.1 \times 0.1) = 3.02$ MPa.

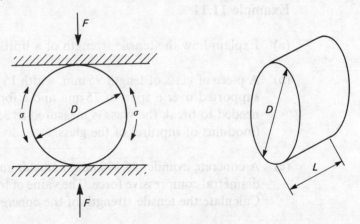

Figure 11.11

11.3 Questions

Question 11.1

Brinell hardness impressions on a sample of annealed copper, using a 5 mm ball indenter, gave the following readings:

Load (kgf)	125	250	375
Indentation diameter (mm)	2.20	2.70	3.10

Determine whether these data obey the Meyer relationship and, if so, evaluate the Meyer constants.

Question 11.2

A consistent value of Brinell hardness for a material can be obtained for different size indenters if the ratio F/D^2 is maintained constant. Examine this statement in the light of the experimental data given.

Test	Indenting force (kgf)	Indenter diameter (mm)	Indentation diameter (mm)
1	30	1	0.473
2	60	2	0.698
3	120	2	0.944
4	750	5	2.35
5	1500	5	3.14
6	3000	10	4.75

Question 11.3

A test-piece of cylindrical cross-section is tested to destruction in a tensile testing machine and extension measurements were taken during the test using an extensometer with a 50 mm gauge length. The readings obtained during the test are given below.

Diameter of test-piece = 7.50 mm. Gauge length = 50 mm. Maximum load = 15.1 kN. Length between gauge marks after test = 66 mm. Diameter after fracture = 5.80 mm.

Force (kN)	Extension (mm)	Force (kN)	Extension (mm)
0.5	0.006	4.0	0.048
1.0	0.012	4.5	0.060
1.5	0.018	5.0	0.082
2.0	0.024	5.5	0.118
2.5	0.030	6.0	0.180
3.0	0.036	6.5	0.290
3.5	0.042	7.0	0.475

(a) Plot a force–extension curve.
(b) Determine: (i) E, (ii) 0.1 per cent proof stress, (iii) tensile strength, (iv) percentage elongation, (v) percentage reduction in area.
(c) What type of material was tested?

(Polytechnic of Central London)

Question 11.4

The following data were obtained in a tensile test on a specimen of 14 mm diameter with a 50 mm gauge length.

Load (kN)	12	25	32	36	40	42	63	80	93	100	101	90
Extension (mm)	0.05	0.10	0.15	0.20	0.25	0.30	1.25	2.50	3.75	5.00	6.25	7.50

Determine: (i) tensile strength; (ii) Young's modulus; (iii) 0.2 per cent proof stress; (iv) percentage elongation.

(Sheffield University)

Question 11.5

The following data were obtained in a tensile test on a specimen of 12 mm diameter. with a 50 mm gauge length.

Load (kN)	20	65	90	110	128	147	183	197	194	180
Extension (mm)	0.10	0.30	0.40	0.50	1.00	2.00	5.00	8.00	11.50	14.00

Determine: (i) tensile strength, (ii) 0.1 per cent proof stress, (iii) Young's modulus, (iv) percentage elongation, (v) maximum uniform true strain, (vi) true stress at a nominal strain of 0.12.

(Sheffield University)

Question 11.6

A test-piece measuring 12.5 mm × 3.2 mm, with a 50 mm gauge length, was tested in tension and gave the following results:

Force (N)	25	50	75	100	125	150	200	250	300
Extension (mm)	0.015	0.035	0.060	0.090	0.125	0.175	0.33	0.58	0.01

The maximum force recorded during the test was 955 N and the maximum total extension was 42 mm. Determine values for: (i) E; (ii) tensile strength; and (iii) percentage elongation at break.

Question 11.7

The true stress–true strain curve is given by $\sigma_t = k\varepsilon_t^n$.
Calculate the tensile strength of a material if $k = 750$ MPa and $n = 0.21$.

Question 11.8

The true stress–true strain relationship for a metal is $\sigma_t = k\varepsilon_t^n$. Find the ratio of plastic strain to elastic strain at the point of instability for a metal with a value of $E = 100\,\text{GPa}$ and for which $n = 0.2$ and $k = 2750\,\text{MPa}$.

Question 11.9

A metal sample of 10 mm diameter was stressed in uniaxial tension and the following information obtained. Over a 40 mm gauge length, a total extension of 2.0 mm was obtained under a load of 30 kN and a total extension of 11 mm was obtained under a load of 34 kN.

Assuming that the relationship between true stress and true strain, $\sigma_t = k\varepsilon_t^n$, applies determine:

(a) the values of the coefficient k and the exponent n, and
(b) the total amount of extension at the maximum load,
(c) the maximum load applied.

Question 11.10

A tensile test-piece of 10 mm diameter gives an elongation value of 24 per cent when measured over a 50 mm gauge length but 32 per cent when measured over a gauge length of 40 mm. What should be the value of the percentage elongation if a sample of the same metal, but of diameter 6 mm and gauge length 25 mm, is tested?

11.4 Answers to Questions

11.1 A plot of log F against log d gives a straight line. Slope $= n = 3.2$; Intercept gives log $a = 1$, $a = 10$.

11.2 The ratio $F/D^2 = 30$ for tests 1, 3, 4 and 6. H_B values are 160.6, 161.3, 162.8 and 159.1. H_B values for tests 2 and 5, with differing F/D^2 ratios are 151.9 and 172.2. Good consistency for constant F/D^2 ratio verifies statement.

11.3 **(b)** (i) 94.3 GPa; (ii) 123.4 MPa; (iii) 341.8 MPa; (iv) 32 per cent; (v) 40.2 per cent. **(c)** E and other values indicate an α brass in the annealed state.

11.4 (i) 660 MPa; (ii) 81.2 GPa; (iii) 266 MPa; (iv) 14.2 per cent.

11.5 (i) 1750 MPa; (ii) 1017 MPa; (iii) 97.3 GPa; (iv) 26.4 per cent; (v) 0.1655; (v) 1881 MPa.

11.6 (i) 1.35 GPa (This is the secant modulus at 0.2 per cent strain); (ii) 23.9 MPa; (iii) 84 per cent.

11.7 448.6 MPa.

11.8 9/1.

11.9 **(a)** $k = 732.8\,\text{MPa}$; $n = 0.2$; **(b)** 8.8 mm; **(c)** 34173 N.

11.10 30.25 per cent.

12 Materials Selection

12.1 Fact Sheet

(a) The Selection Problem

One of the functions of an engineer and designer is to select suitable materials to satisfy specific design, production, operational and maintenance requirements and, in doing this, produce a component or assembly at an acceptable cost. There are many thousands of different materials available to the engineer and the range of mechanical and physical properties possible is extremely wide. However, the proper selection of a material to fit a design requirement is not an exercise which can be carried out in isolation. Selection of a material must involve consideration of design and manufacturing factors. There is a complex inter-dependence between the three elements of design, material and manufacture.

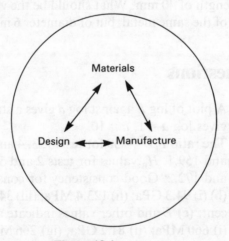

Figure 12.1

(b) Parameters to be Considered

There are many properties of materials, most of them quantifiable, which may need to be considered as part of a selection process. These include;

> elastic moduli,
> yield and maximum strengths,
> hardness and wear resistance,
> ductility,

fracture toughness,
fatigue strength,
creep characteristics,
oxidation and corrosion resistance,
electrical properties,
magnetic properties,
thermal expansion and conductivity,
density.

In addition to the above properties, it is also necessary to consider the formability of a material for ease of manufacture and the factors of cost, both of material and manufacture, and availability.

(c) Properties of materials

The values of E, tensile yield strength, tensile strength, fracture toughness and density for a range of materials is given in the following table. It is very useful often when comparing the relative merits of materials to view *specific properties*, namely the ratio of the property to the density of the material. Specific modulus and specific strength for a number of materials are shown in the form of bar charts.

(d) Costs

The cost of a material is a very important parameter for consideration when selecting a material as it is the aim of the engineer to design and make products which will function adequately for the whole of their design life *at an acceptable cost*. In many cases purchase cost of materials accounts for about one-half of the total works cost of the finished product. It follows from this that the use of a cheaper raw material should have a significant effect on the final product cost. This is not always true as, in some cases, the choice of an expensive material may permit the use of relatively simple and low cost processing methods whereas a cheaper material may require lengthy, complex and expensive production methods.

It is usual to see the cost of materials quoted per unit mass, for example £100 per tonne. This may give a misleading picture as often it is the volume of material which is important rather its mass. The relative positions of materials in a league table of costs change when the criterion is changed from £ per tonne to £ per unit volume. This can be seen in the table below. (The cost figures used in this table are based on 1983 values but in the intervening years the cost of most commodities has risen by similar percentages.) Much of the data for metals in the table are for refined metal in ingot form and it should be realised that the costs of processed products, such as sheet, plate, sections and forgings will be much higher. Every process and every heat treatment will add to the final material cost. Also, the process of alloying will mean that generally the costs of alloys will be higher than those for unalloyed metals. For example, the cost of mild steel cold rolled strip material is approximately three times greater than the cost of mild steel ingot. Similarly, in the aluminium industry, an alloy of aluminium with 2 per cent magnesium is about 25 per cent more expensive than commercial purity aluminium, while an alloy with 4 per cent copper is about twice the cost of pure aluminium.

Properties (at 25°C) of some groups of materials

Material	E (GPa)	Yield strength (MPa)	Tensile strength (MPa)	Fracture toughness (MPa m$^{\frac{1}{2}}$)	Density (kg m^{-3})
steels	200–220	200–1800	350–2300	80–170	7.8–7.9
cast irons	150–180	100–500	300–1000	6–20	7.2–7.6
aluminium alloys	70	25–500	70–600	5–70	2.7–2.8
copper alloys	90–130	70–1000	220–1400	30–120	8.4–8.9
magnesium alloys	40–50	30–250	60–300		1.7–1.8
nickel alloys	180–220	60–1200	200–1400	>100	7.9–8.9
titanium alloys	100–120	800–1400	350–1500	50–100	4.4–4.5
zinc alloys	70–90	50–300	150–350		6.7–7.1
polyethylene (LDPE)	0.12–0.25		1–16	1–2	0.91–0.94
polyethylene (HDPE)	0.45–1.4		20–38	2–5	0.95–0.97
polypropylene (PP)	0.5–1.9		20–40	3.5	0.90–0.91
PTFE	0.35–0.6		17–28		2.1–2.25
polystyrene (PS)	2.8–3.5		35–85	2	1.0–1.1
rigid PVC	2.4–4.0		24–60	2.4	1.4–1.5
acrylic (PMMA)	2.7–3.5		50–80	1.6	1.2
nylons (PA)	2.0–3.5		60–100	3–5	1.05–1.15
PF resins	5–8		35–55		1.25
polyester resins	1.3–4.5		45–85	0.5	1.1–1.4
epoxy resins	2.1–5.5		40–85	0.6–1	1.2–1.4
GFRP	10–45		100–300	20–60	1.55–2.0
CFRP	70–200		70–650	30–45	1.40–1.75
soda glass	74		50*	0.7	2.5
alumina	380		300–400*	3–5	3.9
silicon carbide	410		200–500*		3.2
silicon nitride	310		300–850*	4	3.2
concrete	30–50		7*	0.2	2.4–2.5

*modulus of rupture values

230

Costs of some materials, by mass and by volume

Material	Cost (£/kg)	Material	Cost (£/100 cm³)
tungsten (powder)	24.22	tungsten (powder)	46.75
cobalt	18.1	cobalt	15.75
molybdenum (powder)	13.2	molybdenum (powder)	13.46
tin	8.66	tin	6.32
PTFE	7.0	titanium alloys	2.8
titanium alloys	6.5	chromium	2.63
titanium (99.3%)	4.45	nickel (pellets)	2.58
chromium	3.7	bronze (powder)	2.2
nickel (pellets)	2.9	high speed steel	2.13
bronze (powder)	2.47	titanium (99.3%)	2.0
nylon 6 (PA 6)	2.17	bronze (ignot)	1.73
high speed steel	2.15	PTFE	1.54
dural (sheet)	2.0	copper (powder)	1.51
nylon 66 (PA 66)	2.0	austenitic stainless	1.50
bronze (ingot)	1.94	copper (cathodes)	0.96
austenitic stainless	1.9	brass (ingot)	0.68
copper (powder)	1.7	manganese	0.67
magnesium (ingot)	1.59	dural (sheet)	0.56
acrylic (PMMA)	1.53	zinc (ingot)	0.37
ABS	1.47	lead (ingot)	0.34
copper (cathodes)	1.08	magnesium (ingot)	0.28
aluminium (powder)	1.0	aluminium (powder)	0.27
manganese	0.9	iron (powder)	0.25
brass (ingot)	0.83	nylon 6 (PA 6)	0.24
amino resin thermoset	0.83	mild steel (sheet)	0.24
aluminium (ingot)	0.81	aluminium (ingot)	0.22
natural rubber	0.75	nylon 66 (PA 66)	0.22
P-F thermoset	0.72	acrylic (PMMA)	0.18
polyethylene (HDPE)	0.71	silicon	0.16
polypropylene (PP)	0.7	ABS	0.16
silicon	0.68	amino resin thermoset	0.12
polystyrene (PS)	0.62	P-F thermoset	0.09
zinc (ingot)	0.52	cast iron	0.09
polyethylene (LDPE)	0.51	mild steel (ingot)	0.08
rigid PVC	0.4	polystyrene (PS)	0.07
iron (powder)	0.32	natural rubber	0.07
mild steel (sheet)	0.31	polyethylene (HDPE)	0.07
lead (ingot)	0.3	polypropylene (PP)	0.06
cast iron	0.13	rigid PVC	0.06
mild steel (ingot)	0.1	polyethylene (LDPE)	0.05
concrete (ready mixed)	0.015	concrete (ready mixed)	0.003

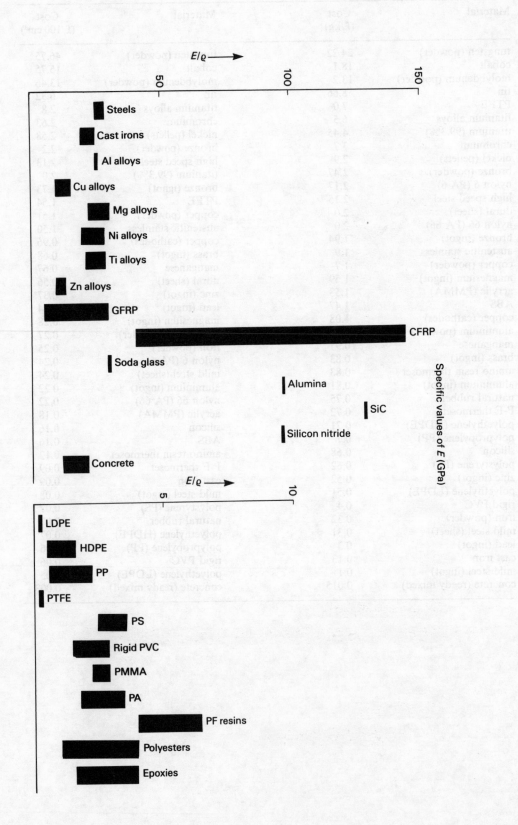

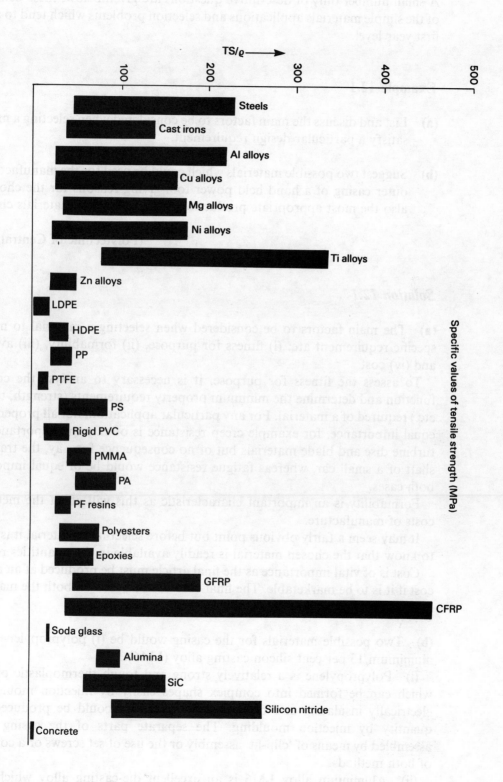

TS/ϱ →

Specific values of tensile strength (MPa)

100

200

300

400

500

Steels
Cast irons
Al alloys
Cu alloys
Mg alloys
Ni alloys
Ti alloys
Zn alloys
LDPE
HDPE
PP
PTFE
PS
Rigid PVC
PMMA
PA
PF resins
Polyesters
Epoxies
GFRP
CFRP
Soda glass
Alumina
SiC
Silicon nitride
Concrete

12.2 Examples

A small number only of descriptive questions are given below, these being typical of the simple materials applications and selection problems which tend to appear at first year level.

Example 12.1

(a) List and discuss the main factors to be considered when selecting a material to satisfy a particular design requirement.

(b) Suggest two possible materials which could be used for the manufacture of the outer casing of a hand held power tool giving reasons for the choice. State also the most appropriate production methods for the materials chosen.

(Polytechnic of Central London)

Solution 12.1

(a) The main factors to be considered when selecting a material to meet some specific requirement are: (i) fitness for purpose, (ii) formability, (iii) availability, and (iv) cost.

To assess the fitness for purpose, it is necessary to analyse the component function and determine the minimum property requirements (strength, toughness, etc.) required of a material. For any particular application, not all properties are of equal importance, for example creep resistance is of extreme importance for gas turbine disc and blade materials but of no consequence for, say, the transmission shaft of a small car, whereas fatigue resistance would be of equal importance in both cases.

Formability is an important characteristic as this will affect the methods and costs of manufacture.

It may seem a fairly obvious point but before selecting a material it is necessary to know that the chosen material is readily available in the quantities required.

Cost is of vital importance as the final article must be produced at an acceptable cost if it is to be marketable. The final cost will be based on both the material cost and the costs of processing.

(b) Two possible materials for the casing would be (i) polypropylene or (ii) an aluminium/13 per cent silicon casting alloy (LM6).

(i) Polypropylene is a relatively strong and tough thermoplastic of low cost which can be formed into complex shapes easily by injection moulding. It is electrically insulating and of low density. Casings could be produced in large quantity by injection moulding. The separate parts of the casing could be assembled by means of 'clip-fit' assembly or the use of set screws or a combination of both methods.

(ii) Aluminium alloy LM6 is an excellent die-casting alloy which can give strong precision castings of simple or intricate shape. The low density of aluminium will give a lightweight product at comparatively low cost (though more expensive than the polypropylene alternative). The method of manufacture would be pressure die-casting for large quantity production.

Conclusions: Either material would be suitable but polypropylene would give the lower cost. Aluminium will give a more robust product and would be better for heavier duty industrial tools while polypropylene is more suited for the domestic DIY market.

Example 12.2

Choose the appropriate material and manufacturing process for each of the five components listed from the following selection of alternatives and give reasons in support of your choices.

Components: (i)   a camshaft for a family car,
                  (ii)   domestic window catches,
                 (iii)   surgical implants,
                 (iv)   patio door frames,
                 (v)   photographic slide containers.

Materials: stainless steel, 70/30 brass, 0.4 per cent C low alloy steel, LDPE, melamine-formaldehyde, aluminium based alloy, zinc based alloy, polystyrene.

Processes: hot chamber die-casting, direct extrusion, investment casting, rolling, compression moulding, press forging, drop forging, injection moulding.

(Trent Polytechnic)

Solution 12.2

(i) A camshaft needs to have high surface hardness, be tough and have a high fatigue strength. These properties can be achieved in a 0.4 per cent C low alloy steel. This material can be shaped from bar stock by drop forging and would require machining to final dimensions and heat treatment after forging. Hardening and tempering will be needed to give the correct combination of properties.

(ii) Domestic window catches may be made from either an aluminium based die-casting alloy or from 70/30 brass, but the use of an aluminium alloy may give slightly reduced costs. For fitment to aluminium window frames, the catches must be of an aluminium alloy otherwise galvanic corrosion may occur. These materials would be selected on the basis of cost, availability and ease of production. The production method in either case would be hot chamber die-casting which would be suitable for large quantity production and give a component with a good surface finish and accurate dimensions requiring no further finishing operations other than, in the case of brass, possibly the provision of an electroplated layer and for aluminium, anodising.

(iii) A surgical implant needs to have excellent corrosion resistance, be biocompatible and, in the case of, say, a femoral head prosthesis, be strong, hard and wear resistant. The stainless steel possesses this combination of properties. A precision component such as a femoral head implant would be produced by investment casting. This is the process most suited to the manufacture of the complex 'one-off' shapes required.

(iv) Patio door frames would be best made from an aluminium-based alloy. This would give a rigid, yet light-weight, frame with excellent corrosion resistance and of pleasing appearance. The relatively complex section from which the frames are made would be manufactured in long lengths by direct extrusion and then anodised to improve corrosion resistance and give a long outdoor life. The extruded sections can then be cut to the appropriate dimensions and assembled to make the door frames.

(v) Photographic slide containers can be made from polystyrene. This will give a low cost, lightweight, yet rigid frame. Polystyrene can be formed into the complex shape of the slide container readily by an injection moulding process. This will be suitable for large quantity production.

Example 12.3

State, giving reasons, the type of steel which should be used for each of the following products and the heat treatment condition it should be in: (i) a hacksaw blade, (ii) sheet for making car body pressings, (iii) a drive half-shaft for a small car, (iv) I-beams for use in building construction, (v) wire for the manufacture of suspension bridge cables.

Solution 12.3

(i) A hacksaw blade is required to be extremely hard. A high carbon steel containing 1.2–1.4 per cent C is needed. The heat treatment will be quench hardening to give martensite followed by tempering to reduce the brittleness slightly. As a reduction in hardness is to be avoided, the tempering temperature will be low, say 220°C.

(ii) Steel sheet for car body pressings is required to have very high ductility so that it may be formed without risk of cracking. A mild steel, containing 0.05–0.1 per cent C should be used. The heat treatment will be full annealing in a controlled atmosphere furnace to give the lowest possible hardness and no surface scaling.

(iii) A drive half shaft is required to be strong, tough, have high fatigue resistance and a high surface hardness, at least at splines and bearing surfaces. A medium carbon steel, 0.4 per cent C, preferably a low alloy steel with 1 per cent Ni for improved fatigue resistance, would be suitable. The steel would be heat treated by normalising to give a fine grain-sized tough structure throughout and then the areas needing to be of high hardness selectively hardened by flame or induction hardening.

(iv) Structural beams would be manufactured from plain carbon or low alloy steels containing about 0.3 per cent C. They are used in the normalised condition. The sectional shapes are produced by hot rolling and the sections are allowed to cool in air from the hot work finishing temperature. No further treatment is given.

(v) The wire used for bridge cables needs to have a very high tensile strength. A high carbon content of about 0.8 per cent C is needed. The wire is produced by a cold drawing process and enters service in the work hardened condition, rather than being hardened by a heat treatment. Tensile strengths of the order of 1600–2000 MPa are obtained in this way.

Example 12.4

Suggest a suitable polymer and the likely manufacturing process for each of the following and give reasons for your choice: (i) rainwater gutters and drainpipes, (ii) a domestic vacuum cleaner body, (iii) a 13 A electrical socket, (iv) a domestic washing-up bowl, (v) lenses for vehicle rear lights.

Solution 12.4

(i) The requirement for gutters and drainpipes is for a rigid, durable material which will withstand an outdoor environment. Unplasticised PVC is a suitable material. This is a low-cost material which has good mechanical properties and is largely resistant to the effects of sunlight, rain etc. Gutters and pipes are best made by the extrusion process, while associated items such as fixing brackets, joining sections etc can be made by injection moulding.

(ii) ABS, the terpolymer of acrylonitrile, butadiene and styrene, is a low-cost material which can be moulded easily into simple or complex shapes, such as a vacuum cleaner body. It is an ideal material for this type of application where the component is unstressed or lightly stressed. The manufacturing process would be injection moulding.

(iii) An electrical socket has to be hard and rigid and be aesthetically pleasing to the eye in a domestic installation. A thermoset will possess suitable properties and a UF resin (urea-formaldehyde) can be made with a light or white colour. The preferred forming process for a thermoset of this type is transfer moulding although compression moulding could be used.

(iv) The ideal material for a domestic washing-up bowl is HDPE (high density polyethylene). It is light, fairly flexible and can be moulded to shape with ease. The manufacturing method for this type of article is injection moulding.

(v) Vehicle rear lenses need to be transparent, and possess a reasonable impact strength. An acrylic material (PMMA) offers an excellent solution. Dyes can be added when the moulding compound is prepared so that transparent red and orange coloured lenses can be produced. Again the forming process for this thermoplastic is injection moulding.

Index